QUESTIONS & ANSWERS:
ADMINISTRATIVE LAW

QUESTIONS & ANSWERS: ADMINISTRATIVE LAW

Multiple Choice and Short-Answer Questions and Answers

Third Edition

LINDA D. JELLUM
Ellison Capers Palmer Sr. Professor of Law
Mercer Univeristy School of Law

KAREN A. JORDAN
Professor of Law
University of Louisville
Louis D. Brandeis School of Law

Print ISBN: 9781630447892
eBook ISBN: 9781630447915

> ## NOTE TO USERS
> To ensure that you are using the latest materials available in this area, please be sure to periodically check the LexisNexis Law School web site for downloadable updates and supplements at www.lexisnexis.com/lawschool.

Editorial Offices
630 Central Ave., New Providence, NJ 07974 (908) 464-6800
201 Mission St., San Francisco, CA 94105-1831 (415) 908-3200
www.lexisnexis.com

MATTHEW◆BENDER

(2015–Pub.3194)

DEDICATION

To Russell Weaver. Thank you for all the opportunities.

-Linda Jellum

ABOUT THE AUTHORS

Linda D. Jellum is the Ellison Capers Palmer Sr. Professor of Law in tax. She teaches Administrative Law, Statutory Interpretation, and Federal Income Taxation. Professor Jellum is a prolific scholar and has written extensively in the areas of Administrative Law, Federal Taxation, and Statutory Interpretation. She has published more than twelve law review articles, three books, and two book chapters.

Professor Jellum serves or has served on many professional committees and boards. For example, Professor Jellum served as the Deputy Director of the Association of American Law Schools and of the Southeastern Association of Law Schools. Additionally, she has been an officer and council member for the American Bar Association Section's on Administrative Law and Regulatory Practice.

Before joining the Mercer Law faculty, Professor Jellum spent five years working for Washington State's Attorney General's office. While there, she served as lead attorney for the Department of Social and Health Services. Professor Jellum received her J.D. from Cornell Law School and her undergraduate degree from Cornell University. She has the unique honor of having sat for and passed five states' bar exams, during which she developed her expertise on multiple choice questions.

Karen A. Jordan is a Professor of Law at the Brandeis School of Law at the University of Louisville. Professor Jordan teaches primarily in the areas of civil procedure, evidence, and administrative law. Her scholarly endeavors focus predominantly on regulatory law and policy issues, especially as they relate to the allocation of power between the federal and state systems. Professor Jordan's articles have appeared in leading journals, and have been cited in federal and state judicial opinions and course textbooks.

Professor Jordan has developed her administrative law expertise primarily in the health law arena. In the past, Professor Jordan has been a speaker at national conferences sponsored by the American Society of Law, Medicine, and Ethics and the Association of American Law Schools; and has contributed to forums such as West Legal News and the employee benefits section of the Association of American Law Schools. More recently, she has focused on issues relating to judicial deference to agency actions and agency preemption.

PREFACE

Administrative Law covers issues relating to the authority and functioning of administrative agencies. What procedures must agencies follow? What rights must they accord to those affected by its action? Administrative Law also addresses issues relating to the relationship between courts and administrative agencies, and judicial review of agency action.

The purpose of this book is to test your understanding of administrative law and procedure and to assist you in preparing for an administrative law exam. This book is not intended to provide a comprehensive explanation of administrative law concepts but as a supplement to class materials.

This book examines the major administrative law topics and concludes with a comprehensive Practice Final Exam. It includes an introduction to the study of administrative law and the Administrative Procedure Act, as well as such topics as rulemaking procedures, adjudication procedures and due process, retroactivity, non-legislative rules, reviewability, agency structure, inspections, reports, subpoenas, the Freedom of Information Act, and Attorneys Fees.

As you utilize these Questions, remember that there may not be a single correct answer, but there might be a "best answer." In other words, you might be asked to make informed judgments based on your knowledge of administrative law and your wisdom.

Professor Linda D. Jellum
Macon, Georgia
April, 2015

Professor Karen A. Jordan
Louisville, Kentucky
April, 2015

TABLE OF CONTENTS

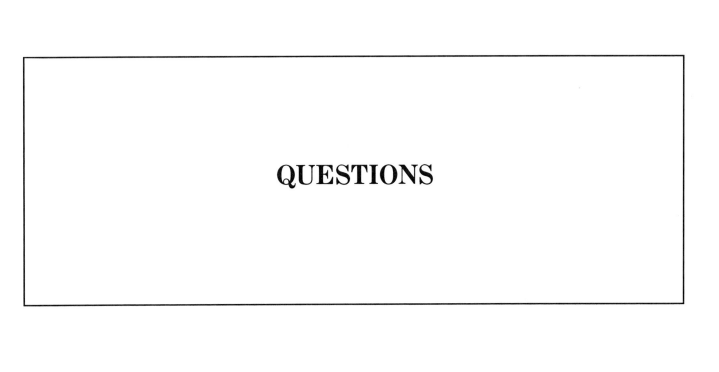

QUESTIONS

The Administrative Procedure Act is hereafter referred to as the "APA."

1.1.   Regarding the history of administrative law, which of the following is an accurate statement?

   (A)   The administrative state did not exist before President Roosevelt's New Deal legislative agenda of the 1930s.

   (B)   The APA was enacted as part of the New Deal agenda to help facilitate the rise of the administrative state.

   (C)   During the New Deal era, judicial review of agency action eroded and the APA was enacted in response to concerns about increasing unfairness in the administrative process.

   (D)   The New Deal led to a significant decrease in the number and power of administrative agencies, and the APA was enacted to empower administrative agencies.

1.2.   Identify and describe the types of agency proceedings expressly recognized by the APA.

ANSWER:

1.3.   The Northern Spotted Owl has been listed as a threatened species under the Endangered Species Act (ESA). The Bureau of Land Management (BLM) wishes to make timber sales on certain land within its jurisdiction but has determined that logging would jeopardize the owl. The ESA prohibits federal agencies from taking any action that would jeopardize a listed species unless they obtain an exemption from the Endangered Species Committee (ESC). The ESC is comprised of six members who are heads of various interested agencies (the Department of the Interior, the Department of Agriculture, the Department of Defense, the Council on Economic Advisors, the Environmental Protection Agency, and the National Oceanic and Atmospheric Administration) and one person appointed by the President to represent the affected State. An exemption may be granted only if the ESC determines that several statutory requirements are satisfied. BLM has petitioned for an exemption.

In determining whether to grant the exemption, must the ESC follow procedures in the APA?

   (A)   The ESC need not follow the APA because the ESC is not an agency.

(B) The ESC need not follow the APA because the proceeding involves an issue relating to public property.

(C) The ESC need not follow the APA because the determination represents a general statement of policy.

(D) The ESC must follow the APA.

1.4. Assume the ESC determines that the statutory requirements are not satisfied and thus, BLM is not entitled to an exemption. Regarding that determination, which of the following is a correct statement?

(A) The determination is a "rule" because the determination has only a future effect.

(B) The determination is an "order" because the determination is a type of licensing.

(C) The determination is not an "agency action" because it is neither a "final rule" nor a "final order."

(D) The determination is "relief" because it is neither a "final rule" nor a "final order."

1.5. Regarding economic justification for administrative regulation, which of the following is NOT an accurate statement?

(A) Administrative agencies generally should address problems associated with natural monopolists through price and profit regulation.

(B) Administrative agencies should only cautiously address problems associated with excessive competition through minimum price regulation.

(C) Administrative agencies often should address problems associated with the adequacy of information available to consumers through a variety of means.

(D) Administrative agencies must have an economic or "efficiency-based" justification for regulation.

1.6. Regarding an agency's rulemaking authority, which of the following is an accurate statement?

(A) Any agency empowered by Congress to promulgate substantive rules implementing a regulatory scheme adopted by Congress has a concurrent power to promulgate interpretive rules.

(B) Any agency empowered by Congress to enforce a regulatory scheme adopted by Congress has a concurrent power to promulgate substantive rules.

(C) Any grant of power by Congress to an agency to promulgate substantive rules implementing a regulatory scheme adopted by Congress forecloses the regulated entity's ability to challenge the agency's rules on the basis of the statutory authority for the rule.

(D)   Any grant of power by Congress to an agency to promulgate substantive rules implementing a regulatory scheme adopted by Congress forecloses the regulated entity's ability to challenge the agency's rules on the basis of the constitutionality of the rule.

1.7.   Regarding an agency's authority generally, which of the following is an accurate statement?

(A)   If an agency is granted both rulemaking and adjudicatory authority, the agency must announce new principles prospectively through rulemaking because making new law through adjudication is inherently unfair and a violation of due process.

(B)   If an agency is granted both rulemaking and adjudicatory authority, the agency generally should announce new principles prospectively through rulemaking, but the agency may proceed on a case-by-case basis if it is addressing an emerging regulatory problem arising from variable industry practices.

(C)   If an agency is granted both rulemaking and adjudicatory authority, the agency is free to use adjudication to announce new principles, and an agency order imposing substantial penalties will not be set aside on the basis of unfair surprise to a regulated person or entity.

(D)   If an agency is granted both rulemaking and adjudicatory authority, the agency is free to use adjudication to announce new principles, and an agency order imposing a penalty will not be set aside on the basis of substantial reliance by a regulated person or entity on the agency's prior practice.

1.8.   Regarding an agency's investigatory powers, which of the following is NOT an accurate statement?

(A)   Agencies may issue subpoenas to compel the production of documents or the testimony of persons with relevant information.

(B)   Agencies cannot compel regulated entities to create and submit compilations of information that would not otherwise exist.

(C)   Agencies may conduct inspections to determine if a regulated entity is in compliance with the law.

(D)   Agencies may compel regulated entities to create and submit compilations of information that would not otherwise exist.

1.9.   Regarding the ways in which an agency keeps the public informed about its actions, which of the following is an accurate statement?

(A)   The *Federal Register*, which is published by the federal government on a weekly basis, is used by agencies to notify the public regarding proposed and final rules and information about other agency actions.

(B)   Each year, agencies publish new regulations promulgated within the previous 12 months in the Code of Federal Regulations.

(C)   Agencies must maintain up-to-date indexes regarding final opinions and other orders made in the adjudication of cases and make such indexes available for public inspection and copying

(D)   Agencies may establish a schedule of fees for the processing of requests for inspection and copying and must consistently adhere to the applicable fee schedule for such requests.

2.1. Administrative agencies are:

   (A) Part of the judicial branch of government.

   (B) Part of the legislative branch of government.

   (C) Part of the executive branch of government.

   (D) An independent fourth branch of government.

2.2. Congress delegates quasi-legislative power to agencies to act. For such a delegation to be valid, what must Congress provide?

   (A) Congress must provide broad discretion to the agency to implement the powers delegated to it.

   (B) Congress must provide an "intelligible principle" to guide the agency in exercising that power.

   (C) Congress must provide express guidelines reining in the agency's delegated authority.

   (D) Congress must identify a named contingency for the executive to know when to act.

2.3. A federal statute directs the Secretary of the Food and Drug Administration (FDA) to maintain a list of ingredients that may be used in infant formulas. The statute further directs the Secretary to ensure that all such ingredients are safe for infant consumption. The FDA promulgates a regulation using notice and comment rulemaking prohibiting Xelentol, a soy alternative, from inclusion in the list. The manufacturer of Xelentol sues, alleging that the statute impermissibly delegates legislative authority to the FDA. How will a court likely rule?

   (A) For the manufacturer; agencies cannot enact regulations with legislative effect.

   (B) For the manufacturer; the statute does not contain an intelligible principle.

   (C) For the FDA; the manufacturer does not have standing.

   (D) For the FDA; the statute contains an intelligible principle.

2.4. The delegation, or non-delegation, doctrine can best be described as:

(A) A doctrine having continuing currency and vitality.

(B) A doctrine, which has never been disavowed, but fails to constrain.

(C) A doctrine that has recently gained relevancy.

(D) A doctrine that constrains Congress from overly broad delegation.

2.5. The Clean Water Act authorizes the Environmental Protection Agency (EPA) to promulgate regulations establishing national ambient air quality standards (standards) for certain air pollutants. The Act further directs that the EPA shall set each standard at a level "requisite to protect the public health within an adequate margin of safety." You represent the EPA, which has concerns about whether this Act would be found to violate the non-delegation doctrine. What do you advise?

ANSWER:

2.6. Congress delegates quasi-adjudicative power to agencies to act. When is such a delegation valid, if ever?

(A) Congress cannot delegate quasi-adjudicative power to agencies because Article III of the United States Constitution vests such powers solely in the judiciary.

(B) Congress must provide an "intelligible principle" to guide the agency in exercising that power.

(C) Congress may delegate *only* when the delegation involves "public rights" rather than "private rights."

(D) Congress may delegate so long as the delegation does not impair an individual's interest in having an impartial Article III judge adjudicate his or her claim and so long as the delegation does not affect the role of an independent Article III judiciary.

2.7. The following factors are all relevant in determining whether Congress validly delegated quasi-adjudicative powers EXCEPT:

(A) The extent to which Congress has provided principles to guide the agency in the exercise of its power.

(B) The extent to which the essential attributes of judicial power are reserved to Article III courts.

(C) The extent to which the non-Article III entity exercises the range of powers normally vested in Article III courts.

(D) The origins and importance of the right to be adjudicated and the concerns that drove Congress to depart from the requirements of Article III.

2.8. Historically, the Supreme Court approved quasi-adjudicative delegations to non-Article III entities when those delegations related to claims involving public rights, or claims against the government, and in limited cases involving private rights, or rights asserted in lawsuits between private parties. Which of the following rationales did the Court use to justify quasi-adjudicative delegation?

(A) In private disputes, non-Article III entities could serve as adjuncts to Article III courts because the legal significance of their findings was subject to review by an Article III court.

(B) Because the government need not allow any public rights claims to be adjudicated at all under sovereign immunity, Congress could choose to allow adjudication in this limited way.

(C) Because the legislative and executive branches historically had decided claims involving public rights, allowing non-Article III courts to resolve such claims made historical sense.

(D) All of the above.

2.9. Examples of cases typically resolved by non-Article III entities include all of the following EXCEPT.

(A) Constitutional claims.

(B) Tax claims.

(C) Military claims.

(D) Patent claims.

2.10. The President and Congress exercise oversight and control over executive agencies. Which of the ways identified below are NOT legitimate methods of oversight?

(A) The line item veto, which authorizes the President to cancel discrete spending provisions.

(B) Executive Order 12866, which requires agencies to identify the costs and benefits of agency regulation.

(C) The Regulatory Flexibility Act, which requires agencies to review regulations for their impact on small businesses and consider less burdensome alternatives.

(D) The Information (Data) Quality Act, which requires agencies to ensure and maximize the quality, objectivity, utility, and integrity of information.

2.11. The Securities and Exchange Commission (SEC) is an independent agency. How does it differ from the Department of Health and Human Services (HHS), which is an executive agency?

(A) While the HHS must follow the APA, the SEC need not abide by the APA.

(B)   The Secretary of the SEC would be a member of the President's cabinet.

(C)   The HHS has a multi-member board, made up of members from both parties, who are removable only for cause.

(D)   The SEC has a multi-member board, made up of members from both parties, who are removable only for cause.

2.12. The Seventh Amendment to the United States Constitution provides that in suits at common law, where the value in controversy shall exceed $20, the right to jury trial shall be preserved. Assume that as a result of an adjudication, an agency fined your client $4,000 for violating the Occupational Safety and Health Act. An administrative law judge presided over the adjudication, but there was no jury. Assume further that you challenged this fine in federal court as violating the Seventh Amendment because the adjudication lacked a jury. How would a court likely rule on the issue of whether the Seventh Amendment applies to non-Article III adjudications?

(A)   A court would likely rule that the Seventh Amendment requires a jury trial before an administrative agency can impose a financial penalty in excess of $20.

(B)   A court would likely rule that when Congress creates a new right the Seventh Amendment does not require a jury trial before an administrative agency can impose a financial penalty in excess of $20.

(C)   A court would likely rule that an agency can choose whether to have a jury trial before imposing a financial penalty in excess of $20.

(D)   A court would likely rule that the APA requires a jury trial before an administrative agency can impose a financial penalty in excess of $20.

2.13. Your client is the Secretary of the Department of Veterans Affairs (VA). Recently, the VA was involved in a scandal involving patient care. Your client has been getting pressure from the President to resign. She would like advice from you regarding whether the President can fire her if she refuses to step down. Write a short answer explaining the appointment and removal rules for principal and inferior officers of the United States.

ANSWER:

2.14. A statute provides as follows: "Regulations promulgated pursuant to this statute shall not take effect for 60 days. During this 60 day period, Congress may prevent any such regulation from taking effect if a majority of both houses expressly disapprove the regulation." A regulated entity files suit to block enforcement of the statute. Assuming reviewability, how would a reviewing court likely rule?

(A)   The court would likely find that the legislative disapproval provision violates the Constitution, but the 60-day waiting period is valid.

(B)   The court would likely find that the 60-day waiting period violates the APA, but the legislative disapproval provision is valid.

(C)   The Court would likely find that both the legislative disapproval provision and the 60-day waiting period are invalid.

(D)   The Court would likely find that both the legislative disapproval provision and the 60-day waiting period are valid.

2.15. Assume you represent a client who overstayed her student visa; hence, she was subject to deportation. Pursuant to the relevant statute, the Immigration and Naturalization Service (INS) can stay deportation for humanitarian reasons. On behalf of your client, you request a stay. The INS grants a stay, but under the relevant statute, reports that decision to Congress. The statute permits either house of Congress to pass a resolution rejecting the INS's stay. The House did exactly that. As a result, your client is now subject to deportation. Assume you file suit challenging the constitutionality of the statute; INS defends. How is a court likely to rule?

(A)   For INS; your client's case is not yet ripe for review.

(B)   For INS; the statute as written and as applied is constitutional.

(C)   For your client; the statute is an unconstitutional delegation.

(D)   For your client; the statute contains an unconstitutional legislative veto.

2.16. Congress has attempted to oversee and control agency action in a number of ways. Which of the following controls identified below are legitimate ways that *Congress* controls agency action?

(A)   Congressional committees oversee agency spending, agency substantive decisions, and agency efficiency.

(B)   Congress has included legislative vetoes in many statutes to reverse and oversee agency actions.

(C)   Congress can appoint and remove members of independent agencies that have multi-member boards.

(D)   Executive Order 12866 requires agencies to perform a cost-benefit analysis for rules that will have a significant impact on the economy.

2.17. For many years, federal legislation provided for the appointment of independent counsel to investigate allegations of misconduct by high ranking governmental officials. The independent counsel served in the United States Department of Justice. Please write a short answer describing whether the independent counsel is an "officer" of the United States and whether Congress can prohibit removal of an independent counsel except for cause.

ANSWER:

2.18. Congress wants to establish the Federal Election Commission (FEC) to enforce federal campaign finance laws. However, Congress does not wish to allow the President to appoint all of the members for fear that the FEC will persecute the President's opponents.

Please write a short answer discussing whether Congress can reserve for itself the power to nominate some commission members.

ANSWER:

2.19. Explain aspects of Executive Order 12866 which tend to curb or provide a safeguard against undue influence by OMB or the President.

ANSWER:

3.1. Describe the key difference(s) between agency rulemaking and agency adjudication.

ANSWER:

3.2. Agency adjudication is sometimes referred to as "quasi-judicial" since the resulting "order" is somewhat akin to a judgment imposed by a court. However, many agency adjudications look nothing like a judicial proceeding. Discuss why agency adjudications very often may lack many procedural safeguards associated with judicial proceedings.

ANSWER:

3.3. The Clean Water Act (CWA) prohibits the discharge of any pollutant into navigable waters unless the point source operator has obtained a permit. However, the CWA also authorizes the Environmental Protection Agency (EPA) to issue exemptions in appropriate cases. Under the CWA, a point source operator is entitled to an exemption if, "after opportunity for public hearing," the operator can demonstrate to the satisfaction of the Administrator that all statutory requirements for the exemption are satisfied. Big O Company applied for and was granted an exemption allowing the discharge of materials in the river adjacent to Big O's property. Shortly thereafter, a regional antipollution group challenged, via judicial review, the EPA decision to grant the exemption. One argument made by the group is that procedures used by the EPA violated APA adjudication requirements. The EPA responded that formal APA adjudication did not apply.

Which of the following statements reflects the best judicial response?

(A)   The EPA will likely win this issue because the Supreme Court has held that formal APA adjudication procedures are required only when Congress expressly requires that the agency's determination be made "on the record after opportunity for an agency hearing."

(B)   It is unclear which side will win this issue because the reviewing court will construe the statute as a whole to determine whether Congress intended to require the APA adjudication requirements.

(C)   The antipollution group will likely win this issue because a presumption exists that formal APA procedures apply whenever Congress imposes a "hearing" requirement unless Congress clearly indicates otherwise.

(D)   The EPA will likely win this issue because the reviewing court regularly defers to the agency determination of the issue.

The following facts apply to questions 3.4–3.10:

Medicare Part B covers physician and outpatient hospital services, including diagnostic tests, laboratory services, durable medical equipment, and many other specialized services for persons eligible to participate in the Medicare program. However, the program will not cover services that are not reasonable and necessary for the diagnosis or treatment of illness or injury. Claims for reimbursement are submitted to entities under contract with the Centers for Medicare and Medicaid (CMM). These contractors make initial determinations regarding whether reimbursement is proper. If the claim is denied, the Medicare beneficiary may seek, from the contractor, reconsideration on the written record. If the denial is affirmed and the claim is over $500, the claimant may appeal the decision to an Administrative Law Judge (ALJ). The ALJ presides over an oral, evidentiary hearing and makes a determination. Claimants can appeal the ALJ decision to a CMM Appeals Council, whose decision is deemed the final agency decision. If the claim is over $1000, a Medicare beneficiary may seek judicial review of final determinations.

Under the statute, the reviewing ALJ has power to enter, upon the pleadings and transcript of the record, a judgment affirming, modifying, or reversing the CMM decision, with or without remanding the cause for a rehearing. However, the findings of the CMM as to any fact, if supported by substantial evidence, shall be conclusive. Assume that the Supreme Court has held that Congress intended that the APA's formal adjudication procedures apply from the point of the ALJ hearing.

3.4.   Assume that Tony, a participant in the Medicare program, was diagnosed with prostate cancer and opted for a treatment called cryosurgical ablation. After the surgery, Tony requested payment from Medicare in the amount of $10,000 to cover physician and outpatient expenses. The Medicare contractor denied payment, stating that the service was considered experimental and thus, was not reasonable and necessary. Upon reconsideration, the denial was affirmed. Tony has requested an ALJ hearing.

Regarding the ALJ hearing, which of the following is an accurate statement?

(A)   The decision of the ALJ may be based in part on facts or information concerning the mortality rate of cryosurgical ablation, even if that information lacks sufficient evidence in the record, as long as Tony is provided a reasonable opportunity to present any contrary evidence he may have.

(B)   In order to affirm the denial of benefits, the ALJ will need to find that the preponderance of the evidence supports the contractor's initial denial.

(C)   The decision of the ALJ will constitute a recommendation to the agency.

(D)   Tony cannot be precluded from presenting his case through the oral testimony of local oncologists.

3.5.   Regarding the ALJ hearing, which of the following is an accurate statement?

(A)   If CMM has issued guidance to all contractors explaining its official position that cryosurgical ablation is experimental, the ALJ is bound to follow CMM's guidance.

(B)   If CMM has issued guidance to all contractors explaining its official position that cryosurgical ablation is experimental, the ALJ may nonetheless issue an order in favor of Tony if Tony presents enough evidence showing that the CMM position is unwarranted.

(C)   Assuming that CMM has no official position and that Tony presents his argument through the oral testimony of local oncologists, the ALJ cannot properly issue an order against Tony if the only contrary evidence in the record consists of affidavits of other equally qualified oncologists.

(D)   If CMM has issued guidance to all contractors explaining its official position that cryosurgical ablation is experimental, the ALJ is free to ignore CMM's guidance.

3.6.   Regarding the appeal to the CMM Appeals Council, which of the following is an accurate statement?

(A)   The CMM Appeals Council can set aside the decision of the ALJ only if it is unsupported by substantial evidence in the record.

(B)   The CMM Appeals Council can set aside the decision of the ALJ only if it is arbitrary, capricious, or an abuse of discretion.

(C)   The CMM Appeals Council may conduct a de novo review of the matter, including presiding over the taking of evidence.

(D)   The CMM Appeals Council may conduct a de novo review of the matter, but will limit its review to the APA § 556(e) record complied by the ALJ and to the written submissions allowed by the APA.

3.7.   Assuming that the ALJ and the CMM Appeals Council issue decisions affirming the initial denial of Tony's claim for reimbursement, which of the following is an accurate statement relating to judicial review?

(A)   If unsupported by substantial evidence in the record, the court is authorized only to set aside the CMM Appeals Council order.

(B)   The court may modify or reverse the CMM Appeals Council's decision, with or without remanding the cause for a rehearing, upon a finding that the agency findings of fact were arbitrary and capricious.

(C)   The court may modify or reverse the CMM Appeals Council's decision, with or without remanding the cause for a rehearing, when appropriate.

(D)   The court may modify or reverse the CMM Appeals Council's decision, with or without remanding the cause for a rehearing, upon a finding that the agency findings of fact were unreasonable under *Chevron*'s step two.

3.8.   In addition to the facts above, now assume that Jane, who also participates in the Medicare program, has been diagnosed with stage III breast cancer. Her physician recommended an expensive treatment involving High Dose Chemotherapy and a Bone Marrow Transplant

(HDC/BMT). Jane agreed to the treatment and has submitted a claim to Medicare for reimbursement of the expenses incurred as a result of the HDC/BMT. The Medicare contractor denied payment, stating that HDC/BMT was considered experimental. Upon reconsideration, the denial was affirmed; and the ALJ affirmed the denial. Jane has appealed the denial to the CMM Appeals Council. While Jane's appeal is pending, the Administrator of CMM sent a memorandum to the persons serving on the CMM Appeals Council. In the memorandum, the Administrator noted her concern about Medicare being obligated to cover HDC/BMT for women with breast cancer, given the high cost of the treatment and the high prevalence of breast cancer in the Medicare population; she urged the members of the CMM Appeals Council to move cautiously.

Regarding the Administrator's memorandum, which of the following is an accurate statement?

(A)   The memorandum constitutes a permissible communication, and CMM's Appeals Council is not required to make the memorandum part of the public record.

(B)   The memorandum constitutes a permissible communication, but CMM's Appeals Council should make the memorandum part of the record.

(C)   The memorandum constitutes a prohibited ex parte communication, which must be disregarded by CMM's Appeals Council.

(D)   The memorandum constitutes a prohibited ex parte communication, but it does not need to be disregarded as long as it is made a part of the public record.

3.9.   In addition to the facts above, assume that the Administrator of CMM attached to her memorandum a letter addressed to the CMM, which was signed by the presidents/CEOs of a number of the nation's largest health insurance providers. The letter explains to the Administrator of the CMM that private insurers have determined that HDC/BMT for women with stage III breast cancer is experimental treatment and thus excluded from coverage under most private health insurance policies.

Regarding the attached letter, which of the following is an accurate statement?

(A)   The attached letter likely constitutes a permissible communication, and the CMM Appeals Council is not required to make the memorandum or the letter part of the public record.

(B)   The attached letter likely constitutes a prohibited ex parte communication, which must be disregarded by the CMM Appeals Council.

(C)   The attached letter likely constitutes a prohibited ex parte communication, but it does not need to be disregarded as long as it is made a part of the public record.

(D)   The attached letter likely constitutes a permissible communication, and the CMM Appeals Council need not make the letter part of the public record.

3.10. In addition to the facts above, assume that CMM's Appeals Council affirmed the ALJ's denial of Jane's claim for Medicare reimbursement for the expenses incurred as a result of the HDC/BMT, agreeing that the treatment was experimental and thus, not reasonable and necessary. Jane learned of the letter sent to the administrator of CMM by the private insurers only after CMM's Appeals Council had issued its order because the letter had not been made a part of the public record. Jane has filed a suit for judicial review, asking the court to set aside the CMM decision as a consequence of the prohibited ex parte communication. CMM has argued that reversal is not necessary or appropriate because each member of CMM's Appeals Council has stated under oath that he or she was not influenced by the letter.

Which of the following is the best judicial response?

(A)   Although the attached letter constitutes a prohibited ex parte communication, the court need not void the CMM order unless it is clear that the agency decision-making process was irrevocably tainted.

(B)   Because the attached letter constitutes a prohibited ex parte communication, the court must void the CMM order.

(C)   Because the attached letter constitutes a prohibited ex parte communication and because the letter was not made part of the record, the court must void the CMM order.

(D)   Although the attached letter constitutes a prohibited ex parte communication, the court need not void the CMM order if the court allows Jane to provide a written response to the letter.

3.11. Assume that an inspector from the Occupational Safety and Health Administration (OSHA) issued a citation against United Motors for a number of substantial workplace safety violations at its Motortown plant. United Motors disputed that it violated any safety standards and requested a hearing before an ALJ. At the hearing, the inspector testified as to conditions at United Motors' plant. Two days after the hearing, while preparing his written findings and conclusions, the ALJ telephoned the inspector to discuss further the evidence relating to conditions at United Motors' plant. United Motors was not a participant in that communication.

Discuss the appropriateness of the telephone communication between the ALJ and the OSHA inspector.

ANSWER:

3.12. Describe the function of a "presiding employee."

ANSWER:

3.13. Identify five procedures required by the APA for an informal adjudication.

ANSWER:

3.14. Discuss the extent to which ALJs are independent and neutral decision-makers when they serve as a presiding officer at an administrative hearing.

ANSWER:

3.15. Explain the scope of review used by an agency when an ALJ's decision is appealed.

ANSWER:

3.16. Regarding federal due process protections, which of the following is an accurate statement?

(A) Due process protections are triggered by all adverse agency adjudications.

(B) Due process protections are triggered by agency rules imposing burdensome costs on regulated businesses.

(C) Due process protections are triggered by agency adjudications terminating government welfare or social services benefits.

(D) Due process protections are triggered only by agency adjudications adversely affecting legally recognized rights and not by agency actions affecting claims to government privileges.

3.17. Assume that the State University hired Susan to fill a "visiting professor" position. The position was for a fixed term of one academic year. At the end of the term, Susan was not re-hired. Further, the University did not provide Susan with any notice that she would not be re-hired and did not provide any reason for the non-retention.

If Susan challenges the University's decision as violating her due process rights because she was not afforded notice and an opportunity to address any possible concerns about her teaching, which of the following represents the best judicial response?

(A) A court would not set aside the determination because courts lack jurisdiction to review university personnel decisions.

(B) A court would not set aside the determination because Susan had no legitimate claim of entitlement to retention, and the determination did not create any impermissible stigma giving rise to a protected liberty interest.

(C) A court would set aside the determination because it will interfere with Susan's liberty interest in finding future teaching positions.

(D) A court would set aside the determination because Susan has been deprived of a property interest.

3.18. Describe when government action creating "stigma" can give rise to a liberty interest worthy of due process protections.

ANSWER:

3.19. Assume that New York has enacted a law requiring convicted sex offenders to register with the New York State Department of Public Safety (DPS) upon their release into the community. Each offender must provide his name, address, photograph, and a DNA sample; notify the DPS of any change in residence; and submit an updated photo periodically. The law requires DPS to post the registry on its website and to make the registry available to the public in certain state offices. The registry contains the following statement. "This registry is intended to facilitate access to publicly available information about persons convicted of sexual offenses."

Regarding due process rights of convicted sex offenders who may be identified and located through the registry, which of the following is an accurate statement?

(A) Convicted sex offenders have no right to have a hearing prior to the agency placing identifying information in the publicly accessible registry because the public has a strong interest in access to this information.

(B) Convicted sex offenders have no right to have a hearing prior to the agency placing identifying information in the publicly accessible registry because there is no dispute as to any relevant fact, and thus, they have nothing to prove or disprove.

(C) Convicted sex offenders have a right to a hearing prior to the agency placing identifying information in the publicly accessible registry because being a part of the registry creates an impermissible stigma without notice and an opportunity to be heard.

(D) Convicted sex offenders have a right to a hearing prior to the agency placing identifying information in the publicly accessible registry because being a part of the registry creates an impermissible stigma without notice and an opportunity to be heard, plus, it adversely impacts their right to privacy and their ability to live in certain communities within the state.

3.20. Professor Markelle of the Alaska State Law School was angry. As hard as he prepared over the years, some of his students never seemed to learn torts. Recently, he noticed that even his research assistant, Michelle Sabbatt, was not competent to analyze complex tort issues. He fired her, and he started a list on the school's website titled "Underperforming and Dishonest Law Students." The list includes Michelle Sabbat's name together with her picture from the law school face book. It notes that he fired Sabbat for "incompetence and possible plagiarism." It further notes that he "would not advise retaining her to perform any legal work." Sabbat is, of course, hurt and angry. She believes that this list and her appearance on it may hurt her employment prospects. Does Sabbat have right to a hearing?

(A) No. Sabbat has no right to have a hearing prior to Professor Markelle placing her name on the website because the public has a strong interest in access to this information.

(B)   No. Sabbat has no right to have a hearing because the Due Process Clause would not apply to actions taken by a private individual in a public law school.

(C)   Yes. Sabbat has a right to have a hearing prior to Professor Markelle placing her name on the website because being fired and listed on the website creates an impermissible stigma without notice and an opportunity to be heard.

(D)   Yes. Sabbat has a right to have a hearing prior to Professor Markelle placing her name on the website because being fired and listed on the website creates an impermissible stigma without notice and an opportunity to be heard, plus, it adversely impacts her right to privacy and her ability to work in her chosen field.

3.21. Regarding the factors a court must consider to determine whether additional procedural protections are warranted by the Due Process Clause, which of the following is the most accurate statement?

(A)   Courts must balance the gravity of the deprivation against the financial burden to agencies associated with additional procedural protections.

(B)   Courts must balance the risk of erroneous deprivation against the value of additional procedural protections.

(C)   Courts must balance the gravity of the deprivation against the risk of error involved using the procedural protections currently used by the agency.

(D)   Courts must balance the gravity of the deprivation and the risk of error associated with the procedural protections currently used by the agency against the burden to agencies that would result from additional procedural protections.

The following facts apply to questions 3.22–3.26:

The Department of Health and Human Services (HHS) regulates the conduct of research for which federal funds are used. Assume that HHS has issued rules that preclude a researcher from participating in the conduct of a clinical trial if the researcher holds a significant financial interest that could be affected by the outcome of the trial, unless the researcher provides to human subjects participating in the trial a full and adequate disclosure of the nature and extent of the financial interest. The disclosure must be made as part of the process of obtaining the human subject's informed consent to participate in the trial. If research is conducted in violation of the HHS rules, HHS may issue a cease and desist order affecting current trials, withhold federal funds from future trials, or prohibit future applications for federal funding. Assume that HHS determined that Dr. Smith had violated the HHS rule by failing to provide an adequate disclosure of her significant financial interest in a drug being tested in a clinical trial for which Dr. Smith is the principal investigator. HHS learned of the violation through complaints provided to HHS from graduate student researchers involved in the clinical trial.

Assume that HHS initiated an enforcement proceeding and that HHS rules require HHS to follow formal APA hearing procedures. During the agency proceeding, the ALJ found in favor of Dr. Smith. Dr. Smith testified that she always provided the required disclosure, that it was always adequate because she read a prepared text, and she demonstrated how she provided the disclosure. The ALJ rejected the testimony of HHS' key witness, John, who stated that he was present on several occasions when Dr. Smith purportedly disclosed her financial interest. According to John, Dr.

Smith's tone of voice and body language were designed to minimize any concerns a potential subject might have about Dr. Smith's financial interest and to maximize the subject's trust in Dr. Smith.

The ALJ's written findings and conclusions explained that Dr. Smith was a sincere and credible witness and that her tone of voice and demeanor would certainly alert a subject to the importance of the information being conveyed. Regarding John, the ALJ explained that he seemed nervous and was unsure of the dates on which he was present during the informed consent process.

HHS reversed the ALJ decision. HHS explained that, although the content of Dr. Smith's prepared text was adequate, the tone and body language used during disclosure could clearly impact the adequacy of the disclosure, and, as in other similar cases, it was very likely that Smith sought to use a tone engendering trust. Further, HHS explained that John's testimony should not have been discounted. As a graduate student researcher, he had reason to be nervous during the hearing. Further, HHS noted that there was no reason to suspect John's testimony simply because he was unclear about precise dates, given that graduate student researchers assisting in clinical trials typically are extremely busy and overworked. Dr. Smith has sought judicial review of the HHS determination.

3.22. Which of the following is an accurate statement regarding the standard of review used by the court?

    (A)   The court may set aside the HHS determination that Dr. Smith's disclosure was not "full and adequate" if the court finds that the determination is unsupported by substantial evidence in the record.

    (B)   The court may set aside the HHS determination that Dr. Smith's disclosure was not "full and adequate" if the court finds that the determination was arbitrary and capricious.

    (C)   The court may set aside the HHS determination that Dr. Smith's disclosure was not "full and adequate" if the court finds that the determination, although having an evidentiary basis in the record, lacks a reasonable basis in law.

    (D)   All of the above.

3.23. Regarding judicial review, which of the following is an accurate statement?

    (A)   In reviewing the record, the court will consider the evidence supporting HHS' determination as well as the body of evidence opposing HHS' determination.

    (B)   In reviewing the record, the court will consider only the evidence supporting HHS' determination.

    (C)   In reviewing the record, the court will give greater weight to the evidence supporting HHS' determination than to the evidence opposing HHS' determination.

    (D)   In reviewing the record, the court will give greater weight to the evidence opposing HHS' determination than to the evidence supporting HHS' determination.

3.24. Regarding Dr. Smith's action for judicial review, which of the following represents the best judicial response?

(A)   HHS' determination that Dr. Smith's disclosure was not "full and adequate" should be set aside because it rests on testimonial evidence discredited by the ALJ, and the ALJ's credibility inferences were based on witness demeanor.

(B)   HHS' determination that Dr. Smith's disclosure was not "full and adequate" need not be set aside. Although the ALJ's credibility inferences were based on witness demeanor, the Commission provided sound reasons, some grounded in experience, for its contrary determination.

(C)   HHS' determination that Dr. Smith's disclosure was not "full and adequate" should be set aside because HHS was bound by the credibility determinations of the ALJ.

(D)   In applying the substantial evidence standard of review, the ALJ's credibility determination is not relevant because it is not part of the record for judicial review.

3.25. In addition to the facts above, assume instead that neither Congress nor HHS requires the determination of whether a disclosure was "full and adequate" to be made pursuant to formal APA procedures, meaning informal adjudication may be used.

Regarding judicial review of HHS' determination, which of the following is an accurate statement?

(A)   The court may set aside HHS' determination that Dr. Smith's disclosure was not "full and adequate" if the court finds that the determination is unsupported by substantial evidence in the record.

(B)   The court may set aside HHS' determination that Dr. Smith's disclosure was not "full and adequate" if the court finds that the determination is arbitrary and capricious.

(C)   The court may set aside HHS' determination that Dr. Smith's disclosure was not "full and adequate" if the court finds that the determination, although having an evidentiary basis in the record, lacks a reasonable basis in law.

(D)   Both (B) and (C).

3.26. If the HHS proceeding constituted informal adjudication and the HHS rules did not require use of formal APA procedures, which of the following is an accurate statement?

(A)   If HHS did not prepare a contemporaneous explanation of the basis for its findings and conclusions, it would be acceptable for HHS to support its action upon judicial review by providing written affidavits of the HHS administrator explaining the basis for the decision.

(B)   If HHS did not prepare a contemporaneous explanation of the basis for its findings and conclusions, the court in an action for judicial review of the action could require the administrator of HHS to give testimony explaining the basis for the decision.

(C)   If HHS did not prepare a contemporaneous explanation of the basis for its findings and conclusions, the court can presume that HHS acted unreasonably and reverse the decision.

(D)   Because the APA does not require agencies to provide a contemporaneous explanation of the basis for their findings and conclusions, agencies generally do not do so.

3.27. When a party seeks judicial review of an agency's order, may the court stay the effectiveness of the order during the pendency of the review?

ANSWER:

3.28. Able Time, Inc. imported a shipment of watches into the United States. The watches bore the mark "TOMMY," which is a registered trademark owned by Tommy Hilfiger Licensing, Inc. The Bureau of Customs and Border Protection (Customs) at the Newark airport in New Jersey seized the watches pursuant to the Tariff Act, which authorizes seizure of any "merchandise bearing a counterfeit mark." Pursuant to the statute, Customs imposed a civil penalty upon Able Time and thereafter filed an *in rem* forfeiture action against Able Time in the local federal district court.

In the judicial action, Able Time argued that because Tommy Hilfiger did not make watches at the time of the seizure, the watches imported by Able Time were not counterfeit, and thus, the civil penalty imposed by Customs was unlawful. The government argues that the Tariff Act does not require the owner of the registered mark to make the same type of goods as those bearing the offending mark. The government acknowledges that such a requirement is commonplace in many related trademark statutes but maintains that Congress did not intend to include such a requirement (known as an "identity of goods or services" requirement) in the Tariff Act. Pointing to its generally conferred authority to promulgate substantive regulations, the government argues that Custom's interpretation is entitled to deference under *Chevron*.

The Tariff Act provides that: "[I]t shall be unlawful to import into the United States any merchandise of foreign manufacture if such merchandise . . . bears a trademark owned by a citizen of, or by a corporation or association created or organized within, the United States . . . unless written consent of the owner of such trademark is produced."

Assuming that the court finds that Congress was silent in the Tariff Act on the precise issue, which of the following is an accurate statement?

(A)   Because Customs is interpreting statutory language, the court must find that Custom's interpretation warrants *Chevron* deference.

(B)   Because Custom's interpretation of the statutory language was formulated in the course of a routine enforcement action, Custom's interpretation is binding on the court.

(C)   Because Custom's interpretation of the statutory language was formulated in the course of a routine enforcement action (an informal proceeding), the court should defer only if the Custom's interpretation reflects thorough consideration, valid reasoning, and consistency with other enforcement actions.

(D)   An agency interpretation advanced only in the course of litigation necessarily lacks the power of persuasion necessary to warrant any form of judicial deference.

4.1. Assume that the snowmobiling industry wants the National Park Service to modify a rule pertaining to use of snowmobiles in national parks. Which of the following is the *least* effective method for the industry to prompt the agency to act?

    (A)   Notify and educate the agency about the burden the current rule imposes on the industry to show the need for a modification of the rule.

    (B)   Notify the media and get it to spotlight the plight of the industry and show the limited impact that a modification of the rule would have on the parks.

    (C)   Lobby congressional representatives and educate them about the plight of the industry and the limited impact that a modification of the rule would have on the parks.

    (D)   Educate the agency about the plight of the industry and the limited impact that a modification of the rule would have on the parks and, concurrently, file a formal, written petition asking the agency to begin a rulemaking proceeding.

4.2. Assume that a judicial action has been filed, asking a court to review an agency's failure to act on a § 553(e) petition for rulemaking. According to the petition, Congress directed the agency to promulgate the requested rules within 18 months. Yet, 24 months have passed, and the agency has not even published the requisite notice of rulemaking. Discuss the effect of the statutory timetable on the court's analysis of whether to compel agency rulemaking under the rule of reason test from *Telecommunications Research & Action Center v. FCC*, 750 F.2d 70 (D.C. Cir. 1984).

ANSWER:

4.3. What remedy would a court likely impose if the court determined that the agency had unreasonably delayed its compliance with a statutory mandate to formulate and promulgate certain rules.

ANSWER:

The following information applies to questions 4.4–4.7:

Assume that the Internal Revenue Service (IRS) decides to update its rules governing the Flexible Spending Account ("FSA") program. Through this program, employees may set aside and use pre-tax earnings for certain qualified expenses. Previously, the IRS had permitted pre-tax earnings to be used for only limited health care expenses. However, in its Notice of Proposed Rulemaking (NPRM) to update the FSA program, the IRS proposed expanding the program to include expenditures for many over-the-counter health care items. However, the IRS explained that it intended to exclude expenses for herbal supplements, given concerns over the safety and efficacy of supplements generally. During the comment period, dozens of consumer advocacy groups submitted comments containing information and testimonials supporting the inclusion of certain popular and safe herbal weight loss supplements.

After the 60-day comment period and shortly before the IRS issued the Final Rule, representatives of two prominent pharmaceutical companies met privately with IRS officials and presented evidence showing various risks associated with the herbal weight loss supplements.

4.4.   Regarding this meeting, which of the following is a correct statement?

(A)   The APA does not expressly prohibit or impose limitations on post-comment communications from interested persons in informal rulemaking. However, the IRS should consider putting a summary of the communications in the public record to ensure fairness.

(B)   The APA does not expressly prohibit or impose limitations on post-comment communications from interested persons in informal rulemaking. Thus, the IRS should communicate with industry lobbyists without including information about the communications in the public record.

(C)   The APA expressly prohibits post-comment communications from interested persons in informal rulemaking, unless a summary of the communication is put in the public record.

(D)   While the APA does not expressly prohibit post-comment communications from interested persons in informal rulemaking, the Constitution would prohibit the post-comment communications in this case because the rulemaking at issue involved competing claims to a valuable privilege.

4.5.   Assume that, in the Final Rule, the IRS reversed its previously stated position of excluding all herbal remedies and allowed expenses for certain, specified herbal weight loss supplements. The IRS explained that many comments noted the value and safety of these herbal weight loss supplements. Pharmaceutical companies challenged the Final Rule, arguing that the IRS's Notice of Proposed Rulemaking did not comply with APA § 553's requirements.

Which of the following is the best judicial response?

(A)   The Final Rule should not be set aside because the Notice of Proposed Rulemaking sufficiently informed interested parties of the issues to be addressed.

(B)   The Final Rule should not be set aside because APA § 553's notice requirement does not apply to rules relating to public benefits.

(C)   The Final Rule should be set aside because it deviates drastically from the Notice of Proposed Rulemaking.

(D)   The Final Rule should be set aside because a complete reversal in the agency's position cannot constitute a logical outgrowth of the original proposed rule.

4.6.   Assume further that in the Final Rule, the IRS reversed the position it offered in the NPRM and allowed expenses for certain, specified herbal supplements. The IRS explained that many consumers commented on the value and safety of certain herbal supplements and treatments for a multitude of health-related conditions and that herbal manufacturers had provided several reports opining to their safety. Further, the IRS noted that its statutory obligation with respect to the Flexible Spending Account program required it to focus primarily on whether it was fair and reasonable, from a tax perspective, to allow certain health-care related expenditures to be paid with pre-tax dollars and not on the safety and efficacy of available health-care items. While the statute did not direct the IRS to consider safety and efficacy issues, it did not prohibit such consideration either.

Because the new rules allow pre-tax dollars to be used for non-herbal over-the-counter first aid items and remedies, the IRS concluded that, in light of the evidence of reasonable safety, it was only fair and reasonable to also allow pre-tax dollars to be used for herbal supplements and treatments, which are also generally available over-the-counter. In both instances, taxpayers are using income to treat health conditions.

Assuming that the pharmaceutical companies challenge the substantive aspects of the IRS's Final Rule, which of the following statements represents the best judicial response?

(A)   The court would likely set aside the Final Rule because the finding of value and safety of herbal supplements and treatments is unsupported by substantial evidence in the record.

(B)   The court would likely NOT set aside the Final Rule because the Final Rule represents a plausible policy decision pursuant to the arbitrary and capricious standard.

(C)   The court would likely NOT set aside the Final Rule because the Final Rule represents a plausible policy decision and the IRS considered appropriate factors, such as fairness and reasonableness, rather than factors Congress did not intend for it to consider.

(D)   The court would likely set aside the Final Rule because the IRS failed to adequately explain why it changed its opinion that herbal supplements and treatments should be treated the same as over-the-counter, non-herbal first-aid items/remedies, given legitimate safety and efficacy concerns.

4.7.   Explain why the "concise general statement of basis and purpose" required by APA § 553(c) is often a complex and detailed explanation of the rationale underlying an agency rule.

ANSWER:

4.8.   What is the primary purpose of the Regulatory Flexibility Act?

(A)   The primary purpose of the Act is to avoid unnecessary federal record-keeping and reporting requirements.

(B)   The primary purpose of the Act is to compel federal agencies to carefully consider the costs and benefits of additional regulations.

(C)   The primary purpose of the Act is to compel federal agencies to carefully consider the potential impacts of additional regulations on small businesses.

(D)   The primary purpose of the Act is to compel federal agencies to carefully consider the costs imposed on states through new regulatory programs or amendments to existing regulatory programs.

4.9.   Which of the following does the Regulatory Flexibility Act authorize?

(A)   The Act authorizes courts to review claims of agency noncompliance and, if found, authorizes courts to remand the rule or defer enforcement of the rule.

(B)   The Act authorizes courts to review claims of agency noncompliance and, if found, requires courts to remand the rule to the agency and order a Regulatory Flexibility Analysis.

(C)   The Act does not authorize judicial review of the content of the Regulatory Flexibility Analysis.

(D)   The Act does not authorize judicial review of agency compliance or noncompliance with the Act.

4.10. Regarding Executive Order 12866, which of the following is an accurate statement?

(A)   The Order authorizes courts to review claims of agency noncompliance and authorizes judicial review of claims regarding the substance of the agency's cost/benefit analysis.

(B)   The Order authorizes courts to review claims of agency noncompliance but does not authorize judicial review of claims regarding the substance of the agency's cost/benefit analysis.

(C)   The Order authorizes courts to review claims regarding the substance of the agency's cost/benefit analysis but does not authorize judicial review of claims of agency noncompliance.

(D)   The Order does not authorize courts to review claims of agency noncompliance and does not authorize judicial review of claims regarding the substance of the agency's cost/benefit analysis.

4.11. Given the many additional sources for procedural requirements (*e.g.*, Executive Orders, the Regulatory Flexibility Act, the Unfunded Mandates Reform Act, and the Paperwork Reduction Action), explain whether the additional procedural requirements enhance or impede administrative regulation.

ANSWER:

4.12. Regarding negotiated rulemaking, which of the following is an accurate statement?

   (A)   Executive Order 12866 requires agencies to use negotiated rulemaking if at all feasible.

   (B)   Whether an agency uses negotiated rulemaking is determined by the agency without input from persons with interests likely to be affected by the rulemaking.

   (C)   If an agency decides to use negotiated rulemaking, the agency must establish a negotiated rulemaking committee; then, the committee must consider the matter proposed and attempt to reach a consensus regarding the matter proposed.

   (D)   If a properly established negotiated rulemaking committee reaches consensus on the matter proposed, the agency may publish the committee's consensus rule in the Federal Register as a final rule.

5.1.   Rules exempt from notice and comment procedures include which of the following:

    (A)   Rules relating to agency management or personnel, public property, loans, grants, benefits, and contracts.

    (B)   Rules for which the agency finds that notice would be impracticable, unnecessary, or contrary to the public interest.

    (C)   Interpretive rules, general statements of policy, and rules of agency organization, procedure, or practice.

    (D)   All of the above.

5.2.   In 1979, when American diplomats were held hostage in Iran, the United States suspended its relationship with Iran. At that time, the Immigration and Naturalization Service (INS) adopted a rule without using notice and comment procedures that altered the number of days for Iranian nationals to voluntarily leave the country or face deportation from 90 to 15 days. Assuming that the INS is sued for failing to use notice and comment procedures, how would a judge likely rule?

    (A)   For INS; the rule would be excepted from notice and comment procedures under the military and foreign affairs exception.

    (B)   For INS; the rule would be excepted from notice and comment procedures as a policy statement.

    (C)   For INS; the rule would be excepted from notice and comment procedures as an interpretive rule.

    (D)   Against INS; the rule is not excepted from notice and comment procedures.

5.3.   Which of the following statements explains why under the APA agencies need not use notice and comment procedures for rules involving agency management or personnel, public property, loans, grants, benefits, and contracts?

    (A)   Such rules do not affect the substantive rights of regulated entities.

    (B)   Most agencies have adopted rules requiring them to follow notice and comment rulemaking in such situations.

    (C)   At the time the APA was enacted, opponents' major concern was that the government not be able to take liberty or property rights without adequate procedures.

(D)   At the time the APA was enacted, this exception was a compromise. Agencies wanted less procedures while regulated entities wanted more.

5.4.   Which of the following statements is correct?

(A)   Regulated entities have a right to comment on all proposed rules.

(B)   Regulated entities need not abide by interpretive rules and rules of agency organization, procedure, or practice because they are advisory only.

(C)   Regulated entities have a right to receive actual notice of all proposed rules.

(D)   Agencies must publish final policy statements and interpretive rules in the Federal Register.

5.5.   Which statement below is accurate?

(A)   Unless an exception applies, administrative agencies must use notice and comment rulemaking procedures if the rule is to have the force and effect of law.

(B)   Unless an exception applies, administrative agencies must use formal rulemaking procedures if the rule is to have the force and effect of law.

(C)   Administrative agencies have discretion to choose whether to use notice and comment rulemaking procedures if the rule is to have the force and effect of law.

(D)   Administrative agencies should use notice and comment rulemaking procedures if the rule is to have the force and effect of law.

5.6.   When a reviewing court determines that an agency's alleged policy statement is invalid because the agency used the wrong procedure, the court is making a determination that:

(A)   Notice was required.

(B)   Notice and comment were required.

(C)   Publication was required.

(D)   Congress did not delegate this power to the agency.

5.7.   A Federal Act directs health institutions to take "necessary precautions to protect client health information." The Act further provides that those facilities failing to take such measure are subject to a fine. The Secretary of the Department of Health and Human Services issues an internal policy, which states, "Privacy violations in health facilities with regard to privacy precautions are on the rise. It is the policy of this office to assure compliance in the most noninvasive manner possible. All health facilities must have at least three systems in place to prevent the unnecessary disclosure of health information or inspectors shall immediately fine the facility for non-compliance."

Assume a regulated entity challenges the rule because the agency failed to use notice and comment rulemaking procedures. Assuming reviewability, will the challenge likely succeed?

(A) No; this rule is a valid policy statement because the agency characterized its rule as such, and the rule does not have present effect.

(B) No; this rule is a valid interpretive rule because the agency characterized its rule as such, and it creates no new rights or duties.

(C) Yes; this rule is not a valid policy statement or valid interpretive rule because it has binding effect, and it does not leave the agency discretion regarding implementation.

(D) Yes; this rule is not a valid policy statement or valid interpretive rule because it substantially alters the rights of the parties and encodes a substantive value judgment.

5.8. There has been debate about whether agencies should be allowed to articulate policy through non-legislative procedures or whether agencies should be required to use legislative procedures (notice and comment rulemaking or formal rulemaking). Many commentators argue that legislative procedures are preferable because they allow greater participation in the rulemaking process by those subject to those rules. Nevertheless, many agencies continue to articulate policy by using non-legislative procedures.

Please write a short answer indicating why agencies might prefer to articulate policy by using non-legislative procedures.

ANSWER:

5.9. If an agency fails to use notice and comment procedures for what it calls an interpretive rule, a court will determine that the agency should have used notice and comment procedures when:

(A) The rule interprets a complex statute for the first time.

(B) The rule creates new rights or duties for regulated entities that do not already exist.

(C) The rule was not published in the Federal Register.

(D) The rule was formulated during formal adjudication.

5.10. Five years ago, the EPA promulgated a regulation via notice and comment procedures that limited ozone emissions. Ozone levels have since decreased significantly in the past five years. The EPA has asked you for advice as to how to rescind the existing rule. What advice do you give?

(A) The EPA need not use notice and comment procedures to rescind its regulation if it provides a reasoned explanation for its determination that the original justification for the rule no longer exists.

(B)   Because the EPA has good cause for rescinding the rule, it need not use notice and comment rulemaking under APA § 553(b).

(C)   The EPA need not use notice and comment procedures if its determination to proceed without using notice and comment procedures is reasonable and supported by substantial evidence.

(D)   Assuming the original decision to proceed by notice and comment rulemaking was correct, then the EPA must proceed by notice and comment procedures to amend or rescind the regulation.

5.11. It is often said that rules promulgated pursuant to notice and comment rulemaking are binding and have the force and effect of law. As a result, those subject to such rules are required to follow them. Are interpretive rules similarly binding? Please write a short answer discussing this issue.

ANSWER:

5.12. An agency issues a rule interpreting a recently enacted statute. You represent a regulated entity that will be expected to follow the new interpretive rule. The regulated entity asks you whether it should conform its conduct to the interpretive rule or wait for the agency to issue a new regulation using notice and comment rulemaking. Please write a short answer advising the regulated entity.

ANSWER:

5.13. An administrative agency issues a valid interpretive rule. Later, the agency changes its mind regarding the interpretation. You represent the agency. How would you advise the agency to change the interpretive rule?

(A)   The agency must use notice and comment rulemaking procedures to change its validly issued interpretive rule.

(B)   The agency must use formal rulemaking procedures to change its validly issued interpretive rule.

(C)   The agency need not use notice and comment or formal rulemaking procedures to change its validly issued interpretive rule.

(D)   The agency must use formal adjudication procedures to change its validly issued interpretive rule.

5.14. Pursuant to the APA, agencies must follow what if any procedures when they issue rules that are exempt from notice and comment rulemaking:

(A)   Notice and comment procedures.

(B)   Publication procedures.

(C)   Formal rulemaking procedures.

(D)   Formal adjudication procedures.

5.15. In determining whether an agency's interpretation of a statute is entitled to *Chevron* or *Skidmore* deference, the reviewing court will consider which of the following the most important factor:

(A)   Whether the agency's interpretation of the statute is reasonable.

(B)   Whether, when promulgating the rule, the agency used "force of law" procedures.

(C)   Whether the agency published its interpretation in the Federal Register or the Code of Federal Regulations.

(D)   Whether the interpretation is a longstanding interpretation.

5.16. When a court reviews the legitimacy of an agency's interpretive rule pursuant to *Skidmore* deference, the court will consider all of the following factors, EXCEPT:

(A)   The consistency of the agency's interpretation over time.

(B)   The thoroughness of the agency's consideration of the issue.

(C)   The reasonableness of the agency's interpretation.

(D)   The soundness of the reasoning offered in support of the interpretation.

5.17. A regulated entity relies on an agency's long-standing policy statement identifying enforcement guidelines for a regulatory scheme. Later, the agency alters its policy statement and brings an enforcement action against the regulated entity. As counsel, what argument would you make that the agency's change in policy is invalid as applied to your client?

ANSWER:

5.18. During the fall of 2012, the Food and Drug Administration (FDA) was notified that a large number of people throughout the southeastern United States were getting sick. From the information the agency had at that moment, it appeared that hamburger processed at any meat processing facility in the Western states from July 1, 2012, to October 31, 2012, was to blame. The FDA immediately implemented a rule without using notice and comment procedures that required all distributors of hamburger from meat processors in California, Montana, Washington, Idaho, and Texas to recall the meat immediately.

Organic Meats, Inc. refused to abide by the rule, claiming that the FDA was required to use notice and comment procedures. When FDA fines Organic Meats, Inc., will a court likely find the rule invalid due to lack of notice and comment procedures?

(A)   No, the court will likely find that the agency can show good cause why notice and comment procedures were impracticable, unnecessary, or contrary to public interest in this case.

(B)   Yes, the court will likely find that this rule encodes a substantive value judgment and substantially alters the rights of the parties; thus, notice and comment procedures are necessary.

(C)   No, the court will likely find that this rule does not impose new rights or obligations or restrict the agency's discretion; thus, notice and comment procedures are unnecessary.

(D)   Yes, the court will likely find that the agency invoked its legislative authority and intended to create new duties; thus, notice and comment procedures are necessary.

5.19. Assume the FDA does NOT use notice and comment rulemaking to adopt a rule. If a regulated entity attacks the validity of the rule based on the lack of notice and comment procedures, and the FDA defends the rule, claiming that the rule is an interpretive rule because the rule interprets the meaning of the statute, then:

I.   If the rule is a valid interpretive rule, then it is not subject to the notice and comment requirements of APA § 553.

II.   If the rule is a valid interpretative rule, then a court would apply *Skidmore* deference to determine whether to defer to the agency's interpretation.

III.   If the rule is a valid interpretative rule, then a court would apply *Chevron* deference to determine whether to defer to the agency's interpretation.

IV.   If the rule is a valid interpretive rule, then it must be published in the Federal Registrar to be enforced against a regulated entity without actual notice.

(A)   I and II only.

(B)   I, III, and IV only.

(C)   I and III only.

(D)   I, II, and IV.

5.20. Regarding the process of rulemaking, which of the following is an *inaccurate* statement?

(A)   Notice of the agency's intent to promulgate a rule must be published in the Federal Register without exception.

(B)   Notice of the agency's intent to promulgate a rule must be published in the Federal Register unless the agency rule is a valid interpretation of a statute or regulation.

(C)   Notice of the agency's intent to promulgate a rule must be published in the Federal Register unless the agency rule is a valid statement of agency policy.

(D) Notice of the agency's intent to promulgate a rule must be published in the Federal Register, unless the agency rule is a valid rule relating to internal agency procedure or practice.

5.21. Discuss the differences between the exemptions in APA § 553(a) and APA § 553(b).

ANSWER:

5.22. Which of the following would be *least likely* to fall within APA § 553(b) exception to notice and comment rulemaking procedures?

(A) The Department of Agriculture issued a rule banning the exportation of fruit from California after declaring an emergency because a Department inspector found a devastating Oriental fruit fly in a trapping device in San Diego.

(B) The United States Coast Guard issued a rule establishing a temporary safety zone following a massive oil spill off the coast of Florida.

(C) The Department of Health and Human Services issued a series of rules detailing when health care providers may release personal health care information. The rules were issued without notice and comment because Congress directed the Department to issue the rules within two years and that statutory deadline could not be met if notice and comment procedures were used.

(D) The Department of Labor issued a series of rules detailing how the Occupational Safety and Health Administration (OSHA) should determine which employers to inspect and when and how to conduct those inspections.

5.23. The Toxic Substances Control Act forbids the manufacture, processing, or use of any polychlorinated biphenyls ("PCBs"). However, the Act also authorizes the EPA Administrator to waive the prohibition by rule if the risk of injury to health or the environment is reasonable. Assume that in 1999, after notice and extensive comment by interested persons, EPA promulgated a rule relating to use of surfaces contaminated by PCB spills. Under that policy, concrete surfaces could be used after a spill of regulated, liquid PCB less than or equal to 50ppm; however, if the spill resulted in a concentration of greater than 50ppm, extensive cleaning, painting, and marking would be required. At that time, EPA explained that the policy would effectively prevent exposure to an unreasonable risk.

Assume further that, five years later, without using notice and comment procedures, EPA amended this rule to require the cleaning, painting, and marking for any spill of a regulated, liquid PCB (i.e., eliminating the threshold trigger). EPA incorporated in the new rule a statement explaining that good cause existed to forego notice and comment procedures.

If the EPA amendment is challenged for failure to follow notice and comment procedures, which of the following represents a court's most likely response to EPA's invocation of the good cause exception?

(A)   The amendment would be set aside because the circumstances did not fall within the scope of the good cause exception to notice and comment.

(B)   The amendment would not be set aside because notice and comment procedures would have been impracticable, given that PCB spills pose an unreasonable risk of injury to health and the environment.

(C)   The amendment would not be set aside because notice and comment procedures were unnecessary, given that the amendment contains only minor, routine clarifications that will not have a significant effect on the industry or the public.

(D)   The amendment would not be set aside because notice and comment procedures would have been contrary to the public interest.

5.24.   In recent years, the Centers for Disease Control and Prevention ("CDC") has become increasing vigilant about the need to rapidly identify the incidence of certain diseases, namely, diseases that might indicate that an act of bioterrorism has occurred. Accordingly, assume that, acting pursuant to its rulemaking authority and using notice and comment procedures, the CDC promulgated a regulation ("Rule 501"), which requires physicians to report to the CDC, within 10 days, the diagnosis of 20 specific diseases referred to as "Potential Bioterrorism Indicators" ("PBIs"). Rule 501 provides that a physician's failure to report such diagnoses could lead to the imposition of substantial civil penalties.

One year after promulgation of Rule 501, the CDC issued, without notice and comment, the "PBI Guidelines." The CDC published the PBI Guidelines in the Federal Register. The PBI Guidelines establish a set of symptoms for each of the 20 PBIs, which, if identified, require a physician to test for the PBIs using specific diagnostic tests, which are also set forth in the PBI Guidelines. The diagnostic tests specified by the Guidelines include some tests beyond those that would otherwise be required by the existing medical standard of care. The PBI Guidelines state that a knowing failure to use the specified diagnostic tests upon identification of the specified symptoms would violate Rule 501 and justify imposition of Rule 501 civil penalties.

Assuming that the American Medical Association has challenged the PBI Guidelines as being an invalid substantive rule, how would a court likely rule?

(A)   The court would likely set aside the PBI Guidelines because neither Rule 501 nor the statute provides an adequate legislative basis for agency enforcement of a duty to use the diagnostic tests specified in the PBI Guidelines.

(B)   The court would likely set aside the PBI Guidelines because the CDC did not intend the Guidelines to have the force and effect of law.

(C)   The court would likely not set aside the PBI Guidelines because the Guidelines simply interpret Rule 501, thereby clarifying for physicians their existing Rule 501 duties.

(D)   The court would likely not set aside the PBI Guidelines because the CDC published the Guidelines in the Federal Register and, therefore, provided adequate notice.

5.25. Since 1937, the statute controlling marijuana has excluded the oil and sterilized seed of hemp from the definition of marijuana. Tetrahydrocannabinol ("THC"), the active agent in marijuana, is found in only trace amounts in hemp seeds and oil. Relying on this exception, U.S. manufacturers have produced and sold consumable products containing sterilized hemp seeds and oil. However, without using notice and comment procedures, the Drug Enforcement Administration (DEA) issued a rule in 2001 that bans all naturally-occurring THC, including THC found in hemp seed and oil. Because the 2001 rule bans the sale of consumable products containing hemp seed or oil, affected manufacturers challenged the rule as being an invalid legislative rule. (Assume no issue exists regarding the DEA's statutory authority to ban all THC, including all naturally-occurring THC, even that found in hemp seed and oil, notwithstanding the 1937 Act's definition of marijuana.)

The DEA has argued that the rule is interpretive and exempt from notice and comment; however, the rule is inconsistent with a rule previously promulgated. Specifically, by 1968 THC was being produced synthetically and DEA promulgated a regulation using notice and comment procedures, which banned "synthetic equivalents" of THC. Then, in response to pending litigation in 1975, the Acting Administrator of the DEA published a non-legislative interpretive rule in the Federal Register that expressly interpreted the 1968 regulation as not covering sterilized hemp seeds or the trace amounts of THC in sterilized seeds and oil.

How would a court likely rule on the manufacturer's challenge?

(A)   The court would likely determine that the 2001 rule is valid. Because the 1975 notice was merely an interpretive rule, it can be changed by a non-legislative rule.

(B)   The court would likely determine that the 2001 rule is invalid. Even though the 1975 rule was merely an interpretive rule, notice and comment procedures are required to change an agency's interpretation of a legislative regulation when the prior interpretation is sufficiently authoritative and when there is a significant reliance interest involved.

(C)   The court would likely determine that the 2001 rule is invalid. Even though the 1975 rule was merely an interpretive rule, once an agency issues an interpretive rule, the agency must use notice and comment procedures to change that rule.

(D)   The court would likely determine that the 2001 rule is valid. Good cause exists for the DEA to avoid using notice and comment procedures because THC is dangerous for public consumption.

5.26   Discuss advantages and disadvantages of an agency's choice to use non-legislative procedures and why an agency may nonetheless elect to use notice and comment for issuing an interpretive rule.

ANSWER:

6.1. Which of the following is a retroactive rule?

(A)   A rule that applies to facts that take place prior to the rule taking effect.

(B)   A rule that applies to facts that take place after the rule takes effect.

(C)   A rule that applies to facts that take place both prior to the rule taking effect and after the rule takes effect.

(D)   A rule that applies only in an adjudication.

6.2. Retroactive rules are objectionable for all of the following reason(s), *except*:

(A)   Because retroactive rules are announced after a regulated entity has engaged in the subject conduct, they deprive regulated entities of advance "notice" regarding the content and meaning of laws.

(B)   Because retroactive rules are announced after a regulated entity has engaged in the subject conduct, they deprive regulated entities of a fair opportunity to bring their conduct into compliance with the law.

(C)   Because retroactive rules are announced after a regulated entity has engaged in the subject conduct, retroactive rules are less likely to meet due process requirements.

(D)   Because retroactive rules are announced after a regulated entity has engaged in the subject conduct, they are *ex post facto* laws.

6.3. Which clause in the United States Constitution impacts an agency's ability to promulgate retroactive rules?

(A)   The Equal Protection Clause.

(B)   The Ex Post Facto Clause.

(C)   The Supremacy Clause.

(D)   The Due Process Clause.

6.4. A court will likely uphold an agency's decision to impose a retroactive rule in an adjudication when:

(A)   The new rule addresses an issue of first impression that the agency has not yet resolved.

(B)   The new rule departs abruptly from the old rule, rather than fills a void in an unsettled area of law.

(C)   The legislative interest in having the new rule applied retroactively outweighs the harm that retroactivity would cause to the regulated entity.

(D)   The new rule was promulgated using formal rather than informal procedures.

The following facts apply to questions 6.5 and 6.6. The United States Department of Agriculture (DOA), which administers the Animal Welfare Act, charges Wild West Puppy Breeders (Wild West) of Dothan, Alabama, with violating the rules under which puppies can be shipped. The relevant statute prohibits the shipment of all animals under "inhumane conditions," which DOA regulations define as including shipments during periods of "excessively hot temperatures." "Excessively hot temperatures" is not defined by statute or by regulation.

6.5.   Wild West shipped puppies in July when the temperature consistently exceeded 90 degrees. You are a legal adviser at the DOA, which believes that Wild West violated the humane treatment statute and its interpretive regulation by shipping puppies during excessively hot weather without providing air conditioning. DOA asks you whether applying a rule that 90 degrees is excessively hot in an adjudication against Wild West would violate the prohibition against retroactive application of rules. How would you respond?

(A)   DOA may NOT apply the 90 degree rule in the adjudication. While adjudicative orders are normally retroactive, in this case applying the new standard retroactively would deprive Wild West of adequate notice to conform its behavior to meet the new standard.

(B)   DOA may apply the 90 degree rule in the adjudication. Adjudicative orders are normally retroactive, and applying the new standard retroactively in this case would be reasonable because the regulation prohibits shipping puppies in "excessively hot temperatures," which implicitly includes 90 degree temperatures.

(C)   DOA may NOT apply the 90 degree rule in the adjudication. While adjudicative orders are normally retroactive, in this case applying the 90 degree rule would unfairly penalize Wild West for its reliance on the prior rule.

(D)   DOA may apply the 90 degree rule in the adjudication. Adjudicative orders are normally retroactive, and applying the new standard retroactively in this case would not be arbitrary and capricious because DOA carefully considered the issue.

6.6.   Assume the DOA decides to issue a new notice and comment regulation defining "excessively hot temperatures" as any temperature higher than 85 degrees. Because DOA believes that this interpretation was already implicit in the existing regulation — shipments during heat in excess of 85 degrees is shipment during "excessively hot temperatures" — DOA wants to apply the new regulation retroactively and fine all puppy suppliers who have violated it in the past. The Secretary has come to you for advice about whether she has the power to apply the new regulation retroactively. What do you advise?

(A)   The Secretary may issue the new regulation as a retroactive rule because retroactivity is the norm for notice and comment regulations.

(B)   The Secretary may issue the new regulation as a retroactive rule so long as Congress has authorized the agency to enact retroactive regulations.

(C)   The Secretary may not issue the new regulation as a retroactive rule because notice and comment rulemaking is prospective only.

(D)   The Secretary may not issue the new regulation as a retroactive rule because the APA specifically prohibits agencies from promulgating retroactive regulations.

6.7.   Assume that the National Highway Traffic Safety Administration (NHTSA) determines that side airbags would greatly reduce traffic fatalities. NHTSA promulgates a regulation, using formal rulemaking procedures, requiring all car and truck manufacturers to install side airbags in new cars effective two years after the regulation's enactment date. Would this regulation be valid?

(A)   No, the regulation is an impermissible retroactive regulation.

(B)   No, NHTSA cannot enact retroactive regulations using formal rulemaking.

(C)   Yes, the regulation is not retroactive because it has prospective effect only.

(D)   Yes, assuming NHTSA has authority in its enabling statute to enact retroactive regulations.

6.8.   Assume again that NHTSA determines that side airbags would greatly reduce traffic fatalities. NHTSA promulgates a regulation using formal rulemaking procedures requiring all car and truck manufacturers to install side airbags in all new cars effective two years from the effective date of the regulation and to retrofit all vehicles currently on the road. Would the regulation be valid?

(A)   No, the regulation is an impermissible retroactive regulation.

(B)   No, NHTSA cannot enact retroactive regulations using formal rulemaking.

(C)   Yes, the regulation is not retroactive because it has prospective effect only.

(D)   Yes, assuming NHTSA has authority in its enabling statute to enact retroactive regulations.

6.9.   The United States Department of Energy (DOE) hears a case as part of its adjudicative process. At the end of the adjudication, DOE issues a new "adjudicative rule" designed to govern that adjudication as well as future adjudications. The defendant in the adjudication objects that the new rule should not be applied to its prior conduct. May DOE apply the new rule retroactively?

    (A)   Yes. DOE has complete discretion to decide whether to apply the new rule retroactively.

    (B)   Yes. DOE may choose to apply the new rule retroactively if the benefits of retroactivity outweigh the "mischief" of retroactivity.

    (C)   Yes. DOE may choose to apply the new rule retroactively so long as the agency's choice is reasonable.

    (D)   Yes. DOE may choose to apply the new rule retroactively so long as the enabling statute grants retroactive authority to DOE.

6.10. Automobile manufacturers petitioned NHTSA and asked the agency to amend fuel economy standards for cars with a retroactive regulation. The manufacturers wanted to avoid paying fines for their past non-compliance. NHTSA denied the petition, indicating that it lacked power to grant the petition. If a court upholds NHTSA's decision for the reason stated, what is the most likely reason?

    (A)   NHTSA's decision is reasonable under *Chevron*.

    (B)   NHTSA's decision lacks the power to persuade.

    (C)   Agencies can only act retroactively by adjudication.

    (D)   The enabling statute does not authorize NHTSA to make retroactive rules.

6.11. Return to question 6.5 regarding the United States Department of Agriculture (DOA), the Animal Welfare Act, and Wild West Puppy Breeders. As you may recall, DOA charged Wild West with violating the rules under which puppies can be shipped. The statute prohibits the shipment of animals under "inhumane conditions," which the regulations define as including shipments during periods of "excessively hot temperatures." Assume there are no other relevant regulations. Wild West shipped puppies during July when the temperature consistently exceeded 90 degrees. Given that Wild West is located in Alabama and that summer temperatures usually exceed 90 degrees in Alabama, Wild West defends by arguing that 90 degrees should not be regarded as an "excessively hot temperature" in Alabama in July. Wild West notes that its puppies are routinely kept during non-shipment periods in 90 degree heat. Suppose that DOA offers proof in the adjudication that it has consistently used 85 degrees as a "cut-off" number for summer shipments. As a result, DOA has cited numerous companies for shipping puppies in heat exceeding 85 degrees and has consistently imposed sanctions on those companies. DOA published these orders.

Under these circumstances, how would a court rule if Wild West challenged the interpretation as impermissibly retroactive?

    (A)   For DOA. Wild West cannot claim undue surprise because DOA's prior decisions were published.

    (B)   For DOA. Wild West cannot claim undue surprise because DOA's prior decisions were consistent.

(C)   For DOA. Wild West cannot claim undue surprise because DOA's prior decisions were consistent and published.

(D)   For Wild West. Even though DOA's prior decisions were consistent and published, Wild West did not have actual notice of them.

6.12. The factors a court will balance to determine whether a new rule may be applied retroactively in an adjudication include all of the following, *except*:

(A)   Whether the new rule represents an abrupt departure from a well-established practice or merely attempts to fill a void in an unsettled area of law.

(B)   Whether and to what extent the party against whom the new rule is applied relied on the former rule.

(C)   Whether the agency issued the new rule using adjudication or rulemaking procedures.

(D)   Whether there is a strong statutory interest in applying a new rule despite the reliance of a regulated entity on the old rule.

6.13. Prior to June 13, 1968, the National Labor Relations Board's (NLRB) case law provided that, when an employee was permanently replaced during a strike, the employer was under no obligation to rehire him or her. Instead, the employer was entitled to treat the replaced employee like any other applicant for employment. Although the employer was not allowed to discriminate against the replaced employee, the employer was not required to give the employee any preference either. However, in 1976, the Supreme Court decided *NLRB v. Fleetwood Trailer Co.*, 389 U.S. 375 (1967). In that case, the Court held that the NLRB's rule was invalid. In response and during a subsequent adjudication, the NLRB changed its rule on June 13, 1968, to require employers to offer former strikers reinstatement.

Two years prior to the NLRB rule change on July 26, 1966, as a result of a bargaining impasse, a union called a strike against a soft drink manufacturer. After the strike was settled, the manufacturer-employer refused to hire back the employees. The NLRB ordered the manufacturer to pay the employees back pay, among other things, pursuant to its new rule, which was not in effect during the strike period. The manufacturer resisted and argued that imposing a back-pay remedy for actions that, when undertaken, were consistent with NLRB policy would be unfair. The manufacturer does not dispute the validity of the new rule, just application of the new rule to its actions.

Please write a short answer indicating whether a court would uphold the NLRB's decision to apply its new rule retroactively. In addition, note whether you would reach a different result if the strike had occurred after *Fleetwood* had been decided, but before the NLRB officially changed its rule.

ANSWER:

7.1. All of the following are elements of reviewability, **EXCEPT:**

(A) Jurisdiction.

(B) Standing.

(C) Ripeness.

(D) Rationality.

7.2. Which of the following statements is **FALSE** regarding statutory grants of jurisdiction to review administrative action?

(A) The general federal question statute, 28 U.S.C. § 1331, can be used to establish jurisdiction.

(B) The APA, 5 U.S.C. § 702, can be used to establish jurisdiction.

(C) The agency's enabling statute may contain a grant of jurisdiction for judicial review.

(D) The applicable statute may contain a grant of jurisdiction for judicial review.

7.3. To seek review of administrative action, a plaintiff must establish that he or she has a cause of action. Which of the following statements correctly reflects the law regarding causes of action to review administrative action?

(A) APA § 702 creates a cause of action for anyone who has suffered a legal wrong, been adversely affected, or been aggrieved by an agency action.

(B) Courts have inherent authority to review administrative actions and can assert common law authority to establish a cause of action.

(C) The agency's enabling statute must contain a cause of action for a court to be able to review the agency's action.

(D) If a court has jurisdiction to review an administrative action, then the plaintiff will necessarily have a cause of action.

7.4. To successfully establish judicial review, a plaintiff must be able to show all of the following, **EXCEPT:**

(A)   That clear and convincing evidence exists to overcome the presumption against judicial review.

(B)   That the enabling statute does not commit the matter to the agency's discretion.

(C)   That the enabling statute does not preclude the matter from review.

(D)   That there is agency action to review, if the APA provides the cause of action.

7.5.   In addition to establishing jurisdiction and a cause of action, plaintiffs must show which of the following elements to be allowed to challenge administrative action:

(A)   That they have exhausted their administrative remedies, if required.

(B)   That the case is "ripe" for review.

(C)   That the agency action is final.

(D)   All of the above.

7.6.   The constitutional standing doctrine is based upon which provision in the U.S. Constitution?

(A)   Article I's Commerce Clause.

(B)   The Fifth Amendment's Due Process Clause.

(C)   Article III's case and controversy requirement.

(D)   Article II's vesting clause.

7.7.   To establish constitutional standing, a plaintiff must show which of the following:

(A)   That the plaintiff suffered or is suffering a concrete, particularized injury; that the allegedly unlawful agency action caused that injury; and that a favorable court decision would redress that injury.

(B)   That the plaintiff suffered or is suffering a generalized grievance; that the allegedly unlawful agency action caused that grievance; and that a favorable court decision would redress that grievance.

(C)   That the plaintiff suffered or is suffering a procedural injury; that the allegedly unlawful agency action caused that injury; and that a favorable court decision would redress that injury.

(D)   That the plaintiff suffered or is suffering a concrete, particularized injury; that the injury is within the zone of interests the statute protects; and that a favorable court decision would redress the injury.

7.8.   The National Bureau of Land Management approved plans to build a ski resort in Arapaho National Forest. The plans call for 200 acres of forest to be clear cut. The Sierra Club believes that clear cutting the forest will endanger a particular species of bird that only lives in this part of the country. The Sierra Club would like to file suit to challenge the agency's decision to approve the construction of the resort. How can the Sierra Club establish standing?

(A)   The Sierra Club can establish standing by showing that it will suffer injury to its environmental, aesthetic, or recreational interests.

(B)   The Sierra Club can establish standing by demonstrating that one of its members lives near the forest and hikes in it regularly.

(C)   The Sierra Club can establish standing by showing that one of its members has studied this particular species of bird in the past but has no plan to do so in the future.

(D)   The Sierra Club can establish standing by joining a senator who believes the agency is acting unconstitutionally or contrary to statutory authority.

7.9.   Environmental and other public interest groups can establish standing to bring suit on behalf of their members' injuries. Please write a short answer indicating what such groups must show to establish standing.

ANSWER:

7.10. For many years, the Internal Revenue Service (IRS) had interpreted a relevant statute by regulation to require hospitals, as a condition of being granted tax exempt status, to accept patients in need of care who were unable to pay for such services. Last year, the IRS changed the regulation via notice and comment rulemaking to allow hospitals to retain their tax exempt status when they turned individuals away for *nonemergency* services so long as the hospitals provided *emergency* services to those who could not pay for the services. The new regulation reduced the amount of free medical care that hospitals would have to provide to qualify for tax exempt status. Assume an organization representing indigent people wished to challenge the new regulation because of its impact on free health care. At trial, the parties conceded that low income people were harmed by the hospitals' failure to treat them for free; however, the organization presented no evidence showing that if the regulation were changed hospitals would begin treating low-income people for free. The IRS moves to dismiss the case for lack of standing. How would a court likely rule?

(A)   The court would likely grant the motion because the organization cannot establish that its members suffered harm.

(B)   The court would likely grant the motion because the organization cannot establish that the harm its members suffered would be redressed by a favorable court ruling.

(C)   The court would likely grant the motion because the organization cannot establish that the harm its members suffered is not a generalized grievance.

(D)   The court would likely dismiss the motion.

7.11. In 2010, Congress authorized a student loan program to be administered by the Department of Education (DOE). After operating the program for four years under an initial set of regulations, DOE issues a notice of proposed rulemaking indicating that DOE plans to make the eligibility requirements more difficult to meet. Specifically, DOE plans to lower the amount of family income a student may have access to before that student may qualify for a loan. The statute is silent regarding exhaustion, and there are no relevant agency rules on exhaustion.

John has received two loans under DOE's original regulation, but has a family income that will be too high to qualify if the proposed regulation is adopted. If John sues to enjoin the Department from promulgating its rule, which of the following reviewability issues would be the strongest barrier to his suit?

(A)   Whether John has standing.

(B)   Whether the case is ripe.

(C)   Whether John must exhaust his administrative remedies.

(D)   Whether a court will have jurisdiction.

7.12. The Fish and Wildlife Coordination Act requires federal agencies, including the U.S. Army Corps of Engineers (Corps), to coordinate with the Fish and Wildlife Service (FWS) before it issues a permit to allow a regulated entity to discharge dredged or fill materials into U.S. waters. The Corps fails to coordinate with FWS and grants a permit to Chuck's Auto Repair Shop. The National Wildlife Federation (NWF) would like to challenge the Corps action. How should NWF establish injury?

(A)   NWF can assert a procedural injury by demonstrating that the Corps failed to follow the procedures required by the Coordination Act.

(B)   NWF can assert direct injury by demonstrating that the Corps' action in approving the permit will directly injure NWF's ability to recruit new members.

(C)   NWF can assert aesthetic injury by demonstrating it has a member who lives near the area who is worried that the discharge will adversely affect the habitat of the birds he likes to watch.

(D)   NWF cannot establish injury because NWF does not have a concrete, particularized injury; rather the injury is simply a generalized, procedural injury.

7.13. The Federal Election Campaign Act requires "political committees" to file certain reports with the Federal Election Commission (FEC). The FEC makes these reports publically available. The FEC concluded that the American Israel Public Affairs Committee (AIPAC) was not a "political committee" within the meaning of the Act. As a result of the FEC's determination, AIPAC was not required to file the reports.

Akins, a voter who wanted access to the reports, first requested the reports from the FEC, then sued when the reports were not provided and challenged the FEC's determination. The Act specifically provides that "any person" may file a complaint with the FEC and that "any party aggrieved" by a FEC denial of its complaint may obtain judicial review of the FEC's decision. The FEC challenged Akin's prudential standing. How would a court likely rule?

(A)   The court would likely deny the FEC's motion because Akin had a concrete and specific, though widely shared, informational injury.

(B)   The court would likely grant the FEC's motion because Akin had a concrete and specific, though widely shared, procedural injury.

(C)   The court would likely grant the FEC's motion because Akin had only an informational or procedural injury.

(D)   The court would likely deny the FEC's motion because Akin had only a generalized grievance.

7.14. The Food and Drug Administration's (FDA) enabling statute ("Act") authorizes the agency to adopt rules of general applicability pursuant to 5 U.S.C. § 553 "as may be necessary or appropriate to implement the purposes of the Act." The Act, among other things, authorizes the agency to regulate persons who sell medical devices by requiring such persons to possess a license to sell such devices. The Act also states that the agency "may deny a license after a hearing." One of the statutory requirements is that a licensee be of good, moral character. The Act is silent regarding exhaustion. The agency promulgated a rule following notice and comment procedures, providing that persons convicted of a felony in the past five years are not of good, moral character. The agency did not provide any opportunity for a hearing or oral testimony on the proposed rule. The rule is silent regarding exhaustion.

Dave submitted an application for a license indicating that he was convicted of a felony within the past five years. The agency denied his application for a license and denied his request for an oral hearing. Under the FDA's rule, Dave may not apply for a license at any time in the future. Dave challenges the agency's decision to deny him a license. Assume Dave files suit under the APA.

Assume the agency argues that Dave's action is non-reviewable. How is a court most likely to rule?

(A)   For Dave because the action is reviewable at this time.

(B)   For the agency because Dave has not exhausted his administrative remedies as required.

(C)   For the agency because its denial of Dave's license is not final agency action.

(D)   For the agency because its denial of Dave's license is not yet ripe for judicial review.

7.15. Cattle ranchers challenge the decision of the U.S. Fish and Wildlife Services to limit grazing on certain federal lands. The ranchers alleged that the agency made a jeopardy determination without using "the best scientific and commercial data available" as required by the Endangered Species Act ("ESA"). The ranchers filed suit under the APA. The ESA specifically requires anyone challenging the agency's action to seek relief from the agency prior to filing suit and to appeal within the agency any adverse decision. There is no stay of the decision during the appeal process. Assuming the ranchers have a direct injury, is the action reviewable at this time?

(A)   The action is likely reviewable, assuming the ranchers are within the zone of interests protected by the ESA.

(B)   The action is likely reviewable, assuming the ranchers are within the zone of interests protected by the APA.

(C)   The action is likely not reviewable, because the ranchers have failed to exhaust their administrative remedies.

(D)   The action is likely not reviewable, because the ranchers have not been injured by agency action.

7.16. Under the Agricultural Marketing Agreement Act of 1937, the Secretary of Agriculture may issue orders that establish the minimum price that handlers (entities that process dairy products) must pay to producers (dairy farmers) for milk products. The Secretary issues an order providing that handlers can pay producers a lower price for "reconstituted milk" (milk that is made from mixing milk powder with water). The Act expressly provides that handlers and producers who are aggrieved by the Secretary's orders may challenge them. The Act does not mention whether consumers may challenge the orders. A consumer group wishes to challenge the order on the basis that, if reconstituted milk can be sold in jugs and cartons like ordinary milk but at a lower price, poor people are more likely to purchase reconstituted milk. Please write a short answer discussing whether APA § 701(a)(1) would preclude review of the Secretary's order.

ANSWER:

7.17. Under the National Security Act, the Secretary of Defense may grant or deny security clearances in his discretion as he deems appropriate for the national security. The Secretary denies a clearance to Rick, who challenges that denial. Rick alleges that he was unconstitutionally denied the clearance on the basis of his ethnic background. He is Arabic. If he files suit, will a court hear the claim at this time?

(A)   A court will likely hear all claims because the court has jurisdiction under the Act, and Rick has a direct injury.

(B)   A court will likely dismiss the claim under the Act because the agency's decision is committed to agency discretion by law, but the constitutional claim may remain.

(C)   A court will likely dismiss the action under the Act because the agency's decision relates to national security matters, but the constitutional claim may remain.

(D)   A court will likely dismiss the claim under the Act because Congress has implicitly precluded the claim from judicial review, but the constitutional claim may remain.

7.18. The Department of Commerce, through its Census Bureau, adjusted the 1990 census' count of the number of people who live in Massachusetts. The Secretary of Commerce submitted the adjusted census to the President, who was supposed to submit the census to Congress for use in reapportioning the House of Representatives. Massachusetts, which under the new census numbers would lose a representative, filed suit against the Department of Commerce alleging that the adjustments to the census were unlawful because the adjustments resulted in Massachusetts' residents being undercounted. The Department of Commerce challenged reviewability, alleging that its adjusted census was not final agency action because the census that mattered was the President's, not the Department's. The President's count led to the reapportionment. In sum, the Department argued that because its adjusted census did not have direct legal consequences, the census was not final agency action. Please write a short answer discussing how the court should rule on the Department's motion. In answering this question, note that the President is not an agency within the meaning of the APA, so his action would be unreviewable. *Franklin v. Massachusetts*, 505 U.S. 788, 796 (1992).

ANSWER:

7.19. The Consumer Product Safety Act authorizes the Consumer Product Safety Commission ("CPSC") to bring suits against toy manufacturers that make unsafe toys. Child Advocates, a public interest group, asked the CPSC to bring suit against Schwinn Corp. for selling an unsafe model of bicycle. The CPSC refused to act, and Child Advocates seeks judicial review. The CPSC's decision would most likely be final agency action that is immediately reviewable if:

(A)   The CPSC's decision violates specific criteria in the Act that specify circumstances in which the agency must take enforcement action.

(B)   The CPSC's decision violates the purposes of the Act and results in injury to a child.

(C)   The CPSC's decision is not supported by substantial evidence.

(D)   The CPSC's regulation requires exhaustion of administrative remedies and stays a penalty.

7.20. Congress amended the Federal Food, Drug, and Cosmetic Act to require manufacturers of prescription drugs to print the "established name" of the drug "prominently and in type at least half as large as that used thereon for any proprietary name or designation for such drug" on labels and other printed material. The underlying purpose of the amendment was to make doctors and patients aware of the fact that many of the drugs sold under familiar trade names are actually identical to drugs sold under their "established" or less familiar trade names at significantly lower prices. Following the amendment, the FDA promulgated the following regulation for the "efficient enforcement" of the Act:

> If the label of a prescription drug bears a proprietary name or designation for the drug or any ingredient thereof, the established name, if such there be, corresponding to such proprietary name or designation, shall accompany each appearance of

such proprietary name or designation.

A group of 37 individual drug manufacturers challenged the regulations on the ground that the FDA exceeded its authority by promulgating an order requiring labels, advertisements, and other printed matter relating to prescription drugs to designate the established name of the particular drug involved every time its trade name was used anywhere. The cost of printing new prescription labels was extremely high. Claiming that they would suffer immediate injury because they would be forced to print new labels, the manufacturers sought preliminary and permanent injunctive relief prohibiting enforcement of the new regulation.

The government sought dismissal of the suit on ripeness grounds. Please write a short answer discussing whether the case should be dismissed on ripeness grounds.

ANSWER:

7.21. The National Forest Management Act ("NFMA") requires the Secretary of Agriculture to "develop, maintain, and . . . revise land and resource management plans for units of the National Forest System." When NFMA adopted a federal land and resource management plan for the Wayne National Forest, the Sierra Club challenged the plan on the ground that the plan permitted excessive logging and clear cutting. The Club sought declaratory and injunctive relief, declaring the plan invalid and prohibiting NFMA from implementing it. Under the plan, no trees could actually be cut until the Forest Service made a timber sale; moreover, each timber sale could be challenged when it occurred. NFMA moved to dismiss the suit on ripeness grounds, arguing that the Sierra Club would not be harmed by delayed review because the Club could challenge the individual timber sales instead.

Please write a short answer describing whether the case is ripe for review.

ANSWER:

7.22. An FDA regulation provided that the FDA could "temporarily suspend" FDA certification to use a product containing a color additive if a manufacturer refused to permit FDA inspectors "free access to all manufacturing facilities, processes, and formulae" involved in the process of producing the product. The penalty would be imposed only if an inspector sought access to a facility and was denied that access. No civil or criminal penalties would attach. Rather, the rule allowed a temporary suspension of the certification, which would be subject to administrative review and, subsequently, judicial review.

The Toilet Goods Association, which represents manufacturers of color additives, seeks pre-enforcement review of the regulation on the ground that the FDA lacked the authority to promulgate the rule. The FDA objects to the suit on ripeness grounds because the regulation does not establish a legal duty or restriction requiring regulated entities to alter their primary conduct.

Please write a short answer discussing whether the case is ripe for review.

ANSWER:

8.01. When is an agency's interpretation of statutory or regulatory text entitled to *Chevron* deference, *Skimore* deference, or *Auer* deference? Is there a difference among these three standards?

ANSWER:

8.02. When is an agency's policy determination reviewed under the arbitrary and capricious standard of review and when is it reviewed under the substantial evidence standard of review? Is there a difference between these standards?

ANSWER:

8.03. When applying the first step in the two-part test identified in *Chevron v. Natural Resources Defense Council, Inc.*, 467 U.S. 837 (1984), what do courts look for?

(A) The clarity of the legislature's intent as identified using the traditional tools of interpretation.

(B) The clarity of the statute as shown by the text.

(C) The statute's legislative history as identified in the statements and drafting history.

(D) The reasonableness of the agency's interpretation.

8.04. When applying the second step in the two-part test identified in *Chevron v. Natural Resources Defense Council, Inc.*, 467 U.S. 837 (1984), what do courts look for?

(A) The clarity of the legislature's intent as identified using the traditional tools of interpretation.

(B) The clarity of the statute as shown by the text.

(C) The statute's legislative history as identified in the statements and drafting history.

(D) The reasonableness of the agency's interpretation.

8.05. Administrative agencies interpret statutes enacted by Congress. Agencies can act in different ways. If an agency sends a letter to a regulated entity in response to a question about the meaning of a statute, is the agency's interpretation of that statute entitled to

Chevron deference?

(A)   Yes, if Congress did not speak to the precise issue before the court and the agency's interpretation is reasonable.

(B)   No, the agency is entitled to *Auer* deference and will be reversed only if the interpretation is plainly wrong.

(C)   No, assuming the agency has not acted with the force of law and the *Barnhart* factors (*Barnhart v. Walton*, 535 U.S. 212 (2002)) are not present, the agency's interpretation is not entitled to *Chevron* deference; however, it may be entitled to *Skidmore* deference.

(D)   No, assuming the agency has not acted with the force of law and the *Barnhart* factors are not present, the agency's interpretation is not entitled to deference of any kind.

8.06.   Assuming a court is applying *Chevron* to an agency's interpretation of a statute, judges should:

(A)   Review the reasonableness of the agency's interpretation regardless of whether the statute's text is ambiguous.

(B)   Review the reasonableness of the agency's interpretation only when the statute's text is ambiguous.

(C)   Review the reasonableness of the agency's interpretation only when the regulation's text is ambiguous.

(D)   Review the reasonableness of the agency's interpretation only when Congress has not directly spoken to the issue.

8.07.   Under the Social Security Act, the Social Security Administration (SSA) is authorized to pay disability insurance benefits to persons with disabilities. The Act defines disability as follows:

> Individuals have a disability only if their physical or mental impairments are of such severity that they are not only unable to perform their previous work but cannot, considering age, education, and work experience, engage in any other kind of substantial gainful work *which exists in the national economy.* (emphasis added).

Using notice and comment rulemaking, the SSA promulgated a regulation interpreting this statutory definition such that an individual is disabled only when that individual can no longer perform his or her prior work (regardless of whether that work continued to exist in the national economy) *and* could not perform any other work that exists in the national economy. The SSA reached its interpretation by applying the rule of last antecedent, which dictates that a limiting clause or phrase (here: "which exists in the national economy") modifies only the antecedent that it immediately follows (here: "any other kind of substantial gainful employment"). Pursuant to the rule of last antecedent, the limiting phrase does not also modify the earlier antecedent (here: "unable to do their previous work.").

Tom has hypertension and cardiac arrhythmia. His job as an elevator operator was eliminated because elevator operators are no longer necessary. While Tom could continue to work as an elevator operator, such jobs no longer exist in the national economy. Tom applied for disability benefits, alleging that he was disabled. An Administrative Law Judge (ALJ) found that his impairments did not prevent him from performing his past work as an elevator operator and thus rejected his argument that he was disabled. The SSA adopted the ALJ's decision. Tom brought suit, challenging the SSA's decision in court.

The issue for the court is whether the phrase "which exists in the national economy" modifies (1) both "previous work" and "substantial gainful work," or (2) just "substantial gainful work." The legislative history is silent on this issue. How would the court likely resolve this issue?

(A)   The court would likely decide the issue de novo because APA § 706 directs "the reviewing court to decide all relevant questions of law."

(B)   The court would likely defer to the SSA's interpretation because Congress has not clearly spoken on this issue and the agency's interpretation is reasonable.

(C)   The court would likely defer to the SSA's interpretation because the agency's interpretation is not plainly wrong.

(D)   The court would likely defer to the SSA's interpretation assuming the SSA was thorough in its consideration, used valid reasoning, and was consistent with earlier and later pronouncements.

8.08. Assume that in the prior question the SSA had issued its regulation as an interpretive rule and had not used notice and comment or formal rulemaking procedures. How would the court likely resolve this issue in light of this change (assume the *Barnhart* factors do not suggested a different result)?

(A)   The court would likely decide the issue de novo because APA § 706 directs "the reviewing court to decide all relevant questions of law."

(B)   The court would likely defer to the SSA's interpretation because Congress has not clearly spoken on this issue and the agency's interpretation is reasonable.

(C)   The court would likely defer to the SSA's interpretation because the agency's interpretation is not plainly wrong.

(D)   The court would likely defer to the SSA's interpretation assuming the SSA was thorough in its consideration, used valid reasoning, and was consistent with earlier and later pronouncements.

8.09. Regarding *Chevron* deference of agency interpretations of the law, which of the following is an accurate statement?

(A)   Courts should cede the judicial task of interpreting statutory language to the executive whenever that language is susceptible to more than one interpretation.

(B)   Courts should cede the judicial task of interpreting ambiguous statutory language because Congress expressly delegated to agencies the power to interpret ambiguities in congressionally created programs.

(C)   Courts should cede the judicial task of interpreting ambiguous statutory language, in part, because the task involves reconciling conflicting policies, the resolution of which is helped by agency, not judicial, expertise.

(D)   Courts should not cede the judicial task of interpreting statutory language because to do so would violate separation of powers.

8.10. Discuss whether an agency is more likely to prevail in a challenge to a legislative rule interpreting a statute at step-one or step-two of the *Chevron v. Natural Resources Defense Council, Inc.*, 467 U.S. 837 (1984), analysis.

ANSWER:

8.11. Explain how the Supreme Court's decisions in *Christensen v. Harris County*, 529 U.S. 576, 587 (2000), *United States v. Mead Corp.*, 533 U.S. 218 (2001), and *Barnhart v. Walton*, 535 U.S. 212 (2002), defined the situations for which *Chevron* deference is due to agency interpretations.

ANSWER:

8.12. Section 706 of the APA sets forth various reasons why courts may set aside agency rules in judicial actions in which agency rules are challenged. Describe when the standard of review used by the court in such actions is *not* deferential (or not fully deferential).

ANSWER:

8.13. In comparing *Chevron*'s second step analysis and "hard look" review of agency action, which of the following is an accurate statement?

(A)   *Chevron*'s second step review is more deferential to an agency than "hard look" review.

(B)   Review under both standards is, in essence, de novo review and is therefore identical.

(C)   "Hard look" review is more deferential to the agency than review under *Chevron*'s second step.

(D)   *Chevron*'s second step review is the same as arbitrary and capricious review.

8.14. Which of the following is *NOT* a valid concern of "hard look" review of agency action?

(A) Hard look review is problematic, because it allows a reviewing court to inject its own biases when reviewing the agency's decision.

(B) Hard look review is problematic, because it does not provide a clear guidance to the agencies to know what they need to do so that courts will sustain their policy choices.

(C) Hard look review is problematic, because it allows a reviewing court to impose a heightened evidentiary standard to factual findings.

(D) Hard look review is problematic, because agencies feel compelled to provide contemporaneous explanations of rules beyond what the APA requires.

8.15. What remedy may a court impose if it determines that when an agency engaged in rulemaking, the agency (1) relied on factors that Congress did not intend for the agency to consider, or (2) failed to articulate a satisfactory explanation for its final rule?

ANSWER:

8.16. In applying the substantial evidence standard, what evidence should a court review?

(A) The entire record upon which the agency based its decision.

(B) The evidence that supports the agency's decision.

(C) The evidence that does not support the agency's decision.

(D) The testimonial and derivative evidence before the ALJ.

8.17. Ignore the *Barnhart* factors. An agency's interpretation of a statute is entitled to deference under *Chevron*'s second step when:
I. The agency is interpreting the APA.
II. The court determines that Congress was clear about its intent.
III. The agency's interpretation was made during an informal adjudication.
IV. The agency's interpretation was contained in a non-legislative rule.

(A) III and IV.

(B) I, II, and III.

(C) II, III, and IV.

(D) None of the above.

8.18. Although there is still some dissension amongst Supreme Court justices, what standard of review do courts typically apply to agency interpretations of statutes contained in non-legislative rules?

(A) *Chevron* deference.

(B) *Skidmore* deference.

(C) *Auer* deference.

(D) No deference.

8.19. The Department of Education (DOE) administers the "Children Are Exceptional" (CARE) program. CARE implements the president's policy of "decreasing drug use, teenage pregnancy, and domestic violence through education." To this end, CARE provides federal funds to schools that meet certain criteria. The statute authorizes DOE to make rules after a hearing. To implement the statute, the DOE published a Notice of Proposed Rulemaking (NPRM) and invited comments on how DOE could best meet the program's objectives.

To decrease teenage pregnancy, the DOE proposed in its NPRM that sex education classes address abstinence-only options. The American Academy of Pediatrics commented that there were no studies that supported the proposition that abstinence-only education decreased teenage pregnancy. Similarly, the American Public Health Association cited multiple studies that concluded that comprehensive sex education programs that include a discussion of abstinence are more effective in decreasing teenage pregnancy than abstinence-only education programs. And the American Medical Association sent the DOE a copy of the numerous studies conducted, none of which supported the agency's proposed rule. A group called Mom's Against Teenagers Having Sex wrote to support the proposed rule because it believed that teens should not have sex.

If the DOE implements a final rule with no changes after the notice and comment period has ended and the American Medical Association files suit, what standard of review should apply?

(A) The substantial evidence standard.

(B) The arbitrary and capricious standard.

(C) *Skidmore* deference.

(D) *Chevron* deference.

8.20. ThinThin, Inc. markets a popular weight loss diet drug. After a number of physicians report to the Department of Health and Human Services (DHHS) that the drug causes unexpected and serious side effects, DHHS issues an order directing the company manufacturing the drug to "cease and desist." Pursuant to the relevant act, ThinThin may contest DHHS's order in a formal adjudication. Assume that after the hearing concludes, the ALJ finds for ThinThin. Assuming the head of DHHS decides to reverse the ALJ's decision, what standard of review will the DHHS apply to the ALJ's decision?

(A) The standard of review would be substantial evidence.

(B) The standard of review would be arbitrary and capricious.

(C) The standard of review would be *de novo*.

(D) The standard of review would be *Chevron* deference.

The following facts apply to questions 8.21–8.23. Congress established Medicare to provide health insurance to the elderly and disabled. Pursuant to 42 U.S.C. § 1395 *et seq.*, the amount Medicare pays for inpatient hospitalization is determined under a prospective payment system. Under that system, Medicare reimburses hospital providers according to predetermined rates, which correspond to a patient's diagnosis at discharge. In creating the payment system, Congress was concerned that teaching hospitals would incur greater costs in treating patients than would non-teaching hospitals. To remedy this inequity, Congress established an Indirect Medical Education ("IME") adjustment to increase Medicare payments to teaching hospitals. Congress delegated responsibility to regulate Medicare to the U.S. Department of Health and Human Services (DHHS). DHHS promulgated regulations using notice and comment procedures to implement the IME adjustment.

One regulation sets forth the type of resident activities DHHS will include in its calculation of a teaching hospital's IME adjustment. To be included in the IME, a resident must "be enrolled in an approved teaching program and be assigned to the portion of the hospital providing patient care . . . ." 42. C.F.R. § 412.105(g)(ii).

State Hospital ("the hospital") has a large graduate medical education program with many residents. Last year, DHHS denied the hospital's request that certain residents be included in the calculation of the hospital's IME based on DHHS's interpretation of its *governing regulation*, identified above. DHHS interpreted language in the regulation to exclude the time residents spent researching, because such time was not providing patient care. The loss to the hospital exceeded one million dollars.

8.21. What language in the regulation did DHHS interpret?

    (A)   "Enrolled."

    (B)   "Approved teaching program."

    (C)   "Providing patient care."

    (D)   "Resident."

8.22. Assuming the hospital sues DHHS for lost reimbursement, the hospital will prevail if:

    (A)   The agency's interpretation is plainly wrong.

    (B)   The agency's interpretation is unreasonable.

    (C)   The agency's interpretation is arbitrary and capricious.

    (D)   The agency's interpretation is clearly erroneous.

8.23. The hospital's best argument, assuming each argument below is accurate, would be which of the following?

    (A)   The agency's interpretation is contrary to the plain meaning of the regulation.

    (B)   The agency's interpretation is contrary to the purpose of the statute.

(C)   The agency's interpretation is contrary to the legislative history of the statute.

(D)   The agency's interpretation violates the rule of lenity.

8.24   Under APA § 706(2)(E), the "substantial evidence" standard of review applies in cases involving which of the following?

(A)   Questions of law in formal adjudication.

(B)   Questions of law in formal rulemaking.

(C)   Questions of fact in non-legislative rulemaking.

(D)   None of the above.

8.25.   The Safe Food Act provides that "the Food and Drug Administration may establish reasonable rules, regulations, and practices with respect to food safety after notice and a full hearing." The Food and Drug Administration Agency concludes that it may enact regulations using notice and comment procedures rather than formal procedures. If a regulated entity brings suit challenging the FDA's decision to use informal rulemaking, how would a court likely rule?

(A)   For the Agency; its interpretation of the Act would likely receive *Chevron* deference.

(B)   For the Agency; its interpretation of the Act does not violate *Vermont Yankee*.

(C)   For the regulated entity; the Agency's interpretation would likely be found to violate the APA.

(D)   For the regulated entity; the Agency's interpretation would likely be found to be arbitrary and capricious.

The following facts apply to questions 8.26 & 8.27. Benjamin Gerson created a revocable trust to benefit his wife, Eleanor. The trust gave Eleanor the right to use the income during her life and to appoint a beneficiary to receive the corpus when she died. By its terms, the trust became irrevocable when Benjamin died in 1983. Eleanor never added any funds to the corpus of the trust. She died in 2000 with a will exercising her power of appointment and leaving the trust corpus to the couple's grandchildren.

Eleanor's executor filed a tax return for the estate. The Internal Revenue Service (IRS) responded with a notice of deficiency, claiming that the transfer to the grandchildren triggered the generation-skipping transfer (GST) tax. According to the IRS, the Gerson Estate owed $100,000 in taxes. The executor of the Gerson Estate sued in the United States Tax Court to challenge the deficiency notice. The Tax Court agreed with the IRS, holding that the deficiency was due. The executor filed suit in federal court.

The Tax Reform Act of 1986 provides that the GST does not apply to "any generation-skipping transfers under a trust that was irrevocable on or before September 25, 1985, but only to the extent that such transfer is not made out of corpus added to the trust after September 25, 1985." The Treasury Department promulgated a regulation that provides that the statute "does not apply to a transfer of property pursuant to the exercise, release, or lapse of a general power of appointment," which is what occurred here. In other words, the IRS argues that testators must include the transfer to the grandchildren in the trust instrument itself or by conferring no more than a limited power of appointment, before 1985. The Estate argues that the IRS's interpretation is contrary to the plain meaning of the text of the statute.

8.26. Assume that Congress has delegated to the Treasury the authority to issue regulations, and this regulation was promulgated after notice and comment rulemaking procedures. How would a court likely to rule?

(A)   If the court disagrees with the executor that Congress spoke to the precise issue before the court at *Chevron* step one, then the court must defer to the IRS's interpretation under *Chevron* step two because the regulation constitutes an agency interpretation of a statute the agency is charged with administering.

(B)   If the court disagrees with the executor that Congress spoke to the precise issue before the court at *Chevron* step one, then the court must defer to the IRS' interpretation if it is reasonable under *Chevron* step two because Congress delegated authority to the agency generally to make rules carrying the force of law and the regulation was promulgated in the exercise of that authority.

(C)   If the court agrees with the executor that Congress spoke to the precise issue before the court at *Chevron* step one, the court must still defer to the IRS's interpretation if it is reasonable under *Chevron*'s second step because Congress delegated authority to the agency generally to make rules carrying the force of law and the regulation was promulgated in the exercise of that authority.

(D)   If the court agrees with the executor that Congress spoke to the precise issue before the court at *Chevron* step one, then *Chevron* deference is not triggered in this case because Congress did not delegate authority to the agency generally to make rules carrying the force of law.

8.27. Assume instead that, although Congress has delegated to the Treasury the authority to issue regulations, unlike in the last example, this rule was issued as a non-legislative interpretive rule. What standard of review would the court apply?

(A)   Regardless of whether the Treasury used notice and comment or formal rulemaking procedures to promulgate its rule, *Chevron* deference is most likely the appropriate standard of review.

(B)   Because the Treasury did not use notice and comment or formal rulemaking procedures to promulgate its rule, *Skidmore* deference is most likely the appropriate standard of review.

(C)   Because the Treasury did not use notice and comment or formal rulemaking procedures to promulgate its rule, *Auer* deference is most likely the appropriate standard of review.

(D)   Because the Treasury did not use notice and comment or formal rulemaking procedures to promulgate its rule, *arbitrary and capricious review* is most likely the appropriate standard of review.

9.1. Agencies conduct inspections, require the submission of reports, and issue subpoenas for which of the following reasons:

(A) To gain information both they and the President need to set policy.

(B) To gain information they and other agencies need to enforce regulations.

(C) To gain information they need to prosecute regulated entities for civil and criminal violations.

(D) All of the above.

9.2. Valid reasons for agencies to perform inspections include which of the following:

(A) Health inspectors enter restaurants to ensure that food storage, preparation, and service areas are clean.

(B) Child welfare officials enter homes when the agency receives a complaint that children in the home are being abused or neglected.

(C) Occupational Safety and Health Administration inspectors examine construction and work sites to make sure that workers are employed in safe and healthy conditions.

(D) All of the above.

9.3. The Fourth Amendment prohibits unreasonable searches and seizures and requires that search warrants be issued only upon a showing of probable cause. In general, does the Fourth Amendment's prohibition against unreasonable searches and seizures apply to administrative inspections of homes and ordinary businesses?

(A) No, the Fourth Amendment's prohibition against unreasonable searches and seizures does not apply, and warrants are unnecessary for administrative searches.

(B) Yes, the Fourth Amendment's prohibition against unreasonable searches and seizures and probable cause requirement apply in the same way as they apply in criminal searches.

(C) Yes, the Fourth Amendment prohibition against unreasonable searches and seizures does apply, but the standard required for a warrant is generally less.

(D)   Yes, the Fourth Amendment prohibition against unreasonable searches and seizures generally applies, but the standard required for a warrant is generally greater.

9.4.   Which of the following searches would require a warrant?

(A)   An administrative search of a business based on an agency's need to respond to an emergency, such as finding poisonous food or fighting a fire.

(B)   An administrative search of a business area that is in plain view.

(C)   An administrative search of a vehicle crossing the U.S. border.

(D)   An administrative search that is a pretext to locate evidence of a violation of a criminal statute.

9.5.   Which of the inspections below would not require a warrant?

(A)   An administrative search of an ordinary business when the search is rationally related to the purpose for the inspection.

(B)   An administrative search of a home when the search is reasonably related to the purpose for the inspection.

(C)   An administrative search of an ordinary business when the statute allows warrantless searches.

(D)   An administrative search of a closely (or pervasively) regulated business whose industry is subject to a licensing system involving intensive regulation.

9.6.   Assume that you represent a closely (or pervasively) regulated business. An inspector has appeared at your client's door asking for permission to inspect the plant. May the inspector inspect the plant?

(A)   The inspector may not inspect the plant without a warrant establishing probable cause to believe that a crime has occurred on the premises.

(B)   The inspector may not inspect the plant without a warrant establishing probable cause to believe that the inspection complies with reasonable legislative or administrative statutory standards.

(C)   The inspector may inspect the plant without a warrant so long as the search serves an important governmental purpose, warrantless searches are necessary to further that purpose, and the statute authorizing the search provides protections substituting for a warrant.

(D)   The inspector may inspect the plant without a warrant so long as the law is detailed enough to put the owner on notice that he or she will be subject to periodic inspections and the law limits the inspector's discretion.

9.7.   Assume that you represent an agency. The agency conducted a warrantless search of a regulated entity based on a good faith belief that no warrant was needed. The agency was wrong. The agency now wants to know whether evidence the agency found during the warrantless search will be admissible pursuant to the exclusionary rule. What do you advise?

(A) The exclusionary rule does not apply to administrative adjudications.

(B) The exclusionary rule does not apply to administrative adjudications that do not impose civil fines.

(C) Pursuant to the exclusionary rule, courts generally exclude evidence obtained in violation of the Fourth Amendment.

(D) Pursuant to the exclusionary rule, the evidence would be admissible during any administrative adjudication, but not as part of any appeal.

9.8. You represent the Occupational Safety and Health Administration (OSHA). A statute specifically authorizes OSHA to conduct "special inspections" when there is an employee complaint that a workplace safety violation exists. The purpose of the inspection is to determine whether a violation occurred. Acme, Inc. manufactures tanks and pressure valves. An employee complained to OSHA, alleging that portable grinders and rollers used in Acme's plant were improperly wired, that compressed gas cylinders were unsecured and not fitted with valve protection caps, and that oil-slick floors and stored materials impeded safe access to workplace aisles and passageways. OSHA asks you whether it must obtain a warrant prior to inspecting the employer and whether the inspection may be comprehensive (a wall-to-wall search) or must be limited to the allegations in the complaint. How do you respond?

(A) OSHA must get a warrant, and the scope of the search may be comprehensive in nature.

(B) OSHA need not get a warrant because the employee's complaint furnishes the requisite emergency for a warrantless search, but the scope of the search must be limited to the allegations in the complaint.

(C) OSHA must get a warrant, and the scope of the search must be limited to the allegations in the complaint.

(D) OSHA need not get a warrant because the employer is a closely (or pervasively) regulated industry, and the scope of the search may be comprehensive in nature.

9.9. The Energy Reorganization Act of 1974 established the Nuclear Regulatory Commission (NRC) to formulate policy, develop regulations, issue licenses, and adjudicate issues, related to nuclear reactors and nuclear material. Businesses that run nuclear reactors must obtain licenses, keep detailed records, and allow inspections of both their facilities and their records. The standards for maintaining such facilities are extremely detailed and are enforced through civil penalties and license suspensions and revocations. Owners of the Tempe Nuclear Reactor refused to let an NRC inspector into the plant on two separate occasions because the inspector did not have a search warrant. Analyze whether an inspector would likely need a warrant under the Court's current approach to closely (or pervasively) regulated industries.

ANSWER:

9.10. Occasionally, agencies want to search individuals in employment or educational settings by imposing drug tests even though the employer has no particularized evidence justifying probable cause. These cases are generally known as "special needs" cases. Which of the following warrantless searches would violate the Fourth Amendment?

(A)   Breath and urine testing of hospital employees working with small children.

(B)   Blood and urine testing of railroad crew members immediately after a major train accident.

(C)   Urine testing of Customs Service employees who were being promoted to positions involving drug interdiction.

(D)   Urine testing of public school athletes where drugs were a confirmed problem.

9.11. You represent the Food and Drug Administration (FDA). An FDA inspector received information that a peanut plant in Georgia was not checking peanuts for a specific toxin. This toxin does not cause life-threatening injuries to people, but it does cause stomach discomfort. The inspector plans to visit the plant tomorrow. She would like to know whether she should obtain a warrant before visiting the plant or just show up and ask for permission to inspect the plant? She also wants to know whether, if she obtains a warrant, she may search for any and all violations or only for circumstances related to the complaint. What would you advise?

ANSWER:

9.12. Agencies may require regulated entities to keep records and to report information to them. Which of the following statements accurately summarizes the authority of administrative agencies to impose such requirements?

(A)   Administrative agencies may impose record keeping and reporting requirements based solely on constitutional authority.

(B)   Administrative agencies can only impose record keeping and reporting requirements when based on express statutory authority.

(C)   Administrative agencies may impose record keeping and reporting requirements based on express or implied statutory authority.

(D)   Administrative agencies may impose record keeping and reporting requirements based on regulatory authority.

9.13. How does the Paperwork Reduction Act affect an agency's ability to obtain information from regulated entities?

   (A)   The Act requires agencies to complete an environmental impact statement if they wish to collect information from the public.

   (B)   The Act requires agencies to analyze the financial impact of any collection requirement that may have a significant impact on the State, local, or tribal government.

   (C)   The Act requires agencies to review regulations relating to collection requirements for their impact on small businesses and consider less burdensome alternatives.

   (D)   The Act prohibits agencies from requiring the collection of information from private persons without first obtaining permission from the Office of Management and Budget.

9.14. You represent the Environmental Protection Agency (EPA). Your client would like to issue a subpoena to a witness who has information about an alleged illegal dumping for an enforcement case. Assume the enabling statute authorizes the EPA to issue subpoenas. What do you advise?

   (A)   Agencies may issue subpoenas and impose sanctions on anyone who fails to abide by a subpoena.

   (B)   Agencies may issue subpoenas to compel witnesses to testify and to produce documents so long as the subpoena is particularized.

   (C)   Agencies may issue subpoenas to search for evidence of legal violations by requesting all of a regulated entity's records.

   (D)   Agencies may issue subpoenas only when less drastic information-gathering techniques are not available.

9.15. The Fifth Amendment assures that no person "shall be compelled in any criminal case to be a witness against himself." Although agencies do not have the power to impose criminal sanctions, they can impose civil penalties. Moreover, specific witnesses may be concerned that testifying in a civil case may lead to criminal consequences. Write a short answer regarding whether the Fifth Amendment applies to regulated entities, to a regulated entity's officers, to its corporate records, and to non-criminal penalties

ANSWER:

9.16. In 1978, Congress enacted legislation that embedded an Inspector General (IG) within each major agency. What is the IG's purpose within the agency?

   (A)   To conduct audits within the agency.

   (B)   To investigate instances of fraud and abuse of the agency's programs.

(C)   To report periodically to Congress about agency activities.

(D)   All of the above.

10.1. Pursuant to the Freedom of Information Act (FOIA), agencies must:

(A) Within 20 days, provide available information at no cost when a requester reasonably describes the records being sought.

(B) Promptly provide available information at no cost when a requester specifically describes the records being sought.

(C) Within 20 days, provide available information at some cost when a requester reasonably describes the records being sought.

(D) Promptly provide available information at some cost when a requester reasonably describes the records being sought.

10.2. The FOIA requires an agency that receives a request for information to:

(A) Decide within 20 days whether to comply with the request.

(B) Provide the requester with an explanation for any refusal to comply.

(C) Decide all appeals of denials within 20 days of the appeal.

(D) All of the above.

10.3. Under the FOIA, an agency may withhold which of the following information?

(A) Classified information.

(B) Internal agency personnel rules.

(C) Trade secrets.

(D) All of the above.

10.4. Under the FOIA, can agencies charge any fees for document search and production?

(A) For non-commercial requests, the agency cannot charge any fees.

(B) For commercial requests, the agency can charge a reasonable fee for searching, duplicating, and reviewing requests.

    (C)   For news media and educational institutions, the agency can charge a reasonable fee for searching, duplicating, or reviewing requests.

    (D)   All of the above.

10.5. If an agency denies a FOIA request and any subsequent appeal, then the requester:

    (A)   May seek judicial review under the FOIA or APA § 706.

    (B)   May seek judicial review under the FOIA.

    (C)   May seek judicial review under APA § 706.

    (D)   May not seek judicial review under either the FOIA or APA § 706.

10.6. Under the FOIA, when a requester seeks review of a denial, which of the following is true?

    (A)   The agency bears the burden of proving that the information is exempt from disclosure.

    (B)   The requester bears the burden of proving that the information is subject to disclosure.

    (C)   The reviewing court applies *Chevron* deference to determine whether the denial is valid.

    (D)   The reviewing court applies arbitrary and capricious review to determine whether the denial is valid.

10.7. Assume you represent a foreign national who claims that he worked for the CIA in the past. He has requested all documents relating to his employment from the CIA, but the agency has provided no information. The agency claims the information is exempt from disclosure because it is classified. You file suit to challenge the CIA's refusal to comply with the FOIA and the agency's claim that the documents are classified (ignore the Privacy Act). The court orders the agency to file a Vaughn index. Explain to your client the purpose and contents of a Vaughn index.

ANSWER:

10.8. To satisfy the "need" requirement in FOIA, a requester:

    (A)   Must show a clear need for the requested information.

    (B)   Must show a likelihood that the requested information will produce needed evidence.

    (C)   Need not make any showing regarding the relevance of the requested information.

    (D)   Must show a clear need for the requested information and that it is not privileged.

10.9. To satisfy the "description" requirement in FOIA, a requester:

(A) Must generally describe the information and records sought.

(B) Must reasonably describe the information and records sought.

(C) Must specifically describe the information and records sought.

(D) Must describe the information and records sought with sufficient particularity.

10.10. The Government in Sunshine Act (Sunshine Act) applies to which of the following agencies?

(A) The Food and Drug Administration.

(B) The Environmental Protection Agency.

(C) The Securities and Exchange Commission.

(D) The Justice Department.

10.11. You work for the Federal Trade Commission (FTC), which is an independent agency subject to the Sunshine Act. The FTC has two, regularly scheduled monthly meetings. At each meeting, all of the commissioners attend. At the first meeting, the commissioners discuss and fully vet issues relevant to agency business in full, but stop short of making any final decisions. Final decisions are made during the second monthly meeting, which can be kept short because of the full vetting that occurred at the first meeting. Currently, the FTC abides by the Sunshine Act for its second monthly meetings, but not for its first. You have been asked whether the agency's meeting practices violate the Sunshine Act. What do you advise the agency (assume none of the exceptions apply)?

ANSWER:

10.12. The Federal Advisory Committee Act (FACA) was enacted to ensure that advice given by advisory committees to government officials would be objective and accessible to the public. FACA imposes a variety of open-meeting and disclosure requirements on entities meeting the definition of "advisory committee." Assume the president establishes a National Genetically Modified Food Policy Development Group to advise and make recommendations to the president about genetically modified foods and public health. The members of the group include a number of agency heads, including the Secretary of the Food and Drug Administration, and assistants, who are all employees of the federal government. The vice president serves as chairperson. The group makes a recommendation to the president, but fails to make public all of the documents it generated. A watch-dog group files suit, alleging that the president's advisory group violated FACA because private lobbyists regularly attended and fully participated in the group's nonpublic meetings; however, the lobbyists did not vote in or veto decisions. Discuss whether the National Genetically Modified Food Policy Development Group is an advisory committee subject to FACA.

ANSWER:

10.13. Regarding attorney's fees in cases against federal agencies, which of the following is *NOT* true?

    (A)   Prevailing parties generally must bear the expense of their own legal representation.

    (B)   Non-prevailing parties generally must bear the expense of both side's legal representation.

    (C)   Citizen suit provisions often include statutory authorization for courts to award costs, including attorney's fees, to prevailing parties.

    (D)   Contingency fee arrangements are permitted.

10.14. The Equal Access to Justice Act (EAJA) applies only to some administrative actions. The EAJA allows prevailing parties (other than the government) to recover reasonable attorney's fees and other expenses, such as expert witness fees and investigation costs. Regarding the types of proceedings to which the EAJA applies, which of the following is *NOT* an accurate statement?

    (A)   The EAJA authorizes judges to award fees and expenses in actions filed in federal court, seeking judicial review of agency actions.

    (B)   The EAJA authorizes judges to award fees and expenses when agencies bring suit to enforce a regulated entity's compliance with a statutory or regulatory requirement.

    (C)   The EAJA does not authorize judges to award fees and expenses in agency proceedings involving ratemaking or the granting or renewing of a license.

    (D)   The EAJA authorizes judges to award fees and expenses in all agency adjudications in which the government is represented by counsel.

10.15. Miss Hattie's Nursing Home, Inc., failed an inspection by the New Carolina State Fire Marshall because some of the residents were incapable of "self-preservation," as defined by a state statute. Miss Hattie's sued for declaratory and injunctive relief, claiming that the State's "self-preservation" law violated the Americans with Disabilities Act. After the lawsuit was filed, the State legislature amended the law by removing the "self-preservation" requirement. Miss Hattie's voluntarily dismissed its lawsuit. Subsequently, Miss Hattie's filed for attorney's fees. Would a court find Miss Hattie's to be a prevailing party?

    (A)   A court would likely find that Miss Hattie's is a prevailing party because the litigation served as a catalyst to encourage the State to change its law.

    (B)   A court would likely find that Miss Hattie's is a prevailing party because the litigation brought about a voluntary change in State's law.

    (C)   A court would likely find that Miss Hattie's is not a prevailing party because it did not succeed on all of its claims against the State.

(D)   A court would likely find that Miss Hattie's is not a prevailing party because it did not receive a litigated judgment or court-endorsed settlement agreement.

10.16. Assume that Arnolds Inc.'s license is revoked by a federal agency. Arnolds' net worth is less than the statutory amount. At an adversarial hearing in which the agency is represented by counsel, the Administrative Judge (AJ) overturns the agency's decision to revoke the license. On appeal to the agency, the agency heads uphold the AJ's determination. Arnolds incurs fees and other expenses in excess of $50,000 to win back his license. Formal APA procedures do not apply to this agency's licensing cases because no statute requires a hearing on the record. Arnolds seeks his fees and other expenses under the EAJA. How should the agency rule?

(A)   The agency should deny the request because the EAJA does not apply to informal adjudications.

(B)   The agency should deny the request because the EAJA does not apply to licensing actions.

(C)   The agency should grant the request because the agency was represented at the hearing by counsel.

(D)   The agency should grant the request because Arnolds was the prevailing party and the type of proceeding is irrelevant.

10.17. Assume that Becky's license is revoked by a different federal agency. Becky's net worth is less than the statutory amount. At an adversarial hearing in which the agency is represented by counsel, the Administrative Law Judge (ALJ) overturns the agency's decision to revoke the license. On appeal to the agency, the agency reverses the ALJ's determination. Formal APA procedures *do* apply to this agency's licensing cases. Becky appeals the agency's determination in federal district court and wins. Becky seeks the fees and other expenses she incurred *both* for the agency process and for the judicial appeal. Assuming only the EAJA applies, how is a court likely to rule?

(A)   The court will likely deny the fees and expenses she incurred at both the agency level and at the district court level.

(B)   The court will likely award the fees and expenses she incurred at the agency level, but deny the fees and expenses she incurred at the trial level.

(C)   The court will likely deny the fees and expenses she incurred at the agency level, but award the fees and expenses she incurred at the trial level.

(D)   The court will likely award the fees and expenses she incurred at both the agency level and at the trial level.

10.18. Assume a federal agency alleges that a business owes a civil penalty of $1,000,000. The statute requires the agency to conduct civil penalty cases "on the record after an opportunity for hearing." After a hearing, the ALJ determines that the business owes a penalty of only $500. The ALJ further determines that the business' conduct was neither willful nor otherwise done in bad faith. The business incurs attorney's fees of $50,000 in resisting the agency's penalty demand. The business owner seeks attorney's fees. Assuming the other requirements of EAJA are met, how is a court likely to rule?

(A)   The court will likely award the fees because the difference between the amount of the penalty assessed and the penalty imposed shows that the agency acted in bad faith.

(B)   The court will likely award the fees because the initial penalty was substantially in excess of the amount the ALJ awarded, regardless of whether bad faith is shown.

(C)   The court will likely deny the fees because the business was not a prevailing party in that it must pay a penalty.

(D)   The court will likely deny the fees because the EAJA does not apply to informal agency actions.

10.19. When an award for attorney's fees and other expenses under the EAJA hinges on whether the position of the United States was substantially justified, which of the following is an accurate statement?

(A)   "Substantially justified" means the agency's position had some substance and a fair possibility of success.

(B)   "Substantially justified" means the agency's position had sufficient support to preclude a finding of frivolousness.

(C)   "Substantially justified" means the agency's position had a reasonable basis in both law and fact.

(D)   "Substantially justified" means the agency's position had sufficient support to preclude Rule 11 sanctions.

10.20. Assume that the Occupational Safety and Health Administration (OSHA) has brought an enforcement proceeding against an employer who has allegedly violated certain safety standards promulgated by OSHA (given OSHA's interpretation of those standards) and that OSHA's proceedings must follow the APA's formal adjudication procedures. Assume further that the employer lost the ALJ hearing but prevailed on appeal to the Occupational Safety and Health Review Commission (OSHRC) (a separate agency that hears all of OSHA's appeals). The employer, as the prevailing party, submitted an application for an award of attorney's fees and other expenses within the 30-day timeframe.

Regarding recovery of fees and other expenses under the EAJA, which of the following is an accurate statement?

(A)   OSHA must award the attorney's fees and expenses to the employer, as the prevailing party, regardless of whether the agency's position was substantially justified.

(B)   OSHA must award the attorney's fees and expenses to the employer, as the prevailing party, unless the agency's position was substantially justified.

(C)   OSHA may defer the decision of whether to award the attorney's fees and other expenses if OSHA appeals OSHRC's determination.

(D)   B & C are both correct.

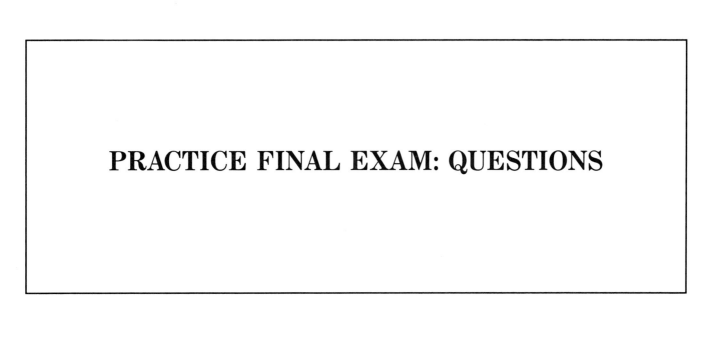

PRACTICE FINAL EXAM: QUESTIONS

INSTRUCTIONS: Suggested time for the examination is 90 minutes.

1. Assume that a food manufacturer successfully argues in court that the Food & Drug Administration's (FDA) informal rulemaking did not comply with the *procedural* requirements for notice and comment rulemaking, how would a court likely rule?

   (A)   A court will likely uphold the FDA rule if the FDA can demonstrate that its failure to follow procedure was reasonable.

   (B)   A court will likely void the FDA rule, and the FDA cannot re-promulgate the proposed rule.

   (C)   A court will likely void the FDA rule, but the FDA can try to re-promulgate the proposed rule.

   (D)   A court will likely void the FDA rule, but the FDA can try to re-promulgate the proposed rule so long as it uses formal rulemaking procedures.

2. Beginning with President Reagan, presidents of the United States have, through Executive Orders, tried to centralize oversight of agency rulemaking and to enhance planning and coordination of rulemaking. Regarding Executive Order 12866 and the roles of the Office of Management and Budget (OMB) and the Office of Information and Regulatory Affairs (OIRA), which of the following is *NOT* an accurate statement?

   (A)   OMB has authority to review an agency's rulemaking plans to ensure consistency with the President's priorities.

   (B)   OIRA has authority to require agencies to assess the potential costs and benefits of significant regulatory actions.

   (C)   OIRA has the authority to disapprove of any regulatory scheme selected by an agency that fails to maximize net benefits.

   (D)   OIRA may require agencies to re-assess the need for, and appropriateness of existing, significant regulations in light of changed circumstances.

3. Regarding agency action, generally, which of the following is a correct statement?

   (A)   When an agency engages in rulemaking, the APA, as judicially interpreted, rarely requires formal, trial-like procedures.

(B)   When an agency engages in adjudication, the APA, as judicially interpreted, usually requires formal, trial-like procedures.

(C)   When an agency engages in rulemaking, the APA, as judicially interpreted, usually requires non-legislative procedures.

(D)   When an agency engages in rulemaking, the APA, as judicially interpreted, allows the agency to choose whether to follow either the formal, trial-like procedures or informal notice and comment procedures.

4.   Explain why non-legislative rules are sometimes referred to as publication rules.

ANSWER:

5.   Assume that a claimant requested a formal APA hearing after the Social Security Administration (SSA) denied her request for Social Security disability benefits. At the hearing, the claimant's physician and oncologist both testified. At the hearing's conclusion, the Administrative Law Judge (ALJ) affirmed the denial. The claimant sought judicial review of the SSA's denial in federal district court. Assuming that the district court upholds the denial of benefits (and assuming no statutory, regulatory, or common law authorization for costs or fees other than the Equal Access to Justice Act (EAJA)), which of the following is an accurate statement?

(A)   Under the EAJA, the court *must* award attorney's fees, other expenses, and costs incurred in the litigation to the SSA — *only if* the court finds that the claimant's position was substantially justified.

(B)   Under the EAJA, the court *must* award attorney's fees, other expenses, and costs incurred in the litigation to the SSA — *unless* the court finds that the claimant's position was substantially justified.

(C)   Under the EAJA, the court *may* award expenses and costs incurred in the litigation to the SSA, *including* attorney's fees — *unless* the court finds that the claimant's position was substantially justified.

(D)   Under the EAJA, the court *may* award expenses and costs incurred in the litigation to the SSA, *other than* attorney's fees — *regardless* of whether the court finds that the claimant's position was substantially justified.

6.   Assume that the automobile industry wants the Department of Transportation to modify a rule pertaining to use of airbags in compact vehicles and that the industry files a formal, written petition requesting such an amendment. Which of the following is an accurate statement regarding the industry's petition?

(A)   The agency may ignore the request because the industry would never have a right to judicial review of the inaction.

(B)   The agency may delay acting on the request for many years before the industry would have a right to judicial review of the delay.

(C)   The agency may deny the industry's request if the agency can demonstrate it has other priorities requiring more immediate attention.

(D)   The agency may deny the industry's request and need not explain its reasons for the denial.

7.   Assume that the National Park Service (NPS) promulgated a rule banning the use of snowmobiles in national parks. The statute required that the NPS promulgate rules "after hearing." The NPS used notice and comment rulemaking procedures. The Final Rule, along with a general statement of basis and purpose, was published in the Federal Register on January 1, 20XX. Less than 30 days later, a snowmobiling group called Freedom Riders led a highly publicized parade of snowmobiles through Yellowstone National Park to protest the ban. NPS rangers issued $300 citations to the 50 riders who participated in the parade, charging them with violating the ban in the newly promulgated regulation.

Regarding the NPS enforcement of the new ban, which of the following is an accurate statement?

(A)   The citations are valid because the NPS published its Final Rule banning snowmobiles in national parks in the Federal Register before the parade occurred.

(B)   The citations are *not* valid because, under the APA, the new rule banning snowmobiles in national parks could not have been effective in less than 30 days.

(C)   The citations are valid because the Freedom Riders had actual notice of the terms of the new rule banning snowmobiles in national parks.

(D)   The citations are *not* valid because the NPS used notice and comment procedures when it should have used formal rulemaking procedures.

8.   Explain the differences between executive agencies and independent agencies.

ANSWER:

9.   Which of the following is *NOT* agency adjudication (for this question only, assume the APA applies to states, cities, and municipalities)?

(A)   A Chicago police officer determined that a car parked on a city street was "parked illegally" and, pursuant to city law, left a notice on the car explaining that if the car was not moved within 72 hours it would be towed.

(B)   A decision by the Federal Housing Authority (FHA) to terminate Capital Mortgage, Inc.'s authority to originate single-family home mortgages insured by FHA.

   (C)   A city's decision (pursuant to and in conformity with a state statute authorizing municipalities to assess taxes) that property owners should pay a special tax for the construction of a road.

   (D)   A determination by the National Transportation Safety Board (NTSB) that a flight instructor's pilot certificate should be suspended for violating statutory aircraft maintenance standards.

10. Please write a short answer describing when warrantless administrative inspections are constitutional.

ANSWER:

11. When the Environmental Protection Agency (EPA) publishes a proposed rule and, after receiving comments, adopts a different final rule, the final rule will be struck down after judicial review unless:

   (A)   The EPA's decision to change the proposed rule is reasonable in light of the comments received.

   (B)   The EPA's decision to change the proposed rule is supported by substantial evidence.

   (C)   The EPA's decision to change the proposed rule is not arbitrary and capricious.

   (D)   The EPA's final rule is a logical outgrowth of the proposed rule.

12. A federal agency is obligated to use rulemaking rather than adjudication in taking a particular action in what situations?

   (A)   When the advantages to the public of rulemaking outweigh the agency's need for flexibility in meeting unforeseen circumstances.

   (B)   When the agency's choice of adjudication over rulemaking is an abuse of discretion, such that the unfairness to the regulated entity outweighs the convenience to the agency.

   (C)   When the agency wishes to announce a policy that will be applied to a broad class of regulated parties.

   (D)   When a large number of parties who would be affected by the new policy request a rulemaking hearing.

13. Under modern administrative law precedent, which of the following statements correctly identifies Congress' authority to delegate power to administrative agencies?

   (A)   The U.S. Constitution prohibits Congress from delegating quasi-legislative power to the executive.

(B) The U.S. Constitution prohibits Congress from delegating judicial-like power to the executive.

(C) The U.S. Constitution allows Congress to delegate only executive power to the executive.

(D) The U.S. Constitution allows Congress to delegate quasi-legislative power so long as Congress provides an intelligible principle cabining the delegation.

14. Jim Worth works for Mobile, Inc. and bought stock for $10/share, allegedly based on inside information. The stock now trades at $20/share. Assume that the Security and Exchange Commission brought an action against Jim to recoup the gain. While his case was pending before an Administrative Law Judge (ALJ), the agency head gave several speeches during which she stressed the evils of insider trading and the need to hold people accountable. The ALJ finds for Jim, but the SEC reverses the decision. Jim files suit, alleging that his constitutional rights were violated. How would the court likely rule?

(A) The court would likely uphold the agency decision unless the court finds the decision to be arbitrary and capricious.

(B) The court would likely uphold the agency decision unless the court finds the decision to not be supported by substantial evidence.

(C) The court would likely uphold the agency decision unless the court finds that the agency head's actions indicated case-specific predisposition.

(D) The court would likely reverse the agency decision due to impermissible ex parte communications.

15. Congress amends a statute administered by the Securities and Exchange Commission (SEC) requiring the SEC to release a public audit of every public accounting firm found to have engaged in criminal misconduct "after a hearing" before the agency. The SEC's procedural rules, adopted without notice and comment procedures, provide for the submission of written evidence but no opportunity for oral testimony or the presentation of witnesses. Author Anderson, Inc., a national accounting firm that was found to have engaged in criminal misconduct, challenges the SEC's rules in federal court arguing that the rules should have been promulgated pursuant to notice and comment procedures and should have provided for both oral testimony and presentation of witnesses because the statute requires formal adjudication. How should the court rule?

(A) For the SEC, because Author Anderson would not have standing.

(B) For the SEC, because neither claim has merit.

(C) For Author Anderson, because the SEC was required to use notice and comment procedures.

(D) For Author Anderson, because the SEC is required to use formal adjudication procedures and must allow oral testimony and witnesses.

16. The Fair Labor Standards Act ("FLSA") defines when employers must pay minimum wages and overtime to employees. Prior to 1966, employees of ordinary laundries and dry cleaning establishments were not subject to the Act's minimum wage and overtime requirements because section 13(a)(3) specifically exempted "any employee employed by any establishment engaged in laundering, cleaning, or repairing clothing or fabrics."

The National Automatic Laundry and Cleaning Counsel ("NALCC") is a national trade association for the coin-operated laundry and dry cleaning industry. In 1963, NALCC sent a letter to the Department of Labor's Wage and Hour Division asking whether coin-operated laundries were included within section 13(a)(3) exemption. The Administrator of the agency responded that, because coin-operated launderettes were "engaged in renting the service of the laundry machines rather than engaged in laundering or cleaning," section 13(a)(3) did not apply. However, the letter continued by explaining that another exception applied, section 13(a)(2)'s exception for conventional retail.

In 1966, Congress amended the FLSA by removing section13(a)(3) and provisions specifying that establishments "engaged in laundering, cleaning or repairing clothing or fabrics" could no longer qualify for the retail exemption of section 13(a)(2). NALCC believed that its members were unaffected by the 1966 amendments because coin-operated laundries had been determined by the Administrator's 1963 letter to be renting the service of laundry machines, not "engaged in laundering, cleaning or repair of clothing or fabrics." NALCC sent a letter to the agency, saying, "We wish to confirm that the 1963 interpretation still applies to our client's business." By letter, the Head of the agency replied, in pertinent part:

>   The legislative history of the 1966 amendments to the FLSA makes it clear that a coin-operated launderette or dry cleaning service is engaged in laundering or cleaning clothing or fabrics within the meaning of the act. The amendments extend the coverage of the act to employees in enterprises engaged in laundering, cleaning or repairing clothing or fabrics. No exception applies.

Employers who violate the FLSA are subject not only to injunctive enforcement proceedings under the Act, but may also be subject to criminal liability. Additionally, such employers are subject to double damages in suits brought by affected employees. Please write a short answer discussing whether the agency's response to the letter is ripe for judicial review.

ANSWER:

17. The Federal Trade Commission (FTC) proposed a rule that would require internet providers to embed a program in their software that blocks transmission of sexually explicit language. During the notice and comment rulemaking, the director of the Office of Management and Budget (OMB) called the FTC rulemaking director for a status report. During the conversation, he mentioned that the President strongly favored such a rule. He also suggested that certain important members of Congress would look fondly on the FTC should it promulgate the regulation. He hinted that OMB would add "substantial" additional enforcement funds to the FTC's budget request if the rule were approved. After notice and comment rulemaking in which the industry raised numerous technical and constitutional objections, the FTC promulgated the rule as proposed. A review of the

record shows that the decision could have gone either way. The National Broadcasting Association has filed suit, challenging the communications. Assuming reviewability, what is the likely result?

(A) A court will find that the regulation is invalid because the FTC failed to docket the ex parte communications with OMB.

(B) A court will find that the regulation is invalid because OMB influenced the decision by offering to increase FTC's budget.

(C) A court will find that the regulation is valid regardless of whether the comments were ex parte.

(D) A court will find that the comments were not ex parte because they involved status reports, which are permissible.

18. Assume that the National Transportation Safety Board (NTSB) sought records from Chrysler Corporation related to the manufacturing of its new ultra sports model automobile. Chrysler refused to comply, claiming that it would suffer injury if it released its records to the agency because federal rules would require the NTSB to disclose the records to Chrysler's competitors should the NTSB receive a Freedom of Information (FOIA) request for the records. Please write a short answer discussing whether the objection is valid. Assume that there are no relevant exceptions within FOIA that would allow the NTSB to withhold the records.

ANSWER:

19. Which of the following is/are *federal* administrative agency(s) under the APA?
   I. National Public Radio
  II. The Central Intelligence Agency
 III. The Republican Party
  IV. The President
   V. The Office of Management and Budget

(A) I, III, and IV.

(B) II and V.

(C) II, IV, and V.

(D) V only.

20. Under the EAJA, which of the following prevailing parties in an agency proceeding would be *ineligible* to recover fees and other expenses?

(A) An individual with a net worth of $1 million.

(B)   A business with 800 employees and a net worth of $8 million.

(C)   A tax-exempt charitable organization with a net worth of $10 million.

(D)   A city government with 400 employees and a net worth of $3 million.

21.   Under the Medicare Act, hospitals are reimbursed for certain services provided to Medicare recipients. The Act authorizes hospitals to appeal reimbursement decisions to the Provider Reimbursement Review Board (the Board) of the Department of Health and Human Services (HHS). The Act further authorizes the Board to establish procedures to implement the providers' right to appeal. The Board issued a rule that provides as follows: "A provider appealing a reimbursement determination must comply with the Board's schedule for submission of one or more position papers. If the provider fails to submit a final position paper to the Board by the scheduled due date, the Board may dismiss the appeal."

Assume that Memorial Hospital filed a timely appeal following a disallowance of approximately $290,000 of the reimbursement Memorial Hospital requested. The Board's schedule of submissions required preliminary position papers by November 1, 2003, and final papers by February 1, 2004. Due to confusion within the hospital's administrative offices, Memorial Hospital failed to file either a preliminary or a final position paper. The Board thus dismissed Memorial's appeal. Memorial Hospital has challenged the Board's rule regarding dismissal of appeals as being invalid because the Board failed to use notice and comment rulemaking procedures. How will a court likely rule on Memorial Hospital's motion?

(A)   A court will likely hold that the Board's rule is valid because it would have been impractical for the Board to use notice and comment procedures for a rule that merely prescribes the manner and time by which the parties present themselves to the agency.

(B)   A court will likely hold that the Board's rule is valid because the Board's rule does not alter the substantive standards the Board uses to review provider claims for reimbursement.

(C)   A court will likely hold that the Board's rule is *not* valid because the Board's rule has a sufficiently grave effect on Memorial Hospital's substantive right to have a hearing pursuant to the Medicare Act.

(D)   A court will likely hold that the Board's rule is *not* valid because choices concerning what "process is due" in adjudicatory agency actions necessarily encode substantive value judgments.

22.   Cattle ranchers challenged the decision of the U.S. Fish and Wildlife Services to limit the number of grazing permits that would be available for 20 identified federal lands. The ranchers allege that the agency made its determination without using "the best scientific and commercial data available" as required by the Endangered Species Act ("ESA"). The ranchers filed suit under the APA. The ESA specifically requires anyone challenging the agency's action to appeal to the agency prior to filing suit and to appeal any adverse agency decision. The ESA does not stay the agency's decision during the appeal process. Assuming

the ranchers have a direct injury, is the action reviewable under the APA?

(A)   No, unless the ranchers exhaust their administrative remedies first.

(B)   No, because there is no discrete agency action to be reviewed.

(C)   No, because the ranchers' claim is not yet ripe for judicial review.

(D)   Yes, because the ranchers are within the zone of interests protected by the APA.

23.   Which of the following is the appropriate "client" of a lawyer in the General Counsel's office of the Department of Transportation?

(A)   The government of the United States.

(B)   The President of the United States.

(C)   The Secretary of the Department of Transportation.

(D)   All of the above.

The following fact pattern applies to Questions 24 and 25.

John and Jane Johnson have been living every parent's nightmare. Accused of abuse by a rebellious child, they were arrested, were criminally charged, and had their other children removed from their care. After a doctor testified that the abuse charges could not be true, the state dismissed the criminal case against them. Upon the Johnsons' petition, the court found the Johnsons factually innocent of the charges for which they had been arrested and ordered the arrest records to be sealed and destroyed. However, the Johnsons still had a problem. They had been placed on the state's Child Abuse Central Index ("CACI"), a database of known or suspected child abusers.

The Child Abuse and Neglect Reporting Act ("CANRA") identifies specific individuals who must report instances of known or suspected child abuse and neglect to either a law enforcement agency or a child welfare agency. These agencies, in turn, are required to conduct "an active investigation" to determine whether the incident is "unfounded or not unfounded." CANRA also provides that these agencies must send a written report of every case of known or suspected child abuse or severe neglect that is determined to be "not unfounded" (Child Abuse Reports) to the state Department of Justice (DOJ). CANRA requires that the DOJ maintain an index of all Child Abuse Reports: this index, the CACI, is maintained by a computerized data bank.

CANRA states that the DOJ shall make the information in the CACI available to a broad range of third parties for a variety of purposes. For example, the information is provided to persons required by statute to make inquiries for purposes of pre-employment background investigations for teachers, those obtaining child care licenses or employment, those seeking adoption, and those seeking to have child placements. Persons obtaining the CACI information are responsible for obtaining a copy of the Child Abuse Report from the reporting agency. Additionally, such persons are responsible for drawing independent conclusions regarding the quality of the evidence disclosed and for determining whether sufficient evidence supports a conclusion that abuse is "not un-founded."

CANRA requires that when an investigating agency forwards a Child Abuse Report to the DOJ, that agency shall also notify the known or suspected child abuser in writing of the report to the

CACI. The agency must also provide information about how the suspected child abuser may obtain a copy of the Child Abuse Report.

CANRA has no provision for removing an individual listed in the CACI. Further, CANRA offers no procedure for challenging a listing on the CACI. CANRA does provide that "if a Child Abuse Report has previously been filed that subsequently proves to be unfounded," the DOJ shall be notified in writing of that fact and shall not retain the report. The statute does not describe who must notify the DOJ of that fact or of how the determination that a report has "subsequently prove[d] to be unfounded" is to be made. CANRA also provides that the CACI "shall be continually updated by the DOJ and shall not contain any reports that are determined to be unfounded." By using the passive voice, CANRA fails to specify who is supposed to determine that a report is unfounded. CANRA also provides that "submitting agencies are responsible for the accuracy, completeness, and retention of Child Abuse Reports," which suggests that the investigating agencies are also somehow responsible for removing reports that are determined to be unfounded.

Although CANRA provides no procedure for an individual to challenge a CACI listing, a listed person could presumably request that the original investigating agency reconsider whether the initial finding was correct. Additionally, such a person could presumably request that any inquiring agencies conduct an independent investigation.

The Johnsons have filed an action in federal court, arguing that this regulatory scheme violates their Fourteenth Amendment right to procedural due process by listing and continuing to list them on the CACI without the existence of any available process to challenge that listing. The Johnsons alleged that listing them on CACI has harmed their reputation and burdened their ability to pursue some of their normal goals and activities. For example, they assert that they would like to work or volunteer at a neighborhood community center offering child care and have proffered an affidavit from the Human Resources Manager at the center stating that all adults must undergo a CACI check prior to obtaining clearance to volunteer or teach at the center.

24.   Would a court likely determine that the Johnsons have a constitutionally protected liberty interest such that due process is triggered?

   (A)   No, the Johnsons do not have a constitutionally protected liberty interest because being placed on the CACI does not mean that the person suspected of child abuse has been found guilty of child abuse or neglect.

   (B)   No, the Johnsons do not have a constitutionally protected liberty interest. Although the agency's action has arguably harmed the Johnsons' reputations, the agency's action has not foreclosed future employment opportunities because information is accessible only to designated types of third parties and because inquiring third parties are cautioned to obtain Child Abuse Reports and to draw independent conclusions.

   (C)   Yes, the Johnsons do have a constitutionally protected liberty interest because agency action has harmed the Johnsons' reputation and has foreclosed future employment opportunities by virtue of the Child Abuse Reports being available to and accessible by third parties required to conduct background checks.

(D)   Yes, the Johnsons do have a constitutionally protected liberty interest because the Johnsons can bring a suit for defamation and thus, have suffered the requisite harm required.

25.   Assume, regardless of your answer to the prior question, that the court determined that the Johnsons had a constitutionally protected liberty interest. Would a court likely find a due process violation?

(A)   The court would likely find a due process violation because unsubstantiated accusations impose a gravely serious burden on persons listed on the CACI and, further, the state does not have an interest in false information being included in the CACI.

(B)   The court would likely not find a violation of due process. Although the Johnsons' interest in not being included on the list in error is very strong, the state has a very strong interest in preventing child abuse. The CACI index furthers the state's interest in an efficient way.

(C)   The court would likely not find a violation of due process. Although the Johnsons' interest in not being included on the list in error is very strong, the state has a very strong interest in preventing child abuse. The CACI index furthers the state's interest in an efficient way. And, assuming the persons listed can ask the original investigating agency to reconsider its finding or ask "inquiring agencies" to conduct an independent investigation, the risk of erroneous deprivation is relatively low.

(D)   The court would likely find a violation of due process. Although the Johnsons' interest in not being included on the list in error is very strong, additional safeguards, such as an informal hearing by which a listed person can ask for reconsideration upon an appropriate showing, would not be too burdensome for the state.

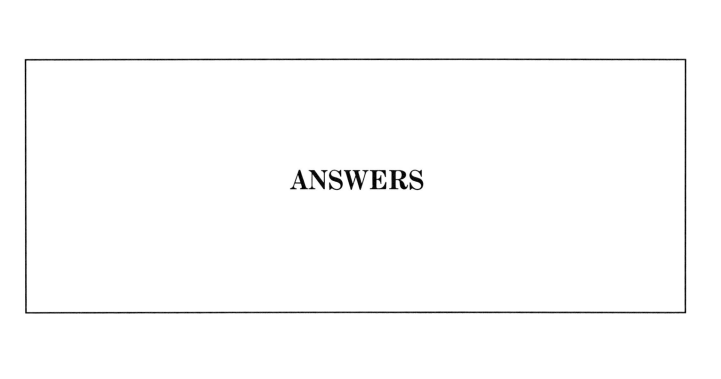

ANSWERS

1.1. **Answer (C) is correct.** During the early years of the New Deal, the federal courts were often hostile to new regulatory programs. However, following President Roosevelt's thwarted "court-packing" plan, the Supreme Court and the lower courts swung from hostility to deference, resulting in a substantial curtailment of rigorous judicial review of agency action. The APA was intended to provide tools to more readily oversee and monitor agency action.

Answer (A) is not correct. American administrative law grew out of the common law. As early as the seventeenth century, writs were used to control a growing number of administrative functions. However, laissez-faire principles prevailed from 1775–1875, when the role of administrative government was far less extensive than it is today. Beginning in 1875, the role of the administrative state grew, largely in the form of rate regulation of railroads and grain elevators. The Interstate Commerce Commission was established in 1887, and the Federal Trade Commission was created in 1914.

Answer (B) is not correct. It is generally understood that the APA was enacted in reaction to the rise of the administrative state which resulted from the New Deal agenda. More specifically, the APA was intended to provide tools to more readily oversee agency action. For example, the APA provided procedural checks on administrative action and reinvigorated judicial review of agency action.

Answer (D) is not correct. The phrase "the New Deal" refers to the ambitious agenda initiated by President Roosevelt in response to the collapse of the economy in the Great Depression. The agenda relied substantially on the need for a strong administrative state. The "New Dealers" created a host of new federal administrative agencies, expanded federal intervention in economic affairs, and laid the foundation for a national welfare state.

1.2. Agency proceedings recognized by the APA include rulemaking, adjudication, and licensing. Section 551(12) of the APA provides that the phrase "agency proceeding" means an agency process as defined by §§ 551(5), (7), and (9). Section 551(5) provides that "rulemaking" is the agency process for formulating, amending, or repealing a rule. Section 551(7) provides that "adjudication" is the agency process for the formulation of an order. And § 551(9) provides that "licensing" includes the agency process relating to licenses.

1.3. **Answer (D) is correct** because the ESC is an agency and because the exemption determination involves an agency proceeding and agency action.

Answer (A) is not correct because the ESC is an agency. The APA § 551(1) defines "agency" as "each authority of the Government of the United States, whether or not it is within or subject to review by another agency . . . . " The ESC is acting as an authority of the United States government. Additionally, the ESC does not fall within the specific exclusions set forth in § 551(1)(A)–(G).

Answer (B) is not correct. Even though the ESC is an agency, certain agency action is exempt from APA procedural requirements. However, this answer is not accurate for two reasons. First, because it appears to be referring to the exemption from rulemaking requirements (*see* APA § 553(a)(2)) and, as is discussed in the following Answer to 1.4, the ESC is not engaging in rulemaking. Second, although the BLM makes decisions relating to public property and thus might in some instances be exempt from the APA pursuant to § 553(a)(2), the determination by ESC relating to an exemption from the ESA prohibition does not fall within § 553(a)(2).

Answer (C) is not correct. Even though the ESC is an agency, certain agency action is exempt from APA procedural requirements. However, this statement is not accurate because it also appears to be referring to an exemption from certain rulemaking requirements (*see* APA § 553(b)(2)(A)); and as is discussed in the following Answer to 1.4, the ESC is not engaging in rulemaking.

1.4.   **Answer (B) is correct.** APA § 551(6) defines "order" as "the whole or a part of a final disposition, whether affirmative [or] negative . . . , of an agency in a matter other than rulemaking but including licensing." Because the determination is not a "rule," the matter was not "rulemaking." *See* APA § 551(5). However, the determination may be characterized as licensing. APA § 551(9) defines "licensing" as the "agency process respecting the grant . . . denial . . . or conditioning of a license"; and § 551(8) defines "license" as the "whole or part of an agency permit, certificate . . . statutory exemption or other form of permission." The BLM was seeking a statutory exemption.

Answer (A) is not correct. APA § 551(4) defines a "rule" as "an agency statement of general or particular applicability and future effect designed to implement, interpret, or prescribe law or policy or describing the organization, procedure, or practice requirements of an agency . . . . " Here, the determination has a more present effect and the determination is not designed to implement, interpret, or prescribe law or policy. The determination is better characterized as an application of the law to particular facts with present effect. The present effect of the determination is that the BLM's petition has been denied, and BLM thus cannot proceed with its plans.

Answer (C) is not correct. The determination may accurately be characterized as "agency action" since APA § 551(13) defines such action as "the whole or part of an agency rule, order, license . . . or the equivalent . . . thereof, ..." However, "agency action" is not limited to actions that are final.

Answer (D) is not correct because APA § 551(11) defines "relief" as a favorable disposition and the ESC denied the BLM's petition for the exemption.

1.5.   **Answer (D) is correct because it is not an accurate statement.** Some administrative regulation is grounded in non-economic justifications. For example, regulatory schemes such as the Social Security Act serve the purpose of redistributing resources from one group to another.

Answer (A) is not correct because it is an accurate statement. A natural monopolist can increase its profits by restricting output and charging higher than competitive prices. Some agencies thus strive to ensure allocative efficiency by setting prices at levels that approximate those that would exist under competitive conditions.

Answer (B) is not correct because it is an accurate statement. Eliminating excessive competition is a debatable justification for administrative regulation. One historical example is the protection previously provided to the airline industry through minimum price regulation. The underlying rationale was that, if prices were allowed to be cut too low through excessive competition, most of the competing firms would go out of business, thereby allowing the few surviving firms to set prices artificially high.

Answer (C) is not correct because it is an accurate statement. For competitive markets to work well, consumers need information with which to evaluate competing products. However, information defects exist in many markets. Government regulation is sometimes designed to compensate for inadequate information or to lower the costs to consumers for obtaining adequate information.

1.6.   **Answer (A) is correct.** Any agency charged with the authority to implement or enforce a regulatory scheme adopted by Congress has the authority to interpret the relevant statutory provisions. The key question is whether an agency has the power to engage in rulemaking or to enforce through adjudications. Thus, a grant of authority to promulgate substantive rules also will inherently authorize promulgation of interpretive rules.

Answer (B) is not correct. An agency has the power to promulgate substantive rules only if Congress has given it that power. The power to enforce a regulatory scheme may not carry with it the power to promulgate substantive rules. *Cf. National Petroleum Refiners Ass'n v. FTC*, 482 F.2d 672 (D.C. Cir. 1973).

Answer (C) is not correct. An agency can only promulgate rules within the scope of its delegated authority. Thus, one possible challenge to a rule promulgated by an agency is that it should be set aside on the grounds that the agency exceeded its authority. *See* APA § 706(2)(C).

Answer (D) is not correct. Even if an agency promulgates a rule within the scope of its delegated authority, that rule must comport with constitutional principles. Thus, one possible challenge to a rule promulgated by an agency is that it should be set aside on the grounds that the rule is contrary to a constitutional right, power, privilege, or immunity. *See* APA § 706(2)(B).

1.7.   **Answer (B) is correct answer because it is an accurate statement.** In *Chenery II*, the Supreme Court noted, among other things, that an agency "may not have had sufficient experience with a particular problem to warrant rigidifying its tentative judgment into a hard and fast rule. Or the problem may be so specialized and varying in nature as to be impossible of capture within the boundaries of a general rule." *See SEC v. Chenery Corp.*, 332 U.S. 194, 202–03 (1947) (*Chenery II*). Thus, using adjudication to make new legal principles is viewed as more acceptable when addressing an emerging regulatory problem arising from variable industry practices.

Answer (A) is not correct because it is not an accurate statement. The Supreme Court has recognized that, although an agency should consider making law as much as possible through rulemaking, agencies must have flexibility to deal with regulatory problems in the manner they deem most appropriate. Certain situations and regulatory problems arguably are better addressed through ad hoc litigation and the decision whether to proceed through rulemaking or adjudication is vested primarily in the informed discretion of the agency. *See Chenery II*.

Answer (C) is not correct because it is not an accurate statement. Although the decision whether to proceed through rulemaking or adjudication is vested primarily in the informed discretion of the agency, courts may set aside an order if the agency's use of adjudication amounts to an abuse of discretion. Imposing a substantial penalty or new liability on a regulated person or entity for violation of a legal principle not previously announced may, in some cases, warrant the setting aside of an agency order. *See, e.g., Nat'l Labor Relations Bd. v. Bell Aerospace Co. Div. of Textron, Inc.*, 416 U.S. 267 (1974).

Answer (D) is not correct because it is not an accurate statement. Although the decision whether to proceed through rulemaking or adjudication is vested primarily in the informed discretion of the agency, courts may set aside an order if the agency's use of adjudication amounts to an abuse of discretion. Substantial reliance by a regulated person or entity on the agency's prior practice may, in some cases, warrant the setting aside of an agency order — especially if the order imposes a substantial penalty or new liability on a regulated person or entity for violation of a legal principle not previously announced. *See, e.g., Nat'l Labor Relations Bd. v. Bell Aerospace Co. Div. of Textron, Inc.*, 416 U.S. 267 (1974).

1.8.   **Answer (B) is correct because it is not an accurate statement.** Congress may grant agencies the power to compel regulated entities to prepare and submit "reports" or other compilations of information.

Answer (A) is not correct because it is an accurate statement. Congress may grant agencies "subpoena power."

Answer (C) is not correct because it is an accurate statement. Congress may grant agencies the power to require regulated entities to permit inspection.

Answer (D) is not correct because it is an accurate statement. Congress may grant agencies the power to compel regulated entities to prepare and submit "reports" or other compilations of information.

1.9.   **Answer (C) is correct because it is an accurate statement.** The Freedom of Information Act, § 552(a)(2), requires agencies to maintain indexes and to make available for inspection and copying not only final opinions and other orders made in the adjudication of cases, but also statements of policy and interpretation not published in the *Federal Register*, administrative staff manuals and instructions to staff that affect the public, and copies of records that have been released to persons and that are likely to become the subject of subsequent requests.

Answer (A) is not correct because it is not an accurate statement. Agencies use the *Federal Register* to notify the public as to many agency actions; however, the *Federal Register* is published on a daily basis.

Answer (B) is not correct because it is not an accurate statement. The *Code of Federal Regulations* (CFR) contains all current agency regulations, not just those promulgated during the preceding 12 months.

Answer (D) is not correct because it is not an accurate statement. Section 552(a)(4)(A)(i) authorizes agencies to promulgate, pursuant to notice and comment, regulations specifying the schedule of fees applicable to the processing of requests under the Freedom of Information Act. However, § 552(a)(4)(A)(iii) authorizes agencies to furnish copies of documents without charge or at a reduced charge if the disclosure of the information is in the public interest because it is likely to contribute significantly to public understanding of the operations or activities of government and is not primarily in the commercial interest of the requester.

2.1.   **Answer (C) is correct.** Administrative agencies are part of the executive branch.

    Answer (A) is not correct. Administrative agencies are not usually located in the judicial branch, although they perform quasi-adjudicatory functions.

    Answer (B) is not correct. Administrative agencies are not usually located in the legislative branch, although they perform quasi-legislative functions.

    Answer (D) is not correct. Although some people think of agencies as an independent fourth branch of government, they are not. They are part of the executive branch of government.

2.2.   **Answer (B) is correct.** The Supreme Court articulated the intelligible principle test in *J.W. Hampton, Jr., & Co. v. United States*, 276 U.S. 394, 409 (1928). The statute at issue in the case allowed the president to increase duties on some foreign goods in identified situations. The Court upheld this delegation because Congress had included within the statute an intelligible principle with which the president was required to conform. The test was refined in *Panama Refining Co. v. Ryan*, 293 U.S. 388 (1935) (the hot oil case) and *A.L.A. Schechter Poultry Corp. v. United States*, 295 U.S. 495 (1935) (the sick chicken case). In both cases, the Court struck down provisions in the National Industrial Recovery Act (NIRA) on delegation grounds. Many believe that these two cases reflected the Court's skepticism of President Roosevelt's New Deal legislation.

    Answer (A) is not correct. Although the Court has never struck down any other statutes despite very broad delegations based on the intelligible principle standard, it is still the applicable standard. Moreover, the Court has neither overruled nor disavowed *Panama Refining Co.* or *A.L.A. Schechter Poultry. Loving v. United States*, 517 U.S. 748, 771 (1996) ("Though in 1935 we struck down two statutes for lack of an intelligible principle [citing these two cases], we have since upheld, without exception, delegations under standards phrased in sweeping terms."). Too broad a delegation would, arguably, violate the non-delegation doctrine.

    Answer (C) is not correct. "Express guidelines" is not the applicable test, as explained in the review of Answer (B).

    Answer (D) is not correct. At one time, the Supreme Court did use the "named contingency test" for delegation issues. *See, e.g., Brig Aurora v. United States*, 11 U.S. (7 Cranch) 382 (1813); *Field v. Clark*, 143 U.S. 649, 693 (1892). However, the Court rejected this test for the intelligible principle test in *J.W. Hampton, Jr., & Co. v. United States*, 276 U.S. 394, 409 (1928).

2.3.   **Answer (D) is correct.** The statute contains an intelligible standard. The statute allows the Secretary of the Food and Drug Administration (FDA) to approve only "ingredients safe for infant consumption." Although this standard does not provide tremendous guidance, the

Supreme Court has upheld the validity of statutes with significantly less guidance. *See Whitman v. American Trucking Assns.*, 531 U.S. 457, 494 (2001) (holding a provision directing the Environmental Protection Agency to regulate at a level "requisite to protect the public health [with an] adequate margin of safety.")

Answer (A) is not correct. An agency can enact a regulation with legislative effect so long as the statute delegating the agency the power contains an intelligible principle.

Answer (B) is not correct. As noted in the response to Answer (D), this statute has an intelligible principle. As noted in *Loving v. United States*, 517 U.S. 748, 771 (1996), the Court generally upholds delegations, even those articulated in sweeping terms.

Answer (C) is not correct. The manufacturer would have standing. The manufacturer makes a product that the FDA prohibited from being included in the list of ingredients that are safe for inclusion in infant formula. Thus, the manufacturer would have direct injury; in a case involving a question about a federal statute, the issue is ripe, and there are no apparent issues with exhaustion.

2.4.   **Answer (B) is correct.** Neither *Panama Refining Co. v. Ryan*, 293 U.S. 388 (1935), nor *A.L.A. Schechter Poultry Corp. v. United States*, 295 U.S. 495 (1935), have ever been explicitly overruled. However, in the 80 or so years since those cases were decided, the Court never rejected any congressional delegation, no matter how broad.

Answer (A) is not correct. As noted in the response to Answer (B), the delegation doctrine currently has no teeth; hence, it has little continued validity.

Answer (C) is not correct. Similarly, the doctrine is unlikely to make a comeback anytime soon.

Answer (D) is not correct. Because the doctrine has no teeth, it cannot constrain Congress from overly broad delegations.

2.5.   The Environmental Protection Agency (EPA) need have no concerns that the Clean Water Act violates the non-delegation doctrine. In determining whether the delegation is too broad, courts apply the intelligible principles test from *J.W. Hampton, Jr., & Co. v. United States*, 276 U.S. 394, 409 (1928). Pursuant to that test, Congress need only provide guidelines to help direct the agency's decisionmaking. In this case, the Act specifically directs the EPA to set standards that are "requisite to protect the public health and within an adequate margin of safety." Such a standard provides sufficient guidance to the agency to meet the intelligible principles test. Indeed, based on these same facts, the Supreme Court held the delegation to be constitutional in *Whitman v. American Trucking Assns.*, 531 U.S. 457 (2001).

2.6.   **Answer (D) is correct.** Currently, the Supreme Court takes a pragmatic approach to this issue. In *Thomas v. Union Carbide Agricultural Products*, 473 U.S. 568, 590 (1985), the Court rejected the prior rule (represented in Answer (C), which required courts to determine whether the right being adjudicated was private or public) to adopt what it called a more practical approach. In that case, the Court focused on the impact of the delegation on the independent role of the judiciary. Then in *Commodity Futures Trading Commn. v. Schor*, 478 U.S. 833, 848 (1986), the Court identified two functions Article III protects: the role of the independent judiciary in our tripartite government and the rights of litigants to have their claims decided by judges who are free from political domination by the other branches.

Answer (A) is not correct. Congress can delegate quasi-adjudicative power despite Article III.

Answer (B) is not correct. The intelligible principles test is used to determine whether delegation of quasi-legislative power is constitutional. It does not apply to delegations of quasi-adjudicative power.

Answer (C) is not correct. This was the old rule under *Crowell v. Benson*, 285 U.S. 22 (1932). Non-Article III entities should adjudicate those cases involving public rights, or claims against the Government. However, the Supreme Court rejected this test and adopted a more practical approach in *Thomas v. Union Carbide Agricultural Products*, 473 U.S. 568, 590 (1985).

2.7. **Answer (A) is correct because it is an inaccurate statement.** In *Commodity Futures Trading Comm. v. Schor*, 478 U.S. 833, 848 (1986), the court identified four factors for determining whether Congress validly delegated quasi-adjudicative powers. Those factors include: (1) the extent to which the essential attributes of judicial power are reserved to Article III courts; (2) the extent to which the non-Article III entity exercises the range of powers normally vested in Article III courts; (3) the origins and importance of the right to be adjudicated; and (4) the concerns that drove Congress to depart from the requirements of Article III. Answers (B), (C), and (D) include all four factors. Answer (A) includes a factor that is irrelevant.

Answer (B) is not correct because it is an accurate statement.

Answer (C) is not correct because it is an accurate statement.

Answer (D) is not correct because it is an accurate statement.

2.8. **Answer (D) is correct** because all of the other answers are correct.

Answer (A) is not correct although it is an accurate statement. This rationale is known as the adjunct theory of delegation. *Crowell v. Benson*, 285 U.S. 22, 53-4 (1932). The adjunct theory currently supports the modern use of federal magistrate judges, who conduct parts of civil and criminal trials. *See* WILLIAM F. FUNK & RICHARD H. SEAMON, ADMINISTRATIVE LAW: EXAMPLES & EXPLANATIONS (3rd ed. 2009).

Answer (B) is not correct although it, too, is an accurate statement. It supported the public rights/private rights test the Court initially used to determine whether the quasi-adjudicative delegation was constitutional. *Northern Pipeline Construction Co. v. Marathon Pipe Line Co.*, 458 U.S. 50, 67–68 (1982). Examples of public rights included tax disputes, disputes regarding licenses and government contracts, and benefits disputes. Under this rationale, modern Article I courts, such as the United States Tax Court and the Court of Federal Claims, are viewed as legitimate.

Answer (C) is not correct although it is an accurate statement. This rationale was articulated in *Crowell v. Benson*, 285 U.S. 22 (1932).

2.9. **Answer (A) is correct.** In *Crowell v. Benson*, 285 U.S. 22 (1932), the Supreme Court held that constitutional claims should be resolved by Article III courts.

Answer (B) is not correct. The United States Tax Court is an Article I court and part of the Executive Branch. *Kuretski v. Commissioner*, 2014 U.S. App. LEXIS 15021 (D.C. Cir. Aug. 1, 2014).

Answer (C) is not correct. The United States Court of Military Appeals for the Armed Forces hears military appeals and other military issues. It is also an Article I court.

Answer (D) is not correct. The Board of Patent Appeals and Interferences is an executive body that adjudicates patent issues.

2.10.   **Answer (A) is correct** because it is not a legitimate method of oversight. In *Clinton v. City of New York*, 524 U.S. 417, 443–44 (1998), the Supreme Court held that the line item veto was unconstitutional because it effectively allowed the president to amend legislation by repealing parts of the legislation. The Constitution does not grant the president the power to amend or repeal legislation.

Answer (B) is not correct because Executive Order 12866 (E.O. 12866) is a legitimate method of oversight. President Reagan issued E.O. 12866 in the 1980s. It has been adopted as amended by every president since. That order requires agencies to make the regulatory process more cost efficient by (1) considering the costs, benefits, and alternatives to regulation; and (2) preparing an annual regulatory agenda summarizing all regulations under development. E.O. 12866 further requires the Office of Information and Regulatory Affairs (OIRA) to review planned regulations for consistency with the president's priorities, other agency actions, and existing law.

Answer (C) is not correct because the Regulatory Flexibility Act is a legitimate method of oversight. The Regulatory Flexibility Act, which was enacted in 1980 and was styled after the National Environmental Policy Act, requires agencies to document the effect that regulations would have on small business entities. OIRA oversees agency compliance with this Act.

Answer (D) is not correct because the Information (Data) Quality Act is a legitimate method of oversight. Congress passed this Act in 2001. It requires the Office of Management and Budget (OMB) to adopt guidelines for agencies related to the integrity and utility of information and data.

2.11.   **Answer (D) is correct.** Independent agencies generally have multi-member boards whose members are from both political parties, and whose members are removable for cause, although not every independent agency follows this model. *See* Kirti Datla & Richard L. Revesz, *Deconstructing Independent Agencies (and Executive Agencies)*, 98 Cornell L. Rev. 769 (2013) (arguing that no single factor or set of factors separates independent from executive agencies).

Answer (A) is not correct. Both executive and independent agencies must abide by the APA.

Answer (B) is not correct. Historically, the heads of the most important executive agencies are members of president's cabinet, or closest advisory group. Hence, the Secretary of HHS would likely be part of the cabinet. The head of the SEC is actually a multi-member body.

Answer (C) is not correct. The HHS is headed up by a single individual, the secretary, who serves at the president's pleasure.

2.12.   **Answer (B) is correct.** The Supreme Court resolved this issue in *Atlas Roofing Co. v. Occupational Safety and Health Review Commission*, 430 U.S. 442, 450 (1977). In that case, the Court held that that the regulated entity's Seventh Amendment rights were not violated by the agency's order despite the lack of a jury because Congress can assign the task of adjudicating violations of the statute to an agency without the need for a jury.

Answer (A) is not correct. *Atlas Roofing* did not hold that the Seventh Amendment requires a jury trial before an administrative agency can impose a fine. It held the opposite.

Answer (C) is not correct. Because a regulated entity has no right to have a jury trial before an administrative agency, a regulated entity would have no right to choose whether to have a jury trial or not.

Answer (D) is not correct. The APA simply says nothing about the right to a jury trial. It is the Constitution that requires a jury trial. Thus, the APA is simply irrelevant.

2.13. **Appointment:** The Appointments Clause of Article II of the Constitution governs the appointment of principal and inferior officers of the United States. U.S. Const. art. II, § 2, cl. 2. The president appoints principal officers, not defined in Article II, with the advice and consent of the Senate. In contrast, the president, without the consent of the Senate, the Courts of Law, or the Heads of the agencies, may appoint inferior officers.

Removal: Additionally, under this clause, "officers of the United States" can be removed only by impeachment. U.S. Const. art. II, § 4. The grounds for impeachment are limited to treason, bribery, and high crimes and misdemeanors. However, agency officials are regularly removed, if not impeached. Because presidents have the responsibility to take care that the laws are faithfully executed, presidents have some power to remove non-performing officials. U.S. Const. art. II, § 1. In two early cases, the Supreme Court created a two-pronged approach. First, Congress could not restrict a president's ability to remove an officer who was appointed with the Senate's consent and who performed purely executive functions. *Myers v. United States*, 272 U.S. 52, 239 (1926). Second, Congress could restrict a president's ability to remove an officer who was appointed with the Senate's consent and who performed quasi-legislative or quasi-judicial functions. *Humphrey's Executor v. United States*, 295 U.S. 602, 628 (1935). This latter restriction has particular force for officers of independent agencies, like the Federal Trade Commissioner in *Humphrey's Executor*.

Recently, the Court has moved away from this two-pronged test to a test focused on whether the removal "impedes the President's ability to perform his constitutional duty." *Morrison v. Olson*, 487 U.S. 654, 691 (1988). Three factors that may be relevant to this analysis are (1) whether the officer performs purely executive functions; (2) whether the officer works for an executive or independent agency; and (3) whether the officer is a principal or inferior officer. Here, although the Secretary of the Department of Veterans Affairs is a principal officer, the president likely has the power to remove her without cause because she performs purely executive functions and heads an executive agency.

2.14. **Answer (A) is correct.** While Congress may delay the effective date of regulations, Congress may not legislatively veto agency regulations. In *INS v. Chadha*, 462 U.S. 919, 951 (1983), the Supreme Court held the legislative veto in that case to be unconstitutional because it violated the bicameralism and presentment clause. To overrule administrative action, Congress must pass legislation bicamerally (in other words, both houses of Congress must pass identical bills) and present it to the president for his or her signature.

Answer (B) is not correct. For the reasons identified in the response to Answer (A), the legislative veto provision is likely unconstitutional. Moreover, the APA does not address waiting periods at all.

Answer (C) is not correct. While the legislative veto provision would be held unconstitutional, there is no constitutional impediment to Congress enacting a waiting period.

Answer (D) is not correct. While there is no constitutional impediment to Congress enacting a waiting period, for the reasons identified in the response to Answer (A), the legislative veto provision is likely unconstitutional.

2.15. **Answer (D) is correct.** These were the facts in *INS v. Chadha*, 462 U.S. 919 (1983). In that case the court held that the provision allowing either house of Congress to pass a resolution rejecting the INS's decision violated the bicameralism and presentment clauses of the U.S. Constitution. U.S. Const. art. I § 7, cl. 2–3 (presentment clauses); U.S. Const. art. I § 1, 7 (bicameralism clauses).

Answer (A) is not correct. This case is ripe for review because your client is about to be deported.

Answer (B) is not correct. For the reasons identified in the response to Answer (D), the legislative veto provision is unconstitutional.

Answer (C) is not correct. The standard the INS must apply in determining whether to stay a deportation is whether the stay is for "humanitarian reasons." Under the Supreme Court's recent delegation doctrine, requiring that Congress provide an intelligible principle, "humanitarian reasons" is likely a sufficient intelligible principle.

2.16. **Answer (A) is correct.** Standing Committees in Congress oversee agency spending, agency substantive decisions, and agency efficiency. Such oversight is legitimate.

Answer (B) is not correct. In *INS v. Chadha*, 462 U.S. 919, 951 (1983), the Supreme Court held the legislative veto to be unconstitutional because it violated the bicameralism and presentment clause. Hence, legislative vetoes are not legitimate methods of congressional oversight.

Answer (C) is not correct. While parts of Congress may have a role in both appointment and removal of the members of independent agencies, Congress as a whole does not have sole power to appoint and remove all such officers. *See Buckley v. Valeo*, 424 U.S. 1, 136 (1976) (holding that Congress cannot reserve for itself the right to appoint FEC members). Rather, the president with the advice and consent of the Senate (not Congress as a whole) appoints principal officers of the United States. U.S. Const. art. II, § 2, cl. 2. In addition, the House and Senate play different roles in the impeachment process.

Answer (D) is not correct. It is true that Executive Order 12866 requires agencies to perform a cost-benefit analysis for certain rules. However, this order is an executive means of oversight, not a congressional means of oversight.

2.17. There is no clear test distinguishing principal officers from inferior officers. However, the Supreme Court has addressed this issue in two cases. In the first case, *Morrison v. Olson*, 487 U.S. 654 (1988), the Court held that an officer was inferior, not principal, when the officer performed only limited duties, had narrow jurisdiction, and was subject to removal by a principal officer. *Id.* at 691 (holding that independent counsels were inferior officers). In the second case, *Edmond v. United States*, 520 U.S. 651(1997), the Court held that an officer was inferior, not principal, when a principal officer closely supervised the other officer's work and had the authority to remove the officer. *Id.* at 662–63 (holding that judges for the Coast Guard Court of Criminal Appeals were inferior officers). Thus, inferior officers are those individuals who are under principal officers, but are also more than mere employees. Officers exercise "significant authority pursuant to the laws of the United States." *Freytag v. IRS*, 501 U.S. 868, 881 (1991). In contrast, employees "are lesser functionaries subordinate to officers of the United States." *Buckley v. Valeo*, 424 U.S. 1, 126 n.162 (1976).

In *Morrison v. Olson*, 487 U.S. 654, 691(1988), the Court held that an independent counsel is an "inferior officer" of the United States. As a result, Congress could limit the officer's removal to cases involving cause.

2.18.   In *Buckley v. Valeo*, 424 U.S. 1 (1976), the Court held that Congress could not reserve to itself the right to appoint some members of the Federal Election Commission (FEC). The Constitution specifically gives that power to the president, who can act only with the advice and consent of the senate. U.S. Const. art. II, § 2, cl. 2. As the Court explained, this omission was deliberate. The Framers specifically chose not to give Congress both the power to create offices and to fill those offices. Were Congress given both powers, it would have the power not only to make laws, but also to enforce those laws.

2.19.   There are three important safeguards. First, the primary safeguard is the requirement that all documents exchanged between OIRA and the agency during OIRA's review be published. Section 6(b)(4) provides that, after a regulatory action has been issued to the public (or after the agency has announced a decision not to issue a regulatory action), OIRA must make available to the public all documents exchanged between OIRA and the agency during OIRA's review. This rule requires disclosure of any written explanations for a decision by OIRA to return a regulatory action to an agency for reconsideration, as well as written responses from the agency head if the agency disagrees with the reasons OIRA provides.

Accordingly, the public should be able to ascertain the substantive changes between a rule as it was submitted to OIRA and the final rule, and the public should be able to identify which changes were due to OIRA influence.

A second safeguard is the requirement in § 4(d) that the Administrator of OIRA convene a regulatory "working group." The working group serves as a forum to assist agencies in analyzing regulatory issues. Section 4(d) provides that the working group shall consist of representatives of the heads of each agency that the Administrator determines to have significant domestic regulatory responsibilities. Because the working group is comprised of agency heads, the working group may help temper the power of the Director of OMB or the Administrator of OIRA.

A third safeguard, arguably, is the vesting of final authority for resolving conflicts between the agency and OIRA with the president, as opposed to with the Director of OMB or the Administrator of OIRA. *See* Section 7. This provision technically enhances the power of the president; however, the president may need to show restraint in exercising that power given that a decision regarding a significant regulatory action can be linked directly back to the president, as opposed to the administrative state generally.

3.1.   Section 551(7) of the APA defines "adjudication" as an "agency process for the formulation of an order." Section 551(6) defines "order" as the "whole or part of a final disposition . . . of an agency in a matter other than rulemaking but including licensing." Section 551(5) defines "rulemaking" as the "agency process for formulating, amending, or repealing a rule." A "rule" is defined by § 551(4) as "the whole or part of an agency statement of general . . . applicability and future effect . . . . " An "adjudication" then, is the agency process for formulating a decision of "particular" applicability and "present" effect. Stated another way, agency rulemaking is akin to legislation enacted by a legislature; whereas, adjudication is akin to a judgment imposed by a court. That is, in rulemaking an agency addresses a problem by crafting a rule that will affect all regulated entities and that takes effect only after its promulgation and publication. In contrast, adjudication permits an agency to address a problem by crafting what is, in essence, a rule that affects only specific entities (those before the agency in the administrative proceeding), and that can, in some instances, affect these entities even if the agency position was not previously known.

3.2.   Most of the procedures set out in the APA that apply to adjudications are not required for the vast majority of agency adjudications. APA § 554 and § 556 apply only to cases of adjudication "required by statute to be determined on the record after opportunity for an agency hearing . . . . " The Supreme Court has not decided what this language means in the adjudication context, but, in the rulemaking context, the Court held that formal APA requirements would be triggered only upon clear congressional intent that the determination be based on a closed record. *See, e.g., U.S. v. Florida Coast Railway Co.*, 410 U.S. 224 (1973). The D.C. and First Circuits have held that agency decisions regarding the formality of the proceeding required are entitled to deference under *Chevron v. Natural Resources Defense Council, Inc.*, 467 U.S. 837 (1984); *Chemical Waste Management, Inc. v. EPA*, 873 F.2d 1477, 1482 (D.C. Cir. 1989); *Dominion Energy v. Johnson*, 443 F.3d 12 (1st Cir. 2006). Some legal scholars disagree: William S. Jordan, *Chevron and Hearing Rights: An Unintended Combination*, 61 ADMIN L. REV. 249 (2009); Melissa M. Berry, *Beyond Chevron's Domain: Agency Interpretations of Statutory Procedural Provisions*, 30 SEATTLE U. L. REV. 541 (2007); William Funk, *The Rise and Purported Demise of Wong Yang Sung*, 58 ADMIN. L. REV. 881 (2006).

3.3.   **Answer (B) is correct.** Whether a congressional requirement of a "hearing" triggers the APA protections is a matter of statutory interpretation, which in turn is a matter of congressional intent as explained in the answer to question 3.2. Further, *Chevron's* second step is not triggered unless the reviewing court cannot ascertain, using traditional tools of statutory interpretation, congressional intent on the issue. *Chevron v. Natural Resources Defense Council, Inc.*, 467 U.S. 837, 843 (1984).

Answer (A) is not correct. APA § 554(a) states that the formal APA adjudication requirements apply in "every case of adjudication required by statute to be determined on the record after opportunity for an agency hearing . . . . " However, it was in the rulemaking context — not the adjudication context — that the Supreme Court held that formal APA requirements would be triggered only upon clear congressional intent that the determination be based on a closed record. *See, e.g., U.S. v. Florida Coast Railway Co.*, 410 U.S. 224 (1973).

Answer (C) is not correct. The Supreme Court decisions in the rulemaking context, noted above, would not support this presumption. It is true that the Court's holding in the rulemaking context was based on the sentiment that trial-like procedures are rarely necessary for fairness in rulemaking, given its more legislative character, and thus, that adjudications may require greater procedural protections. However, it is also well recognized that the full collection of APA's procedural entitlements are not necessary in all adjudications — even if due process is triggered. Due process considerations often demand only limited procedural protections.

Answer (D) is not correct. Although the issue presents a question of statutory interpretation, *Chevron* deference to the agency interpretation is not triggered unless the reviewing court cannot ascertain, using traditional tools of statutory interpretation, congressional intent on the issue. *Chevron v. Natural Resources Defense Council, Inc.*, 467 U.S. 837 (1984).

3.4.   **Answer (A) is correct.** Although the generally understood principle is that an APA adjudication must be based entirely on the exclusive record referred to in § 556(e), § 556(e) recognizes that an ALJ may take "official notice of a material fact not appearing in the record," as long as the opposing party is afforded the opportunity, upon request, to show the contrary. Basic information concerning mortality rates is the type of material that an ALJ may take "official notice" of.

Answer (B) is not correct because it is not an accurate statement. APA § 556(d) provides that the "proponent of a rule or order has the burden of proof," and the Supreme Court has held that this language includes the burden of persuasion. *See Director, Office of Workers' Compensation Programs, Dept. of Labor v. Greenwich Collieries*, 512 U.S. 267 (1994). In this case, Tony is the proponent of the order because he is seeking an order granting him Medicare benefits. Thus, Tony has the burden of persuasion on the issue of reasonable and necessary. Thus, the ALJ will need to find that the preponderance of the evidence supports Tony to reverse the contractor's initial denial.

Answer (C) is not correct because it is not an accurate statement. The facts of the question describe the ALJ decision as one that may be appealed to the CMM Appeals Council. Under § 557(b), a determination by the presiding officer is an "initial decision" and not a "recommended decision" unless the agency requires the ALJ to certify the entire record to the agency for decision.

Answer (D) is not correct because it is not an accurate statement. APA § 556(d) permits the agency to adopt procedures for the submission of all or part of the evidence in written form if the adjudication involves a claim for money or benefits — if the party will not be prejudiced. Tony's claim is for benefits under the Medicare program. Further, Tony likely would not be prejudiced because the evidence that would be provided by Tony's oncologists can be presented via affidavits.

3.5.   **Answer (A) is correct.** ALJs are employees of the agencies for whom they work, and they must apply interpretations and policies of the agency.

Answer (B) is not correct because it is not an accurate statement for the reason stated in the response to Answer A.

Answer (C) is not correct because it is not an accurate statement. Physician opinions presented in the form of affidavits may constitute sufficient evidence to support an agency determination. Tony has the right to subpoena witnesses to preserve his right to cross-examine. No rule precludes an ALJ from relying on evidence in the form of affidavits. The agency cannot, however, base its decision on opinions of oncologists submitted by way of affidavits after the hearing, without re-opening the hearing or otherwise giving Tony an opportunity to rebut the "after-the-fact" evidence. *Richardson v. Perales*, 402 U.S. 389 (1971).

Answer (D) is not correct because it is not an accurate statement. As stated in the Answer A response, ALJs are required to follow agency policies and interpretations.

3.6. **Answer (D) is correct because it is an accurate statement.** Further, § 557(c) requires agencies to allow parties to submit for consideration proposed findings and conclusions, and reasons supporting those findings and conclusions, before a decision on agency review of the decision of subordinate employees.

Answer (A) is not correct because it is not an accurate statement. The substantial evidence standard of § 706(2)(E) applies when courts are reviewing agency factual and policy determinations made pursuant to formal APA procedures. Section 557(b) directs that, "on appeal or review of the initial decision, the agency has all the powers which it would have in making the initial decision." This means that the CMM's Appeal Council may decide the case without deferring to the ALJ's determination.

Answer (B) is not correct because it is not an accurate statement. The arbitrary and capricious standard of § 706(2)(A) applies when courts are reviewing factual and policy determinations promulgated pursuant to informal APA procedures. And, as noted, § 557(b) directs that, "on appeal or review of the initial decision, the agency has all the powers which it would have in making the initial decision." This means that the CMM's Appeal Council may decide the case without deferring to the ALJ's determination.

Answer (C) is not correct because it is not an accurate statement. Section 557(b) directs that, "on appeal or review of the initial decision, the agency has all the powers which it would have in making the initial decision." Although this means that the appeal is conducted, in essence, de novo, the review generally does not include taking additional evidence.

3.7. **Answer (C) is correct because it is an accurate statement**

Answer (A) is not correct because it is an inaccurate statement. Although APA § 706(2) authorizes courts only to "set aside" agency action, findings, or conclusions, the statute specifically authorizing judicial review in the question also allows the court "to modify or reverse" the decision of the agency, with or without remanding the cause for a rehearing.

Answer (B) is not correct because it is an inaccurate statement. According to the facts of the question, the enabling statute states that findings of fact, if supported by substantial evidence, "shall be conclusive." Thus, the statutory authorization to modify or reverse the decision of the agency, with or without remanding the cause for a rehearing, cannot be based upon factual findings unless those facts were unsupported by substantial evidence. The substantial evidence standard is distinct from the arbitrary and capricious standard.

Answer (D) not correct because it is an inaccurate statement. *Chevron*'s reasonableness standard does not apply to agency factual determinations. *Chevron, U.S.A., Inc. v. Natural Res. Def. Council, Inc.*, 467 U.S. 837, 843 (1984). Rather the correct standard is the APA § 706(2)(A)'s arbitrary and capricious standard.

3.8.   **Answer (B) is correct.** The memorandum is an ex parte communication. APA § 551(14). However, it is not *prohibited* by APA § 557(d)(1)(B). This section only prohibits, in cases where formal APA procedures apply, ex parte communications relevant to "the merits of the proceeding" when those communications are made by persons outside of the agency to an agency employee who is involved in the decisional process, or vice versa. Here, the communication was from a person within the CMM. Nevertheless, APA § 556(e) indicates that formal procedures require an "exclusive record for decision." This section shows that Congress intended that any communication or other evidence considered by the decision maker would be made a part of the public record. Thus, the agency should make the memorandum part of the record if the agency wishes to consider the memorandum in its adjudication. But the agency is not required to make the communication public if it pays no attention to it.

Answer (A) is not correct. It is partially correct because the memorandum itself is not a "prohibited" ex parte communication. But the agency should make the memorandum part of the public record if the agency wishes to consider the memorandum as part of the decision making process under APA § 555(e).

Answer (C) is not an accurate statement. The memorandum is not a "prohibited" ex parte communication under APA § 557(d)(1)(B). However, even if it were prohibited by that section, APA § 557(d)(1)(C) does not require that prohibited ex parte communications be disregarded. Rather APA § 557(d)(1)(C) requires the decision maker to place the communication on the public record and to consider whether the interests of justice require some additional sanction.

Answer (D) is not an accurate statement. The memorandum is not a "prohibited" ex parte communication under APA § 557(d)(1)(B).

3.9.   **Answer (C) is correct because it is an accurate statement.** The letter from private insurers likely is a prohibited ex parte communication under APA § 557(d)(1)(B). Section 557(d)(1) prohibits ex parte communications relevant to the merits of the proceeding if made by persons outside the agency, or if the person outside the agency knowingly caused the communication to be made to an agency employee involved in the decisional process. Here, the letter is from persons outside the agency, and, at least arguably, the insurers knowingly caused the communication to be made to the decision maker. The communication is also relevant to the merits of the proceeding — namely, whether to consider HDC/BMT experimental and thus, ineligible for Medicare coverage.

Answer (A) is not correct because it is only a partially accurate statement. Although the memorandum itself is not a "prohibited" ex parte communication and need not be put on the record unless the decision maker wishes to consider it as part of the evidence, the letter from private insurers likely is a prohibited ex parte communication under APA § 557(d)(1)(B). APA § 557(d)(1)(C) requires the decision maker to place the prohibited ex parte communications on the public record and to consider whether the interests of justice require some additional sanction.

Answer (B) is not correct because it is only a partially accurate statement. A reasonable argument exists that the letter from the private insurers constitutes a "prohibited" ex parte communication under APA § 557(d)(1)(B). However, the APA does not require that prohibited ex parte communications be disregarded. Rather § 557(d)(1)(C) requires the decision maker to place the communication on the public record and to consider whether the interests of justice require some additional sanction.

Answer (D) is not correct because it is an inaccurate statement. The letter from private insurers would likely be considered a prohibited ex parte communication under APA § 557(d)(1)(B); thus, it must be made part of the record.

3.10.   **Answer (A) is correct because it is the best judicial response.** Courts have held that prohibited ex parte communications, even when undisclosed during agency proceedings, do not necessarily void an agency decision. *See, e.g., Professional Air Traffic Controllers Organization v. Federal Labor Relations Authority*, 685 F.2d 547 (D.C. Cir. 1982). Rather, courts consider whether the agency decision-making process was "irrevocably tainted so as to make the ultimate judgment of the agency unfair, either to an innocent party or to the public interest." *Id.* Courts consider a number of factors in making this determination: the gravity of the communication; whether the party making or causing the communication benefited from the agency judgment; whether the communication presented information that was unknown to opposing parties; and whether voiding the judgment would serve any useful purpose.

Answer (B) is not correct because it is not the best judicial response. Courts are not required to void the agency order when prohibited ex parte communication takes place.

Answer (C) is not correct because it is not the best judicial response. The fact that the letter was not made part of the record is not, alone, sufficient to warrant a finding that the process of decision making was irrevocably tainted.

Answer (D) is not correct because it is not the best judicial response. The error, if one occurred, occurred at the agency level, not at the judicial level. The agency, not the court, could have cured the issue by placing the communication on the record and allowing Jane to submit a written response.

3.11.   The communication is prohibited by the APA. APA § 554(d) prohibits any participation in the ALJ decision-making process by an employee or agent of the agency who engaged in the performance of investigative or prosecuting functions in the case before the ALJ or in a factually related case. Unlike APA § 557(d), which includes an administrative remedy for violation of the prohibition on ex parte communications in formal agency adjudications, APA § 554(d) does not address the proper remedy at the administrative level. Upon judicial review, however, courts treat violations of APA § 554 similarly to violations of the APA § 557(d)(1) prohibition. A violation of APA § 554 does not necessarily void the agency judgment, but courts will carefully scrutinize the decision for fairness concerns.

3.12.   When an agency adjudication must be conducted pursuant to the "formal procedures," APA § 556 requires that there be a "presiding" officer or employee. APA § 556 provides that an administrative law judge may preside at the taking of evidence; administrative law judges generally are employees of the agency. APA § 556(c) authorizes presiding employees to function much like judges. They are authorized to administer oaths; issue subpoenas; rule on offers of proof and receive relevant evidence; take or order depositions; regulate the course of the hearing; rule on procedural requests or similar matters; make or recommend decisions; hold settlement conferences and compel attendance; and encourage alternative dispute resolution. APA § 556 also provides that the presiding employee must act in an impartial manner.

3.13.   The APA does not specify requirements applicable solely to informal adjudication. However, the minimal requirements of APA § 555 are applicable to all agency proceedings. Those procedures include: (1) the right in any proceeding to be represented by counsel; (2) the right of interested persons to appear before an agency in any proceeding "so far as the orderly conduct or public business permits; (3) the right to have an agency conclude a matter presented to the agency within a "reasonable time"; (4) the right to retain or obtain copies of materials required to be submitted to an agency; (5) the right to utilize agency subpoena power upon a showing of general relevance and reasonable scope of the evidence sought; and (6) the right to receive prompt notice of a denial of a request, application, or petition, as well as a brief statement of the grounds for a denial.

3.14.   Whether ALJs can serve with independence and neutrality is a valid concern given that ALJs are employees of the agency for which they serve as judges (*see* 5 U.S.C. § 3105), and that the agency generally is a party in a proceeding before the ALJ. Accordingly, Congress has adopted important provisions to mitigate that concern. Foremost, agencies are not allowed to rate, evaluate, discipline, reward, punish, or remove ALJs who work for them; rather, adverse personnel actions can only be made by the Merit Systems Protection Board after a formal APA adjudication. *See* 5 U.S.C. § 7521. Additionally, the APA includes specific provisions which help ensure independence and neutrality. For example, with certain exceptions, the APA prohibits an agency employee engaged in investigation or prosecution of a case from participating or advising in the ALJ's decision or recommended decision. *See* APA § 554(d). Further, the APA provides that ALJs are subject to disqualification for personal bias or other reason from hearing a case. *See* APA § 556(b).

3.15.   Appeals within an agency are different in nature from judicial appellate review of a trial court. The APA provides that the agency "has all the powers which it would have in making the initial decision." *See* APA § 557(b). Thus, when an ALJ decision is appealed, the appeals board or agency head decides the case de novo.

3.16.   **Answer (C) is correct because it is an accurate statement.** Although for a number of years the Supreme Court utilized a "rights/privilege" distinction, which would preclude application of the Due Process Clause to agency actions affecting government largesse, the Court in *Goldberg v. Kelly*, 397 U.S. 254 (1970), abandoned that distinction. Today, due process protections are triggered by agency actions that adversely affect legitimate entitlements to government benefits. In *Goldberg*, the Court specifically held that termination of welfare benefits triggers due process protections. *Id.*

         Answer (A) is not correct because it is an inaccurate statement. Due process protections are triggered by agency actions that constitute a deprivation of property or liberty interests. Adjudications, more often than rulemaking, may result in a deprivation of a protected interest. However, not all adverse agency adjudications trigger due process rights, and thus, an initial issue is always whether the Due Process Clause applies at all. *See, e.g., Goldberg v.*

Kelly, 397 U.S. 254 (1970).

Answer (B) is not correct because it is an inaccurate statement. Rulemaking rarely triggers the protection of the Due Process Clause. Agency rulemaking is not based on individualized grounds and, generally, is based on legislative rather than adjudicative facts. Legislative facts are general facts that bear on the subject of the rulemaking. Adjudicative facts concern particular persons and questions such as who did what, when, where, why, and how, etc. *Compare Londoner v. Denver,* 210 U.S. 373 (1908), *with Bi-Metallic Investment Co. v. State Board of Equalization,* 239 U.S. 441 (1915).

Answer (D) is not correct for the reasons noted in the Answer C response above.

3.17.   **Answer (B) is correct** because the University did not make any finding relating to Susan's name, reputation, honor, or integrity, this is not a case where the State has imposed a stigma that would foreclose Susan's freedom to obtain other employment opportunities. *See Board of Regents v. Roth,* 408 U.S. 564 (1972).

Answer (A) is not correct because the facts do not raise any issue relating to jurisdiction to review the decision.

Answer (C) is not correct. Because the University did not make any finding relating to Susan's name, reputation, honor, or integrity, this is not a case where the State has imposed a stigma that would foreclose Susan's freedom to obtain other employment opportunities. *See Board of Regents v. Roth,* 408 U.S. 564 (1972).

Answer (D) is not correct. Because of the terms of Susan's employment contract, the determination did not deprive her of a legitimate property interest. She had no legitimate expectation that her contract would be extended beyond the one year. Further, the facts do not suggest the existence of any university policies that could support Susan's claim of a property interest.

3.18.   The idea that "stigma" resulting from government action could give rise to due process rights arose from language used by the Supreme Court in *Board of Regents v. Roth,* 408 U.S. 564 (1972). In *Roth,* the Court explained that liberty interests "denote[ ] not merely freedom from bodily restraint but also the right of the individual to contract, to engage in any of the common occupations of life, to acquire useful knowledge, []. . . and generally to enjoy those privileges long recognized . . . as essential to the orderly pursuit of happiness by free men." *Id.* at 572. However, the Court in *Roth* found that an assistant professor did not have a protectable liberty interest triggering due process rights because "[t]he [s]tate, in declining to rehire [him], did not make any charge against him that might seriously damage his standing and association[] in his community." *Id.* at 573. The Court stated that where "a person's good name, reputation, honor, or integrity is at stake because of what the government is doing to him, notice and an opportunity to be heard are essential." *Id.* at 573. The Court later clarified that stigma alone was insufficient to trigger due process rights. In *Paul v. Davis,* 424 U.S. 693 (1976), the Court explained that "reputation alone, apart from some more tangible interests such as employment, is [n]either 'liberty' or 'property' by itself sufficient to invoke the procedural protection of the Due Process Clause." *Id.* at 701. The analysis in *Paul* has been described as the "stigma-plus" test. That is, in order to trigger due process protections, the government action must do more than simply harm a person's reputation; the action must also subject the individual to some other significant loss, such as the loss of a job or an invasion of privacy.

3.19.   **Answer (B) is correct.** Disputed facts are essential to a right to a due process hearing. *Codd v. Velger*, 429 U.S. 624, 627 (1977). Because a convicted sex offender cannot dispute the fact of the conviction, the offender would have no right under the Due Process Clause to a hearing. "Plaintiffs who assert a right to a hearing under the Due Process Clause must show that the facts they seek to establish in that hearing are relevant under the statutory scheme." *Connecticut Dep't of Pub. Safety v. Doe*, 538 U.S. 1, 8 (2003).

Answer (A) is not correct because the strength or legitimacy of any governmental or public interest is relevant to what procedures may be necessary, but these factors are not relevant to the question of whether a person's due process rights are triggered. *See Mathews v. Eldridge*, 424 U.S. 319 (1976).

Answer (C) is not correct. Agency action creating a "stigma" (meaning damage to a person's reputation relating to immorality, dishonesty, criminality, etc.) does not itself trigger due process rights. *See Paul v. Davis*, 424 U.S. 693 (1976).

Answer (D) is not correct. Assuming the sex offenders in this situation cannot dispute the existence of the convictions, then there is no need for a hearing under *Codd v. Velger*, 429 U.S. 624, 627 (1977). This is exactly what the Supreme Court held in *Connecticut Dep't of Pub. Safety v. Doe*, 538 U.S. 1, 8 (2003).

3.20.   **Answer (D) is correct.** This answer is in-line with the Supreme Court's decisions holding that "stigma-plus" is essential to trigger a due process hearing. That is, that the government action must both harm the person's reputation and subject the person to some other loss, such as the loss of a government privilege such as a job; loss of a legal right such as the right to purchase alcohol; or loss of another liberty interest such as the interest in privacy or the interest in freedom from restraint. *See Paul v. Davis*, 424 U.S. 693 (1976). Here, Sabbat lost her job and was publically labeled as dishonest.

Answer (A) is not correct because the strength or legitimacy of any governmental or public interest is relevant to what procedures may be necessary, but these factors are not relevant to the question of whether a person's due process rights are triggered, requiring a hearing. *See Mathews v. Eldridge*, 424 U.S. 319 (1976).

Answer (B) is not correct. Although Professor Markell is an individual, he works for a state institution; hence, the Due Process Clause applies. Professor Markell is considered an agency of the institution. Moreover, Professor Markell posted the information on the school's website.

Answer (C) is not correct. This answer is incomplete. Agency action creating a "stigma" (meaning damage to a person's reputation relating to immorality, dishonesty, criminality, etc.) does not itself trigger a due process hearing. *See Paul v. Davis*, 424 U.S. 693 (1976). Stigma plus future harm is required.

3.21.   **Answer (D) is correct.** It best describes the *Mathews* test. The Court in *Mathews v. Eldridge*, 424 U.S. 319, 321 (1976), stated that a court should consider three factors to determine whether additional procedures are required: (i) the private interest, (ii) the risk of erroneous deprivation currently faced given procedural protections and the value of additional protections or safeguards, and (iii) the public interest, including fiscal and administrative burdens that would result from additional protections or safeguards.

Answer (A) is not correct. Although it is a partially accurate statement, it omits one of the three factors: risk of error.

Answer (B) is not correct. These two factors are not balanced against one another; rather, these factors together help reflect the strength or importance of the private interests at stake.

Answer (C) is not correct. Similar to Answer (B), these two factors are not balanced against one another; rather, these factors together help reflect the strength or importance of the private interests at stake.

3.22. **Answer (D) is correct** because Answers (A), (B), and (C) are all accurate statements. Hence, Answer (D), all of the above, is accurate.

Answer (A) is not correct although it is an accurate statement. The facts state that the agency must follow formal APA procedures. Section 706(2)(E)'s substantial evidence standard applies in cases subject to formal APA procedures.

Answer (B) is not correct although it is an accurate statement. A court may always set aside agency action that is arbitrary and capricious. *See Citizens to Preserve Overton Park v. Volpe*, 401 U.S. 402, 413 (1971).

Answer (C) is not correct although it is an accurate statement. A finding of "full and adequate" disclosure in this case is a "mixed" question of the sort discussed by the Supreme Court in *NLRB v. Hearst*, 322 U.S. 111, 131 (1944). Pursuant to the holding in that case, even if the underlying pure factual findings necessary to the determination are supported by sufficient evidence in the record, the court may assess the determination for reasonableness in light of legal principles relevant to when a disclosure is adequate.

3.23. **Answer (A) is correct.** Prior to the enactment of the APA, the Supreme Court applied the substantial evidence standard as requiring only consideration of the evidence supporting the agency decision. *Universal Camera Corp. v. NLRB*, 340 U.S. 474, 477–78 (1951). However, APA § 706 provides that a reviewing court shall review "the whole record or those parts of it cited by a party . . . ." Thus, in *Universal Camera Corp. v. NLRB*, the Court explained that Congress intended to allow courts to set aside agency action if the evidence supporting the agency decision was not substantial when viewed in light of the evidence contrary to the agency's position as well as the evidence in support. *Id.* at 488.

Answer (B) is not correct because it is an inaccurate statement for the reason noted above in the explanation of Answer (A).

Answer (C) is not correct because it is an inaccurate statement. The substantial evidence standard is a deferential standard of review. However, the standard is similar to that used by a court when deciding whether to grant a directed verdict in a civil action. In applying that standard; hence, a court is not "weighing" the evidence.

Answer (D) is not correct because it is an inaccurate statement. As noted in the explanation of Answer (A), the evidence on both sides of the issue should be considered equally.

3.24. **Answer (B) is correct because it represents a better judicial response.** In applying the substantial evidence standard, a difficulty arises when the decision maker on the agency appeal and the ALJ disagree on a finding of fact. A court must proceed carefully when the agency reaches a conclusion opposite from that reached by the "impartial experienced examiner who has observed the witnesses and lived with the case." However, courts have rejected an absolute rule that the finding must be set aside if it rests on testimonial evidence discredited by the ALJ, even if the ALJ's credibility inferences were based on witness demeanor. *See, e.g., Universal Camera Corp. v. NLRB*, 340 U.S. 474, 496 (1951) (noting, "[w]e intend only to recognize that evidence supporting a conclusion may be less substantial" when the agency finding is contrary to the ALJ's credibility determination). Here, the agency gave good reasons for rejecting the ALJ's credibility findings.

Answer (A) is not correct. As noted in the explanation to Answer (A), the agency may reject the ALJ's credibility determinations that are based on demeanor if the agency has good reasons for doing so.

Answer (C) is not correct because the agency is not bound by the ALJ's findings, even those grounded in credibility determinations.

Answer (D) is not correct. The ALJ's findings become a part of the record. APA § 557(c)(3) provides that "all decisions, including initial, recommended, or tentative decisions, are a part of the record . . ." and requires a statement of "findings and conclusions, and the reasons or basis therefor, on all the material issues of fact, law, or discretion presented . . . . "

3.25.   **Answer (D) is correct** because Answers (B) and (C) are accurate statements.

Answer (A) is not correct because it is an inaccurate statement. APA § 706(2)(E)'s substantial evidence standard applies in cases subject to formal APA procedures. In cases of informal adjudication, APA § 706(2)(A) applies, allowing a court to set aside agency findings and conclusions found to be arbitrary and capricious.

Answer (B) is not correct although it is an accurate statement. A court may always set aside agency action that is arbitrary and capricious. *See Citizens to Preserve Overton Park v. Volpe*, 401 U.S. 402, 420 (1971). But Answer (C) is also correct.

Answer (C) is not correct although it is an accurate statement. A finding of "full and adequate" disclosure in this case is a "mixed" question of the sort discussed by the Supreme Court in *NLRB v. Hearst*, 322 U.S. 111, 131 (1944). Thus, even if the underlying pure factual findings necessary to the determination are supported by sufficient evidence in the record, the court may assess the determination for reasonableness in light of legal principles relevant to when a disclosure is adequate.

3.26.   **Answer (B) is correct.** In *Overton Park*, the Court recognized that, in cases of informal adjudication, whatever record existed at the time the agency decision was made might not disclose the factors considered by the agency; thus, the Court concluded that it might be necessary for a court to require some explanation to aid in judicial review of the agency action. Further, the Court did not close the door on mandating testimony in a case where no contemporaneous explanation was made. However, the Court also suggested that other less objectionable means would likely suffice — such as allowing the agency to prepare post hoc "formal findings," as long as the reviewing court viewed them critically. *See Citizens to Preserve Overton Park v. Volpe*, 401 U.S. 402, 420 (1971).

Answer (A) is not correct because it is an inaccurate statement. The Supreme Court in *Overton Park* clarified that this form of post hoc rationalization would be an inadequate basis for judicial review. *See Citizens to Preserve Overton Park v. Volpe*, 401 U.S. 402, 420 (1971). APA § 706 requires courts conducting judicial review to review the whole record — even in cases involving informal adjudication. Litigation affidavits are not part of the record.

Answer (C) is not correct because it is an inaccurate statement. The judicial remedy if an agency fails to provide a contemporaneous explanation of the reasons for its decision is to have the agency provide the information in an acceptable manner. The remedy is not to presume the agency acted impermissibly.

Answer (D) is not correct because it is an inaccurate statement. While the APA does not explicitly require agencies to provide contemporaneous explanations, in light of the Court's sentiment expressed in *Overton Park* regarding the need for an explanation of the basis for an agency's decision in order to properly provide judicial review — and the possibility of being required to submit to examination if necessary — agencies are likely to prepare a contemporaneous explanation of the basis for their findings and conclusions, even in cases involving informal adjudications. *See Citizens to Preserve Overton Park v. Volpe*, 401 U.S. 402, 420 (1971).

3.27. Yes. Section 705 of the APA specifically empowers courts to "issue all necessary and appropriate process to postpone the effective date of an agency action or to preserve status or rights" during the pendency of the judicial review — "on such conditions as may be required and to the extent necessary to prevent irreparable injury." APA § 705.

3.28. **Answer (C) is correct.** The Court in *Gonzales v. Oregon* stated that *Chevron* deference is "warranted only 'when it appears that Congress delegated authority to the agency generally to make rules carrying the force of law, and that the agency interpretation claiming deference was promulgated in the exercise of that authority.'" 546 U.S. 243, 255–56 (2006). Because Customs has pointed to generally conferred authority to promulgate substantive regulations, the requisite congressional delegation exists. However, formulation of an interpretation in a civil enforcement action likely would not be considered an exercise of the authority to make rules with the force of law. The Court in *United States v. Mead Corp.*, 533 U.S. 218, 226–27 (2001) noted that *Chevron* deference has most often been applied to "the fruits of notice-and-comment rulemaking or formal adjudication." Although the Court also stated that the lack of such procedures was not dispositive, the *Mead* Court's application of the standard suggests that formulation of the agency's interpretation of the Tariff Act in a routine in rem forfeiture action in a local federal district court would be insufficient to trigger *Chevron* deference. However, some level of deference may be appropriate, and the factors from *Skidmore v. Swift & Co.*, 323 U.S. 134, 140 (1944), help a court to decide that issue. *See United States v. Able Time, Inc.*, 545 F.3d 824 (9th Cir. 2008) (from which the facts of this question were drawn). *See also Doe v. Leavitt*, 552 F.3d 75 (1st Cir. 2009) (for a case discussing and applying the *Skidmore* factors).

Answer (A) is not correct. The Court has clarified that *Chevron* deference is limited to an interpretation of a statute made by an agency under circumstances that would warrant *Chevron*'s more generous deference. Thus, additional circumstances must be articulated.

Answer (B) is not correct. Although an agency interpretation may carry the force of law — and if valid, it would be binding on a court — whether this particular agency interpretation in fact has the force of law is an issue to be decided in this judicial action. For the reason explained above, formulation in the course of this particular enforcement action likely would not satisfy the standard set forth in *Gonzales*.

Answer (D) is not correct. The Supreme Court has stated that agency interpretations articulated in the course of agency adjudications and enforcement actions may be entitled to some level of judicial deference. *See, e.g., Auer v. Robbins*, 519 U.S. 452 (1997).

4.1.   **Answer (A) is correct** because it is the least effective method to prompt the agency to act. All regulations tend to burden the persons and entities the regulations regulate. Thus, an effective argument for modifying an agency rule should not focus primarily on the burden the industry sustained. Rather, an effective argument would predominantly focus on the agency's statutory mandate: here, protection of the national parks.

       Answer (B) is not correct because it is an effective method to prompt the agency to act. Agencies are aware of public perceptions about the appropriateness or inappropriateness of administrative regulation.

       Answer (C) is not correct because it is an effective method to prompt the agency to act. Members of Congress can exert pressure on agencies or influence administrative agencies to act.

       Answer (D) is not correct because it is an effective method to prompt the agency to act. The argument to the agency combines concerns related to the agency's statutory mandate along with the industry's plight. Further, a formal petition for rulemaking requires the agency to at least consider whether a modification may be warranted. *See* APA § 553(e).

4.2.   In general, courts are cautious when deciding whether to compel an agency to initiate rulemaking and use *TRAC*'s "rule of reason" analysis. *Telecommunications Research & Action Center v. FCC*, 750 F.2d 70, 80 (D.C. Cir. 1984). A statutory timetable supplies content for application of the rule of reason, but courts rarely find timetables to be binding. *See, e.g., Action on Smoking and Health v. Department of Labor*, 100 F.3d 991, 994 (D.C. Cir. 1996) (noting that the statutory deadline was just one of several factors that a court should consider when deciding whether to intervene). Courts may decide not to enforce a statutory deadline when an agency can show that compliance with the deadline would be impossible or when the effect of expediting action may have a negative impact on agency activities with a higher priority. *See, e.g., TRAC*, 750 F.2d at 80.

4.3.   The court likely would order the agency to promptly provide a timetable for the rulemaking and to provide periodic progress reports to the court. The court would also be likely to retain jurisdiction of the case until final agency action in order to monitor and enforce the agency's compliance with its proposed timetable.

4.4.   **Answer (A) is correct.** APA § 551(14) defines an ex parte communication as a communication, other than a status report, which is not on the public record and by which reasonable prior notice to all parties is not given. The communication with the IRS by the pharmaceutical industry representatives may fall within this definition if it is not made part of the rulemaking record. However, the APA expressly prohibits ex parte communications only in the context of formal rulemaking and adjudication. APA § 557(d)(1)(A). The APA does not expressly prohibit ex parte communications in informal rulemaking proceedings.

However some statutes do. *See, e.g., Sierra Club v. Costle,* 657 F.2d 298 (D.C. Cir. 1981) (interpreting the 1977 Amendments to the Clean Air Act, which required the agency to establish a "rulemaking docket"). Additionally, some agencies prohibit ex parte communications by rule because undisclosed ex parte communications impart an air of unfairness. Thus, the IRS should, although it is not required to, consider docketing the ex parte communications.

Answer (B) is not correct. Although the APA does not require agencies to docket ex parte pre- or post-comment communications during informal rulemaking, it is a better practice for agencies to docket such information.

Answer (C) is not correct. The APA expressly prohibits ex parte communications only in the context of formal rulemaking and adjudication. APA § 557(d)(1)(A).

Answer (D) is not correct. The U.S. Court of Appeals for the District of Columbia Circuit has held that, although the APA does not include an express prohibition on ex parte communications in informal rulemaking, such communications should be banned in a rulemaking proceeding that involves "competing claims to a valuable privilege." However, this question involves a typical rulemaking proceeding, involving formulation of a standard for future application in a government program. The question does not involve a rulemaking proceeding that involves competing claims to a valuable privilege, such as an agency decision allocating "VHF channels" among cities. *See, e.g., Sangamon Valley Television Corp. v. United States,* 269 F.2d 221, 222 (D.C. Cir. 1959).

4.5.   **Answer (A) is correct.** APA § 553(b)(3) requires "notice" of a rulemaking to include "either the terms or substance of the proposed rule or a description of the subjects and issues involved." Courts have held that when a final rule deviates from the proposed rule, the notice should be found adequate when the final rule represents "a logical out-growth" of the proposed notice and comments or when the notice was sufficient to serve the policies underlying the notice requirement. *See, e.g., Chocolate Manufacturers Ass'n v. Block,* 755 F.2d 1098, 1105 (4th Cir. 1985). Here, the notice alerted persons that an important issue involved in the rulemaking was whether expenses for herbal supplements should be allowed.

Answer (B) is not correct. APA § 553(a) exempts agency rulemaking that involves public benefits from notice and comment requirements. However, the question involves a rule governing federal taxation of income, not public benefits.

Answer (C) is not correct. A final rule that reverses a position presented in the proposed rule arguably is a drastic deviation from the rule proposed. However, the issue is whether interested parties were sufficiently put on notice of the issue underlying the position.

Answer (D) is not correct because courts have upheld final rules when the agency reached a conclusion directly contrary to the position the agency took in the proposed rule. So long as the notice sufficiently allows interested parties fair opportunity to comment on issues raised by the proposed rule, the parties have no reason to claim they did not know that they should comment. *See, e.g., American Medical Ass'n v. United States,* 887 F.2d 760, 769 (7th Cir. 1989).

4.6.   **Answer (C) is correct.** The Supreme Court has explained that a rule would be arbitrary and capricious if, among other things, the agency relied on factors Congress did not intend for it to consider. *See, e.g., Motor Vehicle Mfrs. Ass'n of United States v. State Farm Mutual Automobile Ins. Co.,* 463 U.S. 29, 43 (1983). The statement of basis and purpose suggests that the IRS considered factors such as safety and efficacy in addition to fairness and reasonableness, but Congress did not preclude consideration of such factors.

Answer (A) is not correct. Section 706(2)(E)'s "substantial evidence" standard of review applies to agency determinations made in formal rulemaking or formal adjudications, not to those made in informal rulemaking.

Answer (B) is not correct. Although the correct standard of review is § 706(2)(A)'s arbitrary and capricious standard, a court using that standard scrutinizes the rule for more than whether an agency has a plausible basis for the policy decision.

Answer (D) is not correct. In *State Farm*, the Court explained that the agency must articulate a satisfactory explanation for its actions, including a rational connection between the facts found and the choice made. *Motor Vehicle Mfrs. Ass'n of United States v. State Farm Mutual Automobile Ins. Co.*, 463 U.S. 29, 43 (1983). Here, the agency supplied a rational connection: in both situations taxpayers are using income to address health conditions. Although not all individuals would agree with the policy choice, it is up to the agency to make that choice, so long as its choice meets the arbitrary and capricious standard, as further defined in *State Farm*.

4.7. APA § 553(c) requires a concise statement of the basis and purpose underlying a final rule. Congress did not intend for this provision to require an elaborate analysis of the rule or detailed discussion of the considerations underlying the rule. However, the standard of review used by courts when reviewing the substantive aspects of rules has resulted in agencies providing much more detailed and extensive explanations than what is technically required by the language of APA § 553(c). Supreme Court decisions have prompted agencies to draft contemporaneous explanations that (i) point to evidence in the rulemaking record supporting the rule, (ii) clarify the factors considered by the agency when deciding on the rule, and (iii) emphasize the logical connection between the evidence, findings of fact, and policy decisions. *See, e.g., Motor Vehicle Mfrs. Ass'n of United States v. State Farm Mutual Automobile Ins. Co.*, 463 U.S. 29, 43 (1983).

4.8. **Answer (C) is correct because it is an accurate statement.** The Act requires a Regulatory Flexibility Analysis when a rule may have a significant economic impact on a substantial number of small businesses, organizations, or governments.

Answer (A) is not correct because it is not an accurate statement. The Paperwork Reduction Act is concerned with unnecessary federal recordkeeping and reporting requirements.

Answer (B) is not correct because it is not an accurate statement. A series of executive orders, such as Executive Order 12,291 and Executive Order 12,866, are the primary sources of the need for cost/benefit analyses by federal agencies for major rules or significant agency action.

Answer (D) is not correct because it is not an accurate statement. The Unfunded Mandates Reform Act of 1995 is concerned with federal mandates requiring significant expenditures by state, local, or tribal governments or by the private sector.

4.9. **Answer (A) is correct because it is an accurate statement.** *See* APA § 611(a)(4)(A) & (B).

Answer (B) is not correct because it is not an accurate statement. Courts are not required to remand the rule. *See* 5 U.S.C. § 611(a)(4)(A) & (B).

Answer (C) is not correct because it is not an accurate statement. The Act provides that, in an action for judicial review of a rule, the Regulatory Flexibility Analysis shall become a part of the "entire record of agency action in connection with such review." *See* 5 U.S.C. § 611(b). Thus, when applying the arbitrary and capricious standard of review (or the substantial evidence standard of review if required by statute), courts will be able to consider the substance of the Regulatory Flexibility Analysis.

Answer (D) is not correct because it is not an accurate statement. The Act authorizes courts to review claims of agency noncompliance and, if found, authorizes courts to remand the rule or to defer enforcement of the rule. *See* 5 U.S.C. § 611(a)(4)(A) & (B).

4.10.   **Answer (D) is correct.** Section 10 of E.O. 12,866 provides that the Order is intended only to improve internal management and that the Order does not create any right or benefit, substantive or procedural, enforceable at law or equity by a party against the United States or its agencies or instrumentalities, or its officers or employees. Hence, neither agency compliance nor analysis substance is reviewable.

Answer (A) is not correct. This answer suggests that courts may review both an agency's noncompliance with the Order and the agency's cost/benefit analysis. As noted in the review of Answer (D), section 10 precludes judicial review of both agency compliance and substance.

Answer (B) is not correct. This answer suggests that courts may review an agency's noncompliance with the Order. As noted in the review of Answer (D), section 10 precludes judicial review of agency compliance.

Answer (C) is not correct. This answer suggests that courts may review an agency's cost/benefit analysis. As noted in the review of Answer (D), section 10 precludes judicial review of substance.

4.11.   On the one hand, several arguments support the view that the additional requirements enhance rulemaking. Centralized coordination helps ensure more efficient rulemaking across the whole of the federal government, and additional assessments, such as cost versus benefit or costs imposed on small businesses, should help ensure a "better" and "more effective" regulatory scheme. On the other hand, an increase in procedural requirements arguably makes rulemaking as to individual regulatory actions less efficient. Additional procedures make it more costly to promulgate individual rules and slow down the rulemaking process — and thus, additional procedures have been blamed, in part, for the stagnation, or ossification, of rulemaking.

4.12.   **Answer (C) is correct because it is an accurate statement.** *See* APA §§ 565(a) and 566(a).

Answer (A) is not correct because it is not an accurate statement. Section 6(a) of Executive Order 12,866 directs agencies to explore and "where appropriate" use consensual methods of rulemaking, including negotiated rulemaking.

Answer (B) is not correct because it is not an accurate statement. Section 563 authorizes an agency to make an initial determination as to whether a negotiated rulemaking committee can adequately represent the interests affected and whether it is feasible and appropriate to use negotiated rulemaking procedures. However, before proceeding, APA §§ 564 and 565 require the agency (1) to publish in the *Federal Register* information about its proposal to use negotiated rulemaking and (2) to solicit and consider comments on the proposal to establish a committee.

Answer (D) is not correct because it is not an accurate statement. The negotiated rulemaking procedures contemplate that the committee's consensus conclusions constitute a proposed rule. *See* APA §§ 562(7) and 566 (a) & (f). Accordingly, the agency must proceed with informal notice and comment procedures when the committee has reached a consensus.

5.1. **Answer (D) is correct.** Answers (A), (B), and (C) are all correct; therefore, Answer (D) is the best answer.

Answer (A) is not correct although it is an accurate statement. Rules relating to agency management or personnel, public property, loans, grants, benefits, and contracts are exempt from notice and comment rulemaking under APA § 553(a)(2).

Answer (B) is not correct although it is an accurate statement. Under APA § 553(b)(3)(B), when an agency has good cause to believe that notice would be impracticable, unnecessary, or contrary to the public interest, notice and comment rulemaking may be avoided. However, the agency must include the basis for the good cause exception in its final rule. Note that some states require agencies to use notice and comment procedures after the rule has been implemented.

Answer (C) is not correct although it is an accurate statement. APA § 553(b)(3)(A) exempts interpretive rules, general statements of policy, and rules of agency organization, procedure, or practice.

5.2. **Answer (A) is correct.** This rule would be exempted from notice and comment rulemaking under APA § 553(a)(1), the military and foreign affairs exemption. *Nademi v. INS*, 679 F.2d 811 (10th Cir. 1982).

Answer (B) is not correct. Although policy statements are exempt from notice and comment rulemaking under APA § 553(b)(3)(A), this rule is not a policy statement. Agencies use policy statements to advise regulated entities regarding how they will prospectively exercise discretionary power. Agencies often use policy statements to indicate how the agency will investigate or enforce its statutory authority. Additionally, agencies use policy statements to provide guidance to its employees. None of these was the case here.

Answer (C) is not correct. Although interpretive rules are exempt from notice and comment rulemaking under APA § 553(b)(3)(A), this rule is not an interpretive rule. Interpretive rules interpret statutory or regulatory language. Based on the facts presented in the question, this rule does not appear to do either.

Answer (D) is not correct. Because Answer (A) is correct, Answer (D) is necessarily incorrect.

5.3. **Answer (D) is correct.** This is an odd exception because the potential breadth is so large. The rationale for the exception lies in the compromise between (1) those who wanted more procedures placed on agencies to slow their ability to act, and (2) agencies who wanted fewer procedures placed on them so that they could act more quickly. At the time, regulated entities most feared government intrusion on liberty and property rights. Hence, Answer (C) is a correct statement and explains why notice and comment rulemaking is required in a large number of situations, but it does not explain the rationale for this particular exception.

Answer (A) is not correct. These rules in many cases affect the substantive rights of regulated entities or the general public. Thus, this statement is incorrect.

Answer (B) is not correct. While Congress by statute and agencies by rule have limited the broad scope of this exception, agencies had not adopted such rules at the time the APA was enacted. Hence, the existence of such rules now cannot support the creation of an exception when the APA was enacted.

Answer (C) is not correct. Although Answer (C) is a correct statement, as noted in Answer (A), this rationale cannot explain the existence of this broad exception.

5.4.   **Answer (D) is correct.** Although agencies are exempt from using notice and comment procedures for policy statements and interpretive rules, agencies must publish such rules pursuant to APA § 552(a)(1)(D). Moreover, if an agency does not publish the rule, then regulated entities cannot be adversely affected by the unpublished rules unless the entity had actual notice of the rules. *Id.* Professor Strauss has suggested for this reason that such rules should be called "publication rules." Peter L. Strauss, *Publication Rules in the Rulemaking Spectrum*, 53 Admin. L. Rev. 803 (2001).

Answer (A) is not correct. APA § 553(b)(A) specifically exempts some rules from the comment requirement.

Answer (B) is not correct. Valid interpretive rules and valid rules of agency organization, procedure, or practice are more than advisory. Agency personnel are required to follow them. Regulated entities are also expected to abide by them.

Answer (C) is not correct. An agency need not provide actual notice to any regulated entities; notice and comment procedures require publication notice only. Moreover, APA § 553(b)(A) specifically exempts policy statements and interpretive rules from this publication notice requirement.

5.5.   **Answer (A) is correct.** Unless an exception applies, agencies *must* use notice and comment rulemaking if they want a rule to have the force and effect of law.

Answer (B) is not correct. This statement is the opposite of the correct statement made in Answer (A) above.

Answer (C) is not correct. While agencies have discretion regarding whether to use notice and comment rulemaking, the ensuing rule will only have the force and effect of law if the agency uses notice and comment rulemaking.

Answer (D) is not correct. Agencies *must*, not should, use notice and comment rulemaking if they want the rule to have the force and effect of law.

5.6.   **Answer (B) is correct.** Agencies are required to use notice and comment rulemaking procedures to promulgate certain rules. When an agency does not use notice and comment rulemaking to issue a rule that will have the force and effect of law, a regulated entity may challenge the rule as invalid based upon the fact that the agency did not use proper procedures. That challenge is likely to be successful.

Answer (A) is not correct because it is incomplete. Both notice and comment procedures are required.

Answer (C) is not correct. While an agency must publish policy statements, failure to publish does not make a policy statement invalid; failure to publish affects enforceability.

Answer (D) is not correct. While Congress must delegate to an agency the power to promulgate legislative rules, agencies have inherent power to promulgate policy statements because such rules do not have binding effect.

5.7.   **Answer (C) is correct.** Pursuant to the binding norm test laid out in *American Hospital Ass'n v. Bowen*, 834 F.2d 1037, 1046 (D.C. Cir. 1987), an agency must use notice and comment procedures when a "policy statement" (1) has present effect, meaning it imposes rights and obligations; (2) restricts the agency's discretion; and (3) is characterized by the agency as legislative. Here, the new policy requires health facilities to have specific systems in place or they will be fined. Further, the rule states that "inspectors shall immediately fine . . . . " Thus, the agency has no discretion. The final factor, while relevant, is not determinative.

Answer (A) is not correct. Although the agency's characterization is a factor in whether a rule is a valid policy statement, it is not determinative. Moreover, contrary to the provided answer, the rule has immediate, present effect.

Answer (B) is not correct. This rule is not an interpretation of any statutory or regulatory language; hence, it cannot be an interpretive rule. Rather, the agency attempted to issue a valid policy statement. *Bowen* is the appropriate test to determine the validity of the agency's choice not to use notice and comment rulemaking.

Answer (D) is not correct. The factors identified in Answer (D) test whether a rule is a valid rule of agency organization, procedure, or practice. This rule is unlikely to be considered a procedural rule; it is a policy statement. As such, the test for determining whether notice and comment rulemaking was required is the test laid forth in *Bowen*, as identified in the analysis of Answer (C) above.

5.8.   There are a number of reasons agencies prefer to not to use notice and comment rulemaking. One of the biggest reasons that agencies prefer to avoid that process is that not using notice and comment rulemaking allows agencies to produce rules much more quickly and enables agencies to change rules more easily. Although notice and comment rulemaking was originally envisioned as a relatively quick process, it has become anything but quick. If powerful entities (*e.g.*, large corporations) will be affected by a proposed rule, these entities can submit detailed reports and comments, which make the notice and rulemaking process much more complex. In addition, procedures beyond those the APA requires also slow down the process. For example, in many instances, the agency must perform a cost-benefit analysis under Executive Order 12866. In short, the agency views notice and comment rulemaking as more onerous and much slower than non-legislative procedures.

5.9.   **Answer (B) is correct.** It can be difficult to discern the difference between a valid interpretive rule, which need not go through notice and comment rulemaking, and an invalid interpretive rule, which must go through notice and comment rulemaking. The Supreme Court has not provided a definitive test yet. Most lower courts have adopted the "legally binding," or "force of law," test. Pursuant to this test, if the challenged rule creates rights, imposes obligations, or changes existing law, the rule is not a valid interpretive rule.

Answer (A) is not correct. An interpretive rule, a rule that interprets a statute or regulation, is valid so long as the underlying law (statute or regulation) contains an adequate basis in the absence of interpretive rule for enforcement action. Whether a statute or regulation is being interpreted for the first time is not decisive in this determination.

Answer (C) is not correct. The validity of a rule is not affected by the agency's failure to publish the rule; however, the agency will be unable to enforce an interpretive rule against a regulated entity that did not have actual notice or publication notice of the rule.

Answer (D) is not correct. Importantly, an agency can never formulate a "rule" as that term is defined in the APA during an adjudication. Under APA § 551(4), a rule is defined as the whole or part of an agency statement of general applicability and future effect. Under APA § 551(5), rulemaking is the process for formulating, amending, or repealing a rule. In contrast, under APA § 551(7), adjudication is the process for formulating an order, which is the whole or part of a final disposition of an agency in a matter other than rulemaking. APA § 551(6). Hence, an adjudication cannot result in an APA rule, only an APA order. However, that order may have rule-like effect because the order may serve as precedent in future adjudications. Terminology is critical. Hence, this answer is essentially nonsense.

5.10.   **Answer (D) is correct.** Assuming that the agency correctly determined that its rule would have the force and effect of law and thus, the agency needed to use notice and comment rulemaking, then the agency can only amend that rule using notice and comment rulemaking. If the agency voluntarily used notice and comment procedures when such procedures were unnecessary, then it is likely that the agency could avoid using notice and comment rulemaking to amend the rule.

Answer (A) is not correct. This answer does not provide the correct test for determining whether the agency needs to use notice and comment rulemaking.

Answer (B) is not correct. If the agency had good cause for avoiding notice and comment rulemaking, then the agency could skip notice and comment rulemaking. Good cause is a valid exception only when notice and comment would be impracticable, unnecessary, or contrary to the public interest. If an agency invokes the good cause exception, the agency must provide its reasoning for such a finding in its final rule. Given the facts in the question, the agency cannot claim good cause.

Answer (C) is not correct. This answer combines two standards not relevant to this issue, arbitrary and capricious review and *Chevron* deference. Neither standard is relevant to the determination of whether an agency can legitimately avoid notice and comment rulemaking.

5.11.   Interpretive rules alone are not binding. Rather, the binding nature of such rules comes from the underlying statutes and regulations that the interpretive rules interpret. Thus, a valid interpretive rule does not by itself create new rights or obligations, but it works within the framework of existing law, and thus, may be binding in that sense.

5.12.   The regulated entity should be advised to follow the interpretive rule. Because an interpretive rule can reflect the view of the agency responsible for a regulatory scheme, and because courts accept such interpretations when the underlying duty can be found in the existing statute or regulation, regulated entities can rely on the interpretive rules and should follow them. Moreover, if the regulated entity relies on the interpretive rule, and the agency subsequently changes its rule, courts may prevent the agency from applying the rule retroactively against a regulated entity that had no notice of the change.

5.13.   **Answer (C) is correct.** Generally, interpretive rules may be amended without notice and comment or formal rulemaking procedures. However, an agency can choose to use more formal processes.

Answer (A) is not correct. Neither notice and comment nor formal rulemaking procedures are necessary to amend a validly issued interpretive rule.

Answer (B) is not correct. Neither notice and comment nor formal rulemaking procedures are necessary to amend a validly issued interpretive rule.

Answer (D) is not correct. The adjudication process is available to the agency should it wish to change its interpretation during the course of an adjudication, but the agency is not required to use this process.

5.14.   **Answer (B) is correct.** Pursuant to APA § 552(a)(1)(D), agencies must publish all rules for the rules to be enforced against a regulated entity that does not have actual notice of the rule.

Answer (A) is not correct. APA § 553(b)(3)(A) specifically exempts certain rules from notice and comment rulemaking procedures.

Answer (C) is not correct. Formal rulemaking procedures are required only when Congress specifically directs an agency to use formal rulemaking procedures. APA § 553(c). Generally, agencies are required to use formal rulemaking "[w]hen rules are required by statute to be made on the record after opportunity for an agency hearing." *United States v. Allegheny-Ludlum Steel Corp.*, 406 U.S. 742, 757 (1972).

Answer (D) is not correct. Generally, formal adjudication procedures are required only when Congress specifically directs the agency to use formal adjudication procedures. APA § 554(a). The magic words to look for are "on the record after opportunity for a hearing." *Chemical Waste Management, Inc. v. EPA*, 649 F. Supp. 347 (D.D.C. 1986).

5.15.   **Answer (B) is correct.** In determining whether *Chevron v. Natural Resources Defense Council, Inc.*, 467 U.S. 837 (1984), deference or *Skidmore v. Swift & Co.*, 323 U.S. 134 (1944), deference should apply in a given case, the Supreme Court places primary emphasis on the procedure the agency used to reach the interpretation. When the agency uses force of law procedures, meaning notice and comment, formal rulemaking, or formal adjudication, the agency earns *Chevron* deference. When the agency uses non-force of law procedures, *Skidmore* deference is generally appropriate pursuant to *United States v. Mead Corp.*, 533 U.S. 218, 237 (2001), and *Christensen v. Harris County*, 529 U.S. 576, 587 (2000).

Answer (A) is not correct. Reasonableness is the second step of *Chevron* deference. It is not relevant to determine whether *Chevron* or *Skidmore* applies.

Answer (C) is not correct. While an agency must publish interpretive rules to enforce them against a regulated entity, publication is not relevant to the determination of whether *Chevron* or *Skidmore* deference applies.

Answer (D) is not correct. Whether the interpretation is a longstanding one is a factor in *Skidmore* deference. It is not relevant to the determination of whether *Chevron* or *Skidmore* deference applies.

5.16.   **Answer (C) is correct because it is an inaccurate statement.** *Skidmore* identified the following factors as relevant to judicial review of the validity of an agency interpretive rule:

(1) the consistency of the agency's interpretation over time, (2) the thoroughness of the agency's consideration of the issue, and (3) the soundness of the reasoning offered in support of the interpretation. *See Skidmore v. Swift & Co.*, 323 U.S. 134, 140 (1944). Reasonableness is the second step of *Chevron* deference. It is not explicitly relevant when *Skidmore* applies.

Answer (A) is not correct because it is an accurate statement. The consistency of the agency's interpretation over time is one of the factors the Court identified in *Skidmore*.

Answer (B) is not correct because it is an accurate statement. The thoroughness of the agency's consideration of the issue is one of the factors the Court identified in *Skidmore*.

Answer (D) is not correct because it is an accurate statement. The soundness of the reasoning offered in support of the interpretation is one of the factors the Court identified in *Skidmore*.

5.17.   The best argument is that it is unfair to apply the new rule retroactively when the regulated entity relied on the prior rule. In the case of regulations, courts have agreed with this argument. *Wholesale and Dep't Store Union v. NLRB*, 466 F.2d 380, 393 (D.C. Cir. 1972). An agency may choose to apply a rule retroactively; however, the agency must evaluate the following factors in doing so: (1) whether the particular case is one of first impression, (2) whether the new rule represents an abrupt departure from well-established practice or merely attempts to fill a void in an unsettled area of law, (3) the extent to which the party against whom the new rule is applied relied on the former rule, (4) the degree of the burden that a retroactive order imposes on a party, and (5) the statutory interest in applying a new rule despite the reliance of a party on the old standard. *Retail, Wholesale & Dep't Store Union v. NLRB*, 466 F.2d 380, 390 (D.C. Cir. 1972). Thus, when the benefits of retroactivity outweigh the costs, then a court will likely uphold an agency's decision to apply the rule retroactively.

5.18.   **Answer (A) is correct.** Because of public safety concerns, the agency should be able to enact the rule quickly. APA § 553(b)(3)(B) permits agencies to avoid notice and comment procedures when good cause can be shown as to why such procedures would be impracticable, unnecessary, or contrary to public interest. The facts in this question present exactly the type of situation Congress anticipated for the good cause exception. Note that the agency need not go back after the crisis is over and use notice and comment rulemaking to promulgate the rule, unlike in some states. However, the agency must incorporate the reasons supporting the good cause finding in the rule.

Answer (B) is not correct. This answer includes the standard for determining whether an agency rule is a valid procedural rule. When a rule encodes a substantive value judgment and substantially alters the rights of the parties, notice and comment procedures are necessary. *See JEM Broadcasting Co., Inc. v. FCC*, 22 F.3d 320, 328 (D.C. Cir. 1994).

Answer (C) is not correct. This answer includes the standard for determining whether an agency rule is a valid policy statement. When a rule imposes new rights or obligations and restricts the agency's discretion, notice and comment procedures are necessary.

Answer (D) is not correct. This answer includes the standard for determining whether an agency rule is a valid interpretive rule. When an agency invokes its legislative authority and intends to create new duties, notice and comment procedures are necessary.

5.19.   **Answer (D) is correct.** Interpretive rules must be published to be enforced against a

QUESTIONS & ANSWERS: ADMINISTRATIVE LAW

regulated entity that lacks actual notice. APA § 552(a)(1)(D). Further, interpretive rules need not go through notice and comment rulemaking to be valid. ABA § 553(b)(3)(A). Finally, a reviewing court applies *Skidmore* deference, rather than *Chevron* deference, to determine whether to adopt the agency's interpretation. *United States v. Mead Corp.*, 533 U.S. 218, 237 (2001); *Christensen v. Harris County*, 529 U.S. 576, 587 (2000). Thus, all of the options, except III, are accurate, so Answer (D) is the correct choice.

Answer (A) is not correct. Answer (A) is incomplete. IV is also correct.

Answer (B) is not correct. Answer (B) is both incomplete and inaccurate. III is inaccurate, and II is omitted.

Answer (C) is not correct. Answer (C) is both incomplete and inaccurate. III is inaccurate, and II and IV are omitted.

5.20. **Answer (A) is correct because it is not an accurate statement.** Generally, notice of the agency's intent must be published in the Federal Register, but exceptions exist.

Answer (B) is not correct because it is an accurate statement. Agencies are not required to follow notice and comment procedures for rules that constitute valid interpretations of a statute or regulation pursuant to APA § 553(b)(2)(A).

Answer (C) is not correct because it is an accurate statement. Agencies are not required to follow notice and comment procedures for rules that are valid statements of general policy pursuant to APA § 553(b)(2)(A).

Answer (D) is not correct because it is an accurate statement. Agencies are not required to follow notice and comment procedures for rules that are valid rules of internal agency organization, procedure, or practice. APA § 553(b)(2)(A).

5.21. APA § 553(a) provides an exemption for matters involving a military or foreign affairs function of the United States and matters relating to agency management or personnel or to public property, loans, grants, benefits, or contracts. APA § 553(b) provides an exemption for interpretive rules; general statements of policy; or rules of agency organization, procedure, or practice; and when the agency for good cause finds that it is impracticable, unnecessary, or contrary to the public interest to engage and notice and its attendant public procedure. Thus, APA § 553(a) provides an exemption based on the subject matter, whereas APA § 553(b) provides exemptions based on the type of rule. A key difference is that subsection (a) provides an exemption from all of APA § 553, whereas subsection (b) provides an exemption from subsection (b)'s notice requirement and, thereby, from subsection (c)'s comment requirement. Thus, for example, a matter exempted by subsection (a) includes an exemption for the agency relating to a petition for rulemaking. Importantly, neither (a) nor (b) exempts agency rules from the requirements of APA § 552.

5.22. **Answer (C) is correct.** Agencies must use notice and comment procedures to promulgate "substantive rules," *i.e.*, rules that create rights or duties, unless an exception applies. A court would not likely find the rules at issue in this answer to be rules of agency organization, procedure, or practice, because the key inquiry in deciding whether a rule falls within this is whether the rule is essentially a "housekeeping measure" — a rule that alters merely the manner in which parties present themselves to the agency — or whether the rule affects, in a more substantive way, the rights and interests of regulated parties. *See, e.g., American Hosp. Ass'n v. Bowen*, 834 F.2d 1037 (D.C. Cir. 1987). These rules likely would be deemed "substantive" because they create new duties relating to private information. Further, a statutory time limit on rulemaking ordinarily is an insufficient excuse for non-compliance with the APA notice and comment procedures. *See, e.g., Air Transport Ass'n of Amer. v. Department of Transportation*, 900 F.2d 369 (D.C. Cir. 1990).

Answer (A) is not correct because this rule likely would fall within APA § 553(b)'s good cause exception. The good cause exception requires an agency to find that the notice and comment procedures are "impracticable, unnecessary, or contrary to the public interest." A situation is "impractical and contrary to the public interest" if the timely execution of agency functions would be impeded or if a safety measure must be put in place immediately. Certain pests, such as the Oriental fruit fly, create substantial risks to agriculture justifying immediate action.

Answer (B) is not correct because the rule likely would fall within APA § 553(b)'s good cause exception as well. An oil spill likely creates risks of injury to health and the environment justifying immediate action by the agency.

Answer (D) is not correct because the rule likely would fall within APA § 553(b)'s exception for rules of agency organization, procedure, or practice. The rules do not impose burdens on employers or change the substantive standards used during inspections carried out by OSHA. The rules apply only internally within the agency, helping to ensure that OSHA uses its inspection resources effectively.

5.23.   **Answer (A) is correct.** The good cause exception requires an agency to find that the notice and comment procedures are "impracticable, unnecessary, or contrary to the public interest." Courts narrowly construe the "good cause" exception. Here, for the reasons explained in answer selections for answers (B), (C), and (D), despite EPA's express finding of "good cause," the facts do not suggest a situation where the agency should be permitted to claim good cause and thereby avoid notice and comment procedures. *See Utility Solid Waste Activities Group v. E.P.A.*, 236 F.3d 749 (D.C. Cir. 2001). Further, amendment of a rule promulgated by notice and comment generally necessitates use of notice and comment procedures.

Answer (B) is not correct. A situation is "impractical" only if the timely execution of agency functions would be impeded or if a safety measure must be put in place immediately. The amendment would seem to promote safety to health and the environment, but the facts do not suggest any need for immediate action. In 1999, after notice and extensive commentary, EPA explained that the rule as originally promulgated would effectively prevent exposure to unreasonable risk.

Answer (C) is not correct. The "unnecessary" exception is allowed for situations in which the rule is a routine, insignificant determination; one that is inconsequential to industry and the public. However, the amendment here is significant — especially to industries that are now subject to an increased regulatory burden. Under the amendment, the clean-up requirements are triggered by any spill of regulated, liquid PCBs since the 50ppm trigger was, in essence, repealed.

Answer (D) is not correct. The "public interest" exception is limited to situations in which the interest of the public would be defeated by any requirement of advance notice. For example, the "public interest" exception would apply to a situation in which notice of a proposed rule would enable regulated persons to perhaps evade the rule or in which a safety measure must be put in place immediately. The facts do not present a situation where evasion of the new rule would be a concern, and, as noted in Answer (C), the facts also do not suggest any need for immediate action.

5.24. **Answer (A) is correct.** A rule is not a valid interpretive rule if, in the absence of a legislative rule, the legislative basis for the enforcement action is inadequate. *See American Mining Congress v. Mine Safety & Health Admin.*, 995 F.2d 1106 (D.C. Cir. 1993). The question is whether the duty to use certain, specified diagnostic tests was imposed by Rule 501 or whether the PBI Guidelines created a new duty. The better analysis of the question is that the PBI Guidelines created a new duty on physicians to use specific tests that are not otherwise required by either Rule 501 or existing medical standards of care. Moreover, the guidelines impose civil penalties for failure to use these tests. Thus, because the duty to use the specified diagnostic tests is created by the PBI Guidelines, § 553(b)'s exemption for interpretive rules does not apply, and the CDC was required to use notice and comment procedures. Thus, because the duty is created by the PBI Guidelines, § 553(b)'s exemption for interpretive rules does not apply.

Answer (B) is not correct. One indicator that the agency should have used notice and comment rulemaking is that the agency intended the rule to have the force and effect of law. *See American Mining Congress v. Mine Safety & Health Admin.*, 995 F.2d 1106, 1111–12 (D.C. Cir. 1993). Thus, a finding that the CDC did not intend the Guidelines to have the force and effect of law would weigh in favor of the rule being interpretive and would not support a finding that the law is invalid. Note, however, that the fact that CDC did not intend the Guidelines to have the force and effect of law is not determinative. Courts will look beyond the agency's characterization to determine whether the law creates new rights or duties.

Answer (C) is not correct. If the PBI Guidelines merely interpret Rule 501, then they are valid interpretive rules and the court should not set them aside.

Answer (D) is not correct. Although required (*see* APA § 552(a)), publication in the Federal Register is not a substitute for APA § 553's notice and comment procedures if the Guidelines should have been promulgated via notice and comment rulemaking.

5.25. **Answer (A) is correct.** As the Supreme Court recently held, the APA § 553(b)(3)(A) does not require an agency to use notice and comment procedures when it issues interpretive rules. *Perez v. Mortgage Bankers Ass'n*, 135 S. Ct. 1199 (2015). Interpretive rules are defined as rules that an agency issues to advise the public on the agency's construction of the statute and rules it administers. *Shalala v. Guernsey Memorial Hospital*, 514 U. S. 87, 99 (1995). Hence, notice and comment rulemaking are not required in this case.

Answer (B) is not correct. Under *Alaska Professional Hunters Ass'n v. F.A.A.*, 177 F.3d 1030 (D.C. Cir. 1999), the D.C. Circuit had held that notice and comment procedures are required to change an agency's interpretation of a legislative regulation when the prior interpretation is sufficiently authoritative and when there is a significant reliance interest involved. The Supreme Court rejected this holding. *Perez v. Mortgage Bankers Ass'n*, 135 S. Ct. 1199 (2015).

Answer (C) is not correct. This statement is incorrect. Generally, an agency may change a valid interpretive rule without using notice and comment procedures. *Alaska Professional Hunters* and *Paralyzed Veterans of America v. D.C. Arena L.P.*, 117 F.3d 579 (D.C. Cir. 1997), were the only cases holding otherwise and they have been overruled.

Answer (D) is not correct. While an agency may, for good cause, avoid notice and comment procedures when it is impracticable, unnecessary, or contrary to the public interest, there are no facts here that would support such a finding.

5.26.   Non-legislative procedures are advantageous because they allow the agency to more quickly and efficiently provide information to the public regarding the agency's views and intentions. Agencies can also use non-legislative procedures to provide centralized guidance to local or regional offices, thereby regularizing agency action that affects the public. Moreover, although interpretive rules and statements of policy are not "binding," regulated entities often comply with such rules. That is, although they are not binding in the sense that legislative rules are binding, regulated entities often comply because the interpretive statements and statements of policy reflect the agency's views regarding, for example, substantive aspects of statutes and future enforcement activities. On the other hand, because such rules are crafted without public input, they may fail to address a particular interest or concern, or otherwise fall short of the best regulatory response. Additionally, regulated entities that believe that a rule is unwise or illegal face a dilemma: they must either comply or risk having to challenge the validity of the agency's procedural choice in an enforcement proceeding. Further, even a complying regulated entity may find itself subject to an enforcement proceeding if the agency changes its mind. Although the advantages of non-legislative procedures generally inure to the benefit of agencies, an agency may nonetheless elect to use notice and comment procedures to issue an interpretive rule because the agency wants input from the regulated industry for policy and political reasons.

TOPIC 6:	ANSWERS
RETROACTIVITY	

6.1.   **Answer (A) is correct.** It represents the classic statement of retroactivity. A retroactive rule applies to facts that occurred prior to its enactment.

Answer (B) is incorrect. It represents a classic statement of prospectivity. A rule is prospective when it applies only to future activities.

Answer (C) is incorrect. This answer combines both A and B above; therefore, the rule is both prospective and retroactive.

Answer (D) is incorrect. A rule applied in an adjudication, while typically retroactive, may be either prospective or retroactive, depending on what actions the rule applies to. For example, a cease and desist order would be prospective.

6.2.   **Answer (D) is the correct answer because it is an inaccurate statement.** Retroactive laws are not *ex post facto* laws.

Answer (A) is not correct because it is an accurate statement. Retroactive rules deprive regulated entities of advance "notice" regarding the content and meaning of laws and how to conform their behavior to the laws.

Answer (B) is not correct because it is an accurate statement. Retroactive rules deprive regulated entities of the opportunity to bring their conduct into compliance with the law before they are penalized.

Answer (C) is not correct because it is an accurate statement. Because retroactive rules deprive regulated entities of advance "notice" regarding the content and meaning of laws and because retroactive rules deprive regulated entities of the opportunity to bring their conduct into compliance with the law before being penalized, retroactive rules are less likely to be consistent with due process.

6.3.   **Answer (D) is correct.** The Fifth and Fourteenth Amendments to the United States Constitution each contain a Due Process Clause. Due Process protects citizens from arbitrary denial of life, liberty, or property by the Government. While retroactivity is not explicitly prohibited in either clause, courts have interpreted these clauses to require that citizens have fair notice of laws limiting their conduct and to require that citizens have an opportunity to conform their conduct to those laws.

Answer (A) is not correct. The Equal Protection Clause provides that no state shall deny to any person within its jurisdiction "the equal protection of the laws." Retroactivity is not related to equal treatment.

Answer (B) is not correct. In the United States, *ex post facto* laws are *criminal* laws that apply retroactively by criminalizing conduct that was legal when originally performed. *Calder v. Bull*, 3 U.S. 386 (1798). Administrative rules are not criminal laws; rather they are regulatory, even if they have a penal element. Hence, although *ex post facto* laws are retroactive, retroactive administrative rules are not *ex post facto* laws.

Answer (C) is not correct. The Supremacy Clause establishes that federal law is "the supreme law of the land." It is not related to retroactivity.

6.4.   **Answer (C) is correct.** Despite the problems with retroactive rules, agencies may apply retroactive rules during an adjudication. Courts use a balancing test to determine whether the harm of retroactivity outweighs the benefits. Among the considerations that courts consider when evaluating an agency's choice to apply a rule retroactively are the following: (1) whether the particular case is one of first impression; (2) whether the new rule represents an abrupt departure from well-established practice or merely attempts to fill a void in an unsettled area of law; (3) whether and to what extent the party against whom the new rule is applied relied on the former rule; (4) whether and to what extent retroactivity imposes a burden on a party; and (5) whether there is a strong statutory interest in applying a new rule despite the reliance of a party on the old standard. *Retail, Wholesale & Dep't Store Union v. NLRB*, 466 F.2d 380, 390 (D.C. Cir. 1972). Thus, when the legislative interest in having the new rule applied retroactively is high and the regulated entity would not be substantially harmed by retroactivity, a court will likely uphold an agency's decision to apply the rule retroactively.

Answer (A) is not correct. Courts are reluctant to uphold an agency's decision to apply a retroactive rule in an adjudication when the issue before the agency is one of first impression because the regulated entity would have no way of knowing what the rule would be.

Answer (B) is not correct. Courts are very unlikely to uphold an agency's decision to apply a retroactive rule in an adjudication when that rule abruptly departs from the old rule, rather than simply fills a void, because a regulated entity is likely to rely on the prior rule.

Answer (D) is not correct. The formality of the procedures used to promulgate a rule does not affect the validity of a retroactive rule.

6.5.   **Answer (B) is correct.** Judicial decisions are normally retroactive. In contrast, there has been much litigation about whether, and when, administrative agencies are allowed to apply their decisions in adjudications *prospectively*. *See NLRB v. Wyman-Gordon Co.*, 394 U.S. 759 (1969). As a result, administrative decisions are usually applied retroactively unless doing so would deprive a regulated entity of adequate notice (and an opportunity to comply) or perpetuate unfairness. Neither would occur here because the rule refers to "inhumane conditions," and a court would likely interpret temperatures in excess of 90 degrees as "excessively hot temperatures."

Answer (A) is not correct. Because a court would likely conclude that temperatures in excess of 90 degrees are "excessively hot temperatures" and, thus, shipping puppies in such weather is "inhumane," Wild West should have known to conform its behavior accordingly.

Answer (C) is not correct. Because a court would likely conclude that temperatures in excess of 90 degrees are "excessively hot temperatures" and, thus, shipping puppies in such weather is "inhumane," Wild West should have known to conform its behavior accordingly. Importantly for this answer, there was no prior rule upon which Wild West could have relied.

Answer (D) is not correct. Arbitrary and capricious review generally applies to agency findings of fact and policy. While this deference standard might apply to an agency's decision to apply a rule retroactively, the standard in the case of retroactivity is further defined by the balancing factors identified in *Retail, Wholesale & Dep't Store Union v. NLRB*, 466 F.2d 380, 390 (D.C. Cir. 1972). Those factors are identified in the answer to question 6.4. Whether the agency carefully considered the issue is not one of those factors.

6.6.   **Answer (B) is correct.** For regulations, the norm is prospective application. However, an agency may issue a regulation with retroactive effect if Congress specifically gives the agency the power to enact retroactive regulations.

   Answer (A) is not correct. This statement is simply inaccurate. Retroactivity is the norm for adjudication, not rulemaking.

   Answer (C) is not correct. This statement is incomplete. While prospectivity is the norm for rulemaking, agencies can promulgate regulations with retroactive effect when Congress provides the agency with such authority.

   Answer (D) is not correct. This statement is simply incorrect.

6.7.   **Answer (C) is correct.** The regulation has prospective, not retroactive effect, because it applies to new cars two years after the effective date.

   Answer (A) is not correct. This statement is inaccurate. The regulation has no retroactive effect.

   Answer (B) is not correct. This statement is inaccurate. The process used for rulemaking, formal or informal, is irrelevant to whether a regulation can have retroactive effect.

   Answer (D) is not correct. This statement would be correct if the regulation had retroactive effect, but because the regulation does not, the statement is inaccurate.

6.8.   **Answer (D) is correct.** This regulation has both prospective and retroactive effects. The prospective piece — requiring all car and truck manufacturers to install side airbags in all new cars in two years — is not an issue. The retroactive piece — requiring retro-fitting — would be invalid unless Congress gave NHTSA authority to enact regulations with retroactive effect.

   Answer (A) is not correct. This statement is incomplete. Yes, the regulation has retroactive effect, but if Congress gave NHTSA the authority to promulgate retroactive regulations, then the regulation would be valid.

   Answer (B) is not correct. The statement is inaccurate. Whether a rulemaking is formal or informal (notice and comment) is irrelevant to the validity of retroactivity.

   Answer (C) is not correct. This statement is inaccurate. The regulation has both retroactive and prospective effects.

6.9.   **Answer (B) is correct.** An agency may choose to apply a rule retroactively; however, the agency must evaluate the following factors in doing so: (1) whether the particular case is one of first impression; (2) whether the new rule represents an abrupt departure from well-established practice or merely attempts to fill a void in an unsettled area of law; (3) the extent to which the party against whom the new rule is applied relied on the former rule; (4) the degree of the burden which a retroactive order imposes on a party; and (5) the statutory interest in applying a new rule despite the reliance of a party on the old standard. *Retail, Wholesale & Dep't Store Union v. NLRB*, 466 F.2d 380, 390 (D.C. Cir. 1972). Thus, when the benefits of retroactivity outweigh the costs, then a court will likely uphold an agency's decision to apply the rule retroactively.

Answer (A) is not correct. An agency has discretion to apply a rule retroactively; however, the agency must evaluate the *Retail, Wholesale* factors when doing so or its decision will be reversed on appeal.

Answer (C) is not correct. This statement is inaccurate. It refers to *Chevron's* second step. *Chevron U.S.A., Inc. v. Natural Resources Defense Council, Inc.*, 467 U.S. 837 (1984). When an agency applies a rule retroactively in an adjudication, the agency's decision is evaluated using the balancing test identified in *Retail, Wholesale. Chevron* is not the appropriate standard.

Answer (D) is not correct. Agencies may only promulgate retroactive rules through rulemaking when Congress specifically grants that power. Agencies have inherent power to apply new rules retroactively in adjudications. Retroactive effect is the norm in adjudications.

6.10. **Answer (D) is correct.** Agencies may promulgate regulations with retroactive effect only when Congress grants the agency that authority.

Answer (A) is not correct. *Chevron* is not the appropriate standard to apply to retroactivity issues. *Chevron* is the appropriate standard to apply to agency interpretations of statutory language arrived at using more procedurally prescribed processes.

Answer (B) is not correct. *Skidmore's* power to persuade test is not the appropriate standard to apply to retroactivity issues. *Skidmore* is the appropriate standard to apply to agency interpretations of statutory language arrived at using less procedurally prescribed processes. *Skidmore v. Swift & Co.*, 323 U.S. 134 (1944).

Answer (C) is not correct. This statement is inaccurate. Agencies may promulgate retroactive rules using rulemaking or using adjudication.

6.11. **Answer (C) is correct.** In this case, the harm to the regulated entity of applying the "new rule" retroactively is minimal. Wild West could easily have learned what DOA's rule was by looking at the published orders. Moreover, DOA consistently applied its rule. Given that the legislative interest in protecting puppies from inhumane treatment is high, retroactivity is appropriate in this case. In other words, the regulated entity should have been aware of the agency's position and cannot claim surprise.

Answer (A) is not correct. This statement is true, but incomplete.

Answer (B) is not correct. This statement is true, but incomplete.

Answer (D) is not correct. Publication notice will generally suffice for due process concerns. An agency must provide actual notice only when it otherwise fails to publish its rules.

6.12. **Answer (C) is correct because it is an inaccurate statement.** According to *Retail, Wholesale & Dep't Store Union v. NLRB*, 466 F.2d 380, 390 (D.C. Cir. 1972), a court will balance the following factors: (1) whether the particular case is one of first impression; (2) whether the new rule represents an abrupt departure from well-established practice or merely attempts to fill a void in an unsettled area of law; (3) the extent to which the party against whom the new rule is applied relied on the former rule; (4) the degree of the burden which a retroactive order imposes on a party; and (5) the statutory interest in applying a new rule despite the reliance of a party on the old standard.

Answer (A) is not correct because it is an accurate statement. When a new rule is an abrupt departure from the old rule, it is less likely that a regulated entity would know to change its behavior. When, however, the new rule fills a void, it is more likely that the regulated entity knew or should have known the rule was possible because the void existed.

Answer (B) is not correct because it is an accurate statement. When a regulated entity relies on a prior rule to its determent, then it is generally unfair to penalize the regulated entity unless the reliance was unjustified.

Answer (D) is not correct because it is an accurate statement. When applying rules retroactively would further an important statutory interest, such as protecting the public or (in this case) animals, then retroactivity may be appropriate.

6.13. These are the facts from *Retail, Wholesale and Department Store Union v. NLRB*, 466 F.2d 380 (D.C. Cir. 1972). In that case, the Court held that the NLRB should not be allowed to apply the decision in *NLRB v. Fleetwood Trailer Co.*, 389 U.S. 375 (1967) retroactively because the regulated entity would have had no notice of the rule change.

The Court stated that:

> The standard to which the Company attempted to conform its conduct in this case was well established and long accepted by the Board. Unlike *Chenery*, this is not the kind of case where the Board "had not previously been confronted by the problem" and was required by the very absence of a previous standard and the nature of its duties to exercise the "function of filling in the interstices of the Act." Rather it is a case where the Board had confronted the problem before, had established an explicit standard of conduct, and now attempts to punish conformity to that standard under a new standard subsequently adopted.

Retail, Wholesale and Department Store Union v. NLRB, 466 F.2d at 391. In contrast, if the strike had occurred after the Supreme Court handed down the *Fleetwood* decision, then the soft drink manufacturer would have had notice that its behavior had to conform to the *Fleetwood* standard. In that case, the NLRB could likely apply its rule retroactively.

7.1 **Answer (D) is correct** because it is not an accurate statement. Rationality is irrelevant to the availability of judicial review.

Answer (A) is not correct because it is an accurate statement. A court must have a statutory grant of jurisdiction to hear any case, including administrative cases. Generally, the federal question statute, 28 U.S.C. § 1331, or the applicable statute provide statutory grants of jurisdiction. The APA does not provide jurisdiction.

Answer (B) is not correct because it is an accurate statement. One plaintiff (and only one of possibly many plaintiffs) must have standing for a court to hear a case pursuant to the cases and controversies requirement in Article III of the United States Constitution.

Answer (C) is not correct because it is an accurate statement. A case must be ripe for judicial review for a court to hear it. The ripeness doctrine predates the APA, and, unlike finality and exhaustion, ripeness was not codified in the APA. Hence, it remains a common law issue. Ripeness issues generally arise in pre-enforcement review cases.

7.2. **Answer (B) is correct** because it is not an accurate statement. The APA is not a jurisdictional statute, and a court must have a statutory grant of jurisdiction to hear a case.

Answer (A) is not correct because it is an accurate statement. Because lawsuits against agencies invariably raise questions about federal law, the general federal question statute can be used to establish jurisdiction. Suit is filed in a district court.

Answer (C) is not correct because it is an accurate statement. Often, the enabling statute will contain a statutory grant of jurisdiction. For example, the Hobbs Act, 28 U.S.C. § 2342, directs that most orders from the Federal Communications Commission be reviewed directly by a court of appeals, bypassing the district court.

Answer (D) is not correct because it is an accurate statement. Often, the applicable statute will contain a statutory grant of jurisdiction. For example, the Clean Air Act provides that judicial challenges to rules promulgated under the Act must be brought in the United States Court of Appeals for the District of Columbia. Not only is the district court bypassed, but only one appellate court is appropriate.

7.3. **Answer (A) is correct.** Under prudential standing, a plaintiff must have a cause of action to bring a case. Pursuant to APA § 702, any person who is "adversely affected or aggrieved by agency action within the meaning of a relevant statute" has a cause of action. Pursuant to this language, courts require plaintiffs to be within the zone of interests that the relevant statute protects. The zone of interests test is resolved using statutory interpretation analysis: who or what did Congress intend to protect when it enacted the statute? For example, in *Air Courier Conference of America v. American Postal Workers Union, AFL-CIO*, 498 U.S. 517, 526 (1991), the Supreme Court held that postal workers were not within the zone of interests of a statute that created the United States Postal Service as a monopoly.

Answer (B) is not correct. Courts do not have inherent authority to review administrative action, and there is no common law (non-statutory) right of review

Answer (C) is not correct. Because the APA can be used as the basis for creating a cause of action, the agency's enabling statute need not include a cause of action.

Answer (D) is not correct. The elements of jurisdiction and cause of action are separate and cannot be conflated. A court must have jurisdiction. A plaintiff must have constitutional standing and prudential standing, the latter of which includes a cause of action.

7.4.   **Answer (A) is correct because it is not an accurate statement.** Although the Supreme Court, in *Abbott Laboratories v. Gardner*, 387 U.S. 136, 141 (1967), stated that the APA embodies a presumption of judicial review that must be overcome only upon a showing of "clear and convincing evidence" that Congress intended to preclude review, the Court has backed away from this high standard. Today, the presumption can be overcome with a showing that congressional intent to preclude review is "fairly discernible in the statutory scheme." *Block v. Community Nutrition Institute*, 467 U.S. 340, 351(1984).

Answer (B) is not correct because it is an accurate statement. APA § 702(a)(2) provides that APA §§ 701–06 do not apply to the extent that agency action is "committed to agency discretion by law." To determine whether agency action is committed to agency discretion, a court will look to the relevant statute to determine whether there are meaningful standards for the court to review the agency's decision. This test is known as the "no law to apply test." *See, e.g., Heckler v. Chaney*, 470 U.S. 821, 831 (1985) (holding that the decision of whether to enforce a particular law was committed to prosecutorial discretion).

Answer (C) is not correct because it is an accurate statement. APA § 702(a)(1) provides that APA §§ 701–06 do not apply to the extent that the applicable statute precludes judicial review. In essence, when Congress intends that agency decisions made pursuant to a particular statute are non-reviewable or are reviewable only for specific issues, then that congressional intent controls. *See, e.g., Block v. Community Nutrition Institute*, 467 U.S. 340, 351 (1984) (holding that review was precluded in specific situations where the relevant statute expressly provided for review by specific groups but not by all).

Answer (D) is not correct because it is an accurate statement. Most administrative law cases are brought under the APA. APA § 702 creates a cause of action, but only for persons suffering legal wrong or adversely affected or aggrieved by *agency action*. APA § 551(13) defines agency action to include, "the whole or a part of an agency rule, order, license, sanction, relief, or the equivalent or denial thereof, or failure to act." While the requirement that there be agency action is generally met, in *Lujan v. National Wildlife Federation*, 497 U.S. 871, 899 (1990), the Supreme Court held that the Bureau of Land Management's refusal to adopt a plan to protect public lands from off-road vehicle use was not agency action. While an agency's failure to act can be considered agency action, the agency's failure to act must relate to a discrete act, for example a failure to adopt a particular regulation or order. An agency's general failure to protect public lands is not discrete.

7.5.   **Answer (D) is correct because it includes all of the choices.** In order to challenge administrative action, a plaintiff must show that he or she has exhausted the administrative remedies, that the case is ripe for review, and that the agency action is final. Answer (D) includes all of these options.

Answer (A) is not correct although it is an accurate statement. The requirement that plaintiffs exhaust administrative remedies gives the agency a chance to correct its decision, if necessary. This requirement predated the APA; however, in *Darby v. Cisneros*, 509 U.S. 137, 147–48 (1993), the Supreme Court held that APA § 704 includes a statutory exhaustion requirement that supersedes the common law requirement when suit is brought under the APA. Exhaustion is required in two circumstances: (1) when a statute expressly requires exhaustion, and (2) when an agency rule requires exhaustion and provides for an automatic stay of the agency's decision pending the appeal.

Answer (B) is not correct although it is an accurate statement. A case must be ripe for judicial review for a court to hear it. The ripeness doctrine predates the APA, and, unlike finality and exhaustion, ripeness was not codified in the APA. Hence, it remains a common law issue. Ripeness issues generally arise in pre-enforcement review cases.

Answer (C) is not correct although it is an accurate statement. Before the APA was enacted, the Supreme Court had held that only final agency action was reviewable. The requirement reflects that courts are reluctant to review interim steps because the choices at those steps may change. APA § 704 codified this requirement. Agency action is final when (1) it is the consummation of the agency's decision-making process, and (2) it is one by which rights or obligations have been determined or from which legal consequences will flow. *Bennett v. Spear*, 520 U.S. 154, 177–78 (1997).

7.6.   **Answer (C) is correct.** To the extent that the standing doctrine is constitutionally based, rather than prudentially based, it is premised upon Article III's case and controversy requirement. *See United States v. Richardson*, 418 U.S. 166, 171 (1974); *Sierra Club v. Morton*, 405 U.S. 727, 754 (1972).

Answer (A) is not correct. The commerce clause is irrelevant to the standing doctrine.

Answer (B) is not correct. The due process clause is irrelevant to the standing doctrine.

Answer (D) is not correct. While Article II's vesting clause establishes the powers of the president, it is irrelevant to the standing doctrine.

7.7.   **Answer (A) is correct.** In *Lujan v. Defenders of Wildlife*, 504 U.S. 555 (1992), the Supreme Court identified the elements for constitutional standing:

> [T]he irreducible constitutional minimum of standing contains three elements[:] First, the plaintiff must have suffered an injury in fact — an invasion of a legally-protected interest which is (a) concrete and particularized, and (b) actual [and] imminent, not conjectural or hypothetical. Second, there must be a causal connection between the injury and the conduct[,] complained of — the injury has to be fairly . . . trace[able] to the challenged action of the defendant, and not . . . the result [of] the independent action of some third party not before the court. Third, it must be likely, as opposed to merely speculative, that the injury will be redressed by a favorable decision.

Id. at 560–61 (internal quotations omitted). Answer (A) includes all three elements.

Answer (B) is not correct. When a plaintiff suffers only a generalized grievance, meaning that the injury does not affect the plaintiff in a personal and individual way, the plaintiff does not have standing because the plaintiff does not have injury in fact. The legislature, rather than the courts, is the appropriate place to resolve generalized grievances. *BiMetallic*

Investment Co. v. State Board of Equalization, 239 U.S. 441, 445 (1915).

Answer (C) is not correct. Procedural injury, an agency's failure to follow a required procedure, is considered a generalized grievance and thus, is insufficient by itself to establish the requisite particularized injury for standing. *Lujan v. Defenders of Wildlife*, 504 U.S. 555, 573 n.8 (1992).

Answer (D) not incorrect. Answer (D) is both incomplete and contains an element of prudential standing. The question asked about constitutional standing. The missing element is causation. The prudential element is the zone of interests. Hence, this answer is inaccurate.

7.8.   **Answer (B) is correct.** Recreational, aesthetic, and environmental injuries are sufficient for constitutional standing requirements. *See Sierra Club v. Morton*, 405 U.S. 727, 734 (1972). Prudential standing, associational standing, requires that the Sierra Club have a member with constitutional injury. In this case, the member's interest in continuing to hike in the area would count as an injury in fact, specifically a recreational injury.

Answer (A) is not correct. In *Sierra Club v. Morton*, 405 U.S. 727, 730 (1972), the Sierra Club sought to challenge administrative action that it viewed as having an adverse effect on the environment. It did so based on its status as an organization interested in the environment. The Court rejected that argument. The Sierra Club would need to establish direct injury to itself, for example that the Club cannot attract new members, or injury in fact to one of its members.

Answer (C) is not correct. While a member who had studied birds in the past in this particular area and planned to do so again in the future would have a direct injury, a member who has no plan to return in the future does not. *See Animal Legal Defense Fund, Inc. v. Espy*, 23 F.3d 496, 500–01 (D.C. Cir. 1994).

Answer (D) is not correct. While only one plaintiff need have standing, neither the Sierra Club nor the senator would have standing. The Sierra Club would need either a direct injury or a member with injury. Members of Congress do not have a particularized injury to challenge a statute's constitutionality. *Raines v. Byrd*, 521 U.S. 811, 830 (1997); *see also, Harrington v. Bush*, 553 F.2d 190, 206 (D.C. Cir. 1997) (holding that members of Congress do not have particularized injury when they challenge agency action that deviates from the statute even though the legislator helped pass the statute).

7.9.   Generally, plaintiffs must assert their own injuries and not those of a third party. *See Tileston v. Ullman*, 318 U.S. 44, 46 (1943). However, in the case of an association, the association can sue on behalf of its members if (1) one of its members had injury in fact, (2) if the lawsuit relates to the purpose of the organization, and (3) if the lawsuit does not require individual members' participation, meaning that the lawsuit seeks injunctive or declaratory relief. The member's required injury need not be financial, but can involve injury to environmental, aesthetic, or recreational interests. *Sierra Club v. Morton*, 405 U.S. 727, 734 (1972).

7.10.   **Answer (B) is correct.** The facts of the question indicated that the organization did not present any evidence that if the regulation were changed, the harm would be redressed. Hence, the organization cannot show redressibility. Arguably, the organization has also failed to show that the harm is fairly traceable to the new regulation (causation), which is what the

Supreme Court held in *Simon v. Eastern Kentucky Welfare Rights Organization*, 426 U.S. 26, 62 (1976).

Answer (A) is not correct. The facts of the question specifically indicate that the parties conceded that low income people would be harmed by the new regulation; hence, the organization can establish injury.

Answer (C) is not correct. The harm the indigent individuals will suffer is not sufficiently generalized, although this is a close question.

Answer (D) is not correct. Because the organization cannot establish one and possibly two elements of constitutional standing, causation and redressibility, a court will likely grant the motion and dismiss the case.

7.11.   **Answer (B) is correct.** Because John has not suffered an injury yet and he continues to receive loans under the old regulations, his case would not be ripe.

Answer (A) is not correct. Assuming the case was ripe, John would have an injury in fact because he would likely lose his loans. John's injury would be fairly traceable to the regulation change; hence, John can show causation. And, a favorable court ruling would likely redress the injury; therefore, John can demonstrate redressibility, the third element of constitutional standing. Because John's injury is particularized and not generalized, he can also show prudential standing.

Answer (C) is not correct. Under APA § 704, exhaustion is required in two circumstances: (1) when a statute expressly requires exhaustion, and (2) when an agency rule requires exhaustion and provides for an automatic stay of the agency's decision pending the appeal. *Darby v. Cisneros*, 509 U.S. 137, 148 (1993).

Answer (D) is not correct. A court would have a statutory grant of jurisdiction under the general federal question statute, 28 U.S.C. § 1331, because the lawsuit questions the validity of a federal regulation.

7.12.   **Answer (C) is correct.** NWF needs to show that it has a member who has an injury in fact. The only option that shows a member with injury in fact is Answer (C). Aesthetic injury is sufficient for constitutional injury under *Lujan v. Defenders of Wildlife*, 504 U.S. 555, 562–63 (1992)

Answer (A) is not correct. Under *Lujan v. Defenders of Wildlife*, 504 U.S. 555, 573 n.8 (1992), procedural injury alone cannot serve as injury in fact.

Answer (B) is not correct. If NWF could show that the Corps' action would actually affect its ability to recruit new members, then Answer (B) would be accurate. However, it is highly unlikely that the Corps' decision to issue the permit would have any impact on NWF's ability to recruit new members.

Answer (D) is not correct. While NWF does not have a concrete particularized injury, a member, such as the member identified in Answer (C), would have a particularized injury and could help NWF establish standing.

7.13.   **Answer (A) is correct.** This is a very hard question. In *Federal Election Commission v. Akins*, 524 U.S. 11, 26 (1998), the Court held that Akins had standing. The injury in fact was his inability to obtain information. Although the Court acknowledged that the grievance was widely shared, the Court reasoned that because the statute specifically provided that "any party" could file a complaint with the FEC and that "any person aggrieved" by a FEC denial of its complaint could obtain judicial review, Congress had overridden prudential standing in this case. Prudential standing, unlike constitutional standing, can be overridden.

Answer (B) is not correct. Under *Lujan v. Defenders of Wildlife*, 504 U.S. 555, 573 n.8 (1992), procedural injury alone cannot serve as injury in fact.

Answer (C) is not correct. While a procedural injury is not sufficient alone to serve as injury in fact, an informational injury can be sufficient.

Answer (D) is not correct. As noted in Answer (A), generally, Akins' injury would appear to be universally shared and thus, not sufficient for prudential standing. But in this case, the Court concluded that Congress had chosen to override prudential standing because the statute gave voters both a right to challenge FEC decisions and a right to appeal denial of those challenges. Without this unique set of circumstances, Akins would likely have had only a generalized grievance.

7.14.   **Answer (A) is correct.** Dave meets all the elements for reviewability. Dave has constitutional and prudential standing. A court would have jurisdiction under the federal question statute. Dave would have a cause of action because he is likely within the zone of interests the statute was designed to protect. The action is final agency action, and there are no timing issues.

Answer (B) is not correct. Under APA § 704, exhaustion is required in two circumstances: (1) when a statute expressly requires exhaustion, and (2) when an agency rule requires exhaustion and provides for an automatic stay of the agency's decision pending the appeal. *Darby v. Cisneros*, 509 U.S. 137, 148 (1993). Here, neither the Act nor the regulation requires exhaustion.

Answer (C) is not correct. Before the APA was enacted, the Supreme Court had held that only final agency action was reviewable. The requirement reflects that courts are reluctant to review interim steps because the choices at those steps may change. APA § 704 codified this requirement. Agency action is final when (1) it is the consummation of the agency's decision-making process, and (2) it is one by which rights or obligations have been determined or from which legal consequences will flow. *Bennett v. Spear*, 520 U.S. 154, 177–78 (1997). Here, the agency's act in denying the license is final agency action.

Answer (D) is not correct. A case must be ripe for judicial review for a court to hear it. The ripeness doctrine predates the APA and, unlike finality and exhaustion, ripeness was not codified in the APA. Hence, it remains a common law issue. Ripeness issues generally arise in pre-enforcement review cases. Here, the agency has denied Dave's request for a license, so there are no pre-enforcement issues. The case is ripe.

7.15.   **Answer (C) is correct.** In this case, the relevant Act, the ESA, specifically requires the ranchers to exhaust their administrative remedies. It does not matter that there is no stay of the decision during the appeal process. Were the exhaustion requirement found in an agency rule, then the existence of a stay would be relevant. Hence, exhaustion is required.

Answer (A) is not correct. Although the correct statute for determining whether the ranchers have a cause of action is the ESA and not the APA, the ranchers must meet all reviewability requirements. In this case, they must exhaust their administrative remedies pursuant to the ESA.

Answer (B) is not correct. The relevant statute for determining a cause of action in this case is the ESA, not the APA.

Answer (D) is not correct. Assuming this case was brought under the APA, APA § 702 creates a cause of action for persons suffering legal wrong or adversely affected or aggrieved by *agency action*. APA § 551(13) defines agency action to include, "the whole or a part of an agency rule, order, license, sanction, relief, or the equivalent or denial thereof, or failure to act." Here, the agency's decision to limit grazing on federal lands would likely be considered a discrete agency action. *Bennett v. Spear*, 520 U.S. 154, 177–78 (1997).

7.16.   APA § 702(a)(1) provides that APA §§ 701–06 do not apply to the extent that the applicable statute precludes judicial review. In essence, when Congress intends that agency decisions made pursuant to a particular statute are non-reviewable or are reviewable only for specific issues, that decision controls. In *Block v. Community Nutrition Institute*, 467 U.S. 340, 351 (1984), the Court reasoned that dairy handlers and producers would have standing to challenge the Secretary's milk market orders because the statute specifically provided an appeal process for them. In contrast, the Court held that the consumers could not challenge the Secretary's milk market orders because they were not mentioned in the appeal process. The Court concluded that congressional intent to preclude consumers from suing was fairly discernable in the statutory scheme.

7.17.   **Answer (B) is correct.** APA § 702(a)(2) provides that APA §§ 701–06 do not apply to the extent that agency action is "committed to agency discretion by law." To determine whether agency action is committed to agency discretion, a court will look to the relevant statute to determine whether there are meaningful standards for the court to review the agency's decision. This test is known as the "no law to apply test." Here, there are no standards, and the Act specifically indicates that the decision of whether to issue security clearances is committed to the Secretary's discretion. However, any constitutional challenge would remain because Congress cannot give the Secretary discretion to violate the Constitution. *Webster v. Doe*, 486 U.S. 592, 603 (1988).

Answer (A) is not correct. While Rick does have direct injury and otherwise likely meets the reviewability requirements, the Act specifically commits decisions relating to security clearances to the Secretary's discretion and provides no law by which to evaluate the Secretary's decision.

Answer (C) is not correct. Reviewability is unrelated to whether the case involves national security issues.

Answer (D) is not correct. To overcome the presumption of reviewability, congressional intent to preclude review must be fairly discernible in the statutory scheme. There is no indication in this fact pattern that the Act addresses this issue at all.

7.18.   While the Department's adjusted census would be the Department's final action, the Department's count would not lead to reapportionment. Rather, the President's count would lead to reapportionment; however, the President cannot be sued under the APA. Thus, the Department's action is not final agency action because direct legal consequences will not flow from the Department's action, so the court should grant the motion. In *Franklin v. Massachusetts*, 505 U.S. 788 (1992), the Court held exactly that.

7.19.   **Answer (A) is correct.** APA § 702 creates a cause of action for persons suffering legal wrong or adversely affected or aggrieved by *agency action*. APA § 551(13) defines agency action to include, "the whole or a part of an agency rule, order, license, sanction, relief, or the equivalent or denial thereof, or failure to act." The facts in this question indicated that the CPSC failed to act. The Supreme Court has reasoned that an agency's failure to act can be considered agency action when the action is "discrete agency action that [the agency] is required to take." *Norton v. Southern Utah Wilderness Alliance*, 542 U.S. 55, 64 (2004).

Answer (B) is not correct. The question asks about reviewability, not about the validity of the CPSC's decision. The facts in Answer (B) relate to the validity of the decision.

Answer (C) is not correct. The question asks about reviewability, not about the validity of the CPSC's decision. The substantial evidence test is applicable when either a statute required this standard or when the agency's decision-making process involved formal procedures. APA § 706(2)(E).

Answer (D) is not correct. This statement is incorrect. If the CPSC's regulation requires exhaustion and stays the action pending that appeal, then the action would not be immediately reviewable. Rather, Child Advocates would need to seek administrative review before filing its action in court.

7.20. The ripeness doctrine "prevent[s] the courts, through avoidance of premature adjudication, from entangling themselves in abstract disagreements over administrative policies, and also [protects] the agencies from judicial interference until an administrative decision has been formalized and its effects felt in a concrete way by the challenging parties." *Abbott Laboratories v. Gardner*, 387 U.S. 136, 148 (1967). The two-part test requires courts to evaluate both (1) the fitness of the issues for judicial determination, and (2) the hardship to the parties of withholding the issue from judicial consideration. Applying that test to the facts in this question, a court would likely find that this issue is ripe. First, the relevant issue — whether the FDA exceeded its statutory authority — is purely legal and thus, fit for judicial determination. Second, the drug manufacturers would face substantial hardship. Although the drug manufacturers could obtain judicial review in response to an enforcement action, they would be required to choose whether to incur criminal sanctions for refusing to follow the regulation or to pay the substantial costs of complying with a regulation they view as unlawful. Because the drug manufacturers would have to make an immediate and significant change or face serious penalties for non-compliance, the action is ripe. In *Abbott Labs*, the Court held that the matter was ripe for review because the plaintiffs would be faced with the choice of incurring immediate compliance costs or facing the risk of criminal sanctions. The Court held that the plaintiffs should not be required to undergo this risk.

7.21. The ripeness doctrine "prevent[s] the courts, through avoidance of premature adjudication, from entangling themselves in abstract disagreements over administrative policies, and also [protects] the agencies from judicial interference until an administrative decision has been formalized and its effects felt in a concrete way by the challenging parties." *Abbott Laboratories v. Gardner*, 387 U.S. 136, 148 (1967). The two-part test requires courts to evaluate both (1) the fitness of the issues for judicial determination, and (2) the hardship to the parties of withholding the issue from judicial consideration. Applying that test to the facts in this question, a court would likely find that this issue is not ripe. First, the relevant issue — whether the plan permits excessive logging and clear cutting — is not purely legal, like the issue in *Abbott Labs*, but is factual. Second, the Club will suffer no hardship in delaying judicial review. The plan itself does not authorize the cutting of any trees. Thus, no timber cutting can take place until the Forest Service actually makes a timber sale. When it does, the Club can then challenge the timber sale. In *Ohio Forestry Association, Inc. v. Sierra Club*, 523 U.S. 726 (1998), the Court held that the case was not ripe for review. The Court noted that if the Club had sued under National Environmental Policy Act (NEPA), alleging that the Environmental Impact Statement was inadequate, the action would have been ripe. "NEPA, unlike the NFMA, simply guarantees a particular procedure, not a particular result . . . . Hence a person with standing who is injured by a failure to comply with the NEPA procedure may complain of that failure at the time the failure takes place, for the claim can never get riper." *Id.* at 737.

7.22. The ripeness doctrine "prevent[s] the courts, through avoidance of premature adjudication, from entangling themselves in abstract disagreements over administrative policies, and also [protects] the agencies from judicial interference until an administrative decision has been formalized and its effects felt in a concrete way by the challenging parties." *Abbott Laboratories v. Gardner*, 387 U.S. 136, 148 (1967). The two-part test requires courts to evaluate both (1) the fitness of the issues for judicial determination, and (2) the hardship to the parties of withholding the issue from judicial consideration. Applying that test to the facts in this question, a court would likely find that this issue is not ripe. First, the relevant issue — whether the FDA exceeded its statutory authority — is purely legal and thus, fit for judicial determination.

However, unlike *Abbott Labs*, the color additives manufacturers would not face substantial hardship if judicial review were delayed because no civil or criminal penalties will attach. The manufacturers will simply lose their certification temporarily. Moreover, that loss can be challenged both at the administrative and the judicial level. Hence, the issue is not ripe. In *Toilet Goods Association v. Gardner*, 387 U.S. 158 (1967), the Court held that the case was not ripe for review; the analysis for the first issue was slightly different because the facts presented differed from those presented here.

8.01. An agency's interpretation of regulatory text is generally entitled to *Auer* deference. When an agency interprets its own regulation, a different form of deference applies: *Auer* deference. Under *Auer*, courts defer to an agency's interpretation of its own *regulation* unless the interpretation is "plainly wrong." While judicial deference to agency interpretations of statutes has varied widely through time, judicial deference to an agency's interpretation of its own regulations has remained relatively constant. Traditionally, courts defer almost completely to an agency's interpretation of its own regulation. This high level of deference should come as no surprise; after all, it was the agency that drafted the regulation in the first place. Thus, in 1945, the Supreme Court held that an agency's interpretation of its regulation has "controlling weight unless it is plainly erroneous or inconsistent with the regulation." *Bowles v. Seminole Rock & Sand Co.*, 325 U.S. 410, 414 (1945). The Supreme Court reasoned that when Congress delegates the authority to promulgate regulations, it also delegates authority to interpret those regulations; such power is a necessary corollary to the former. This substantial level of deference is generally known as either *Seminole Rock* or *Auer* deference. The latter term refers to the Supreme Court case of *Auer v. Robbins*, 519 U.S. 452 (1997), which came after *Chevron* and confirmed that *Seminole Rock* deference had survived *Chevron*. *Id.* at 461–63. There is at least one limit on when an agency will receive this high level of deference. When an agency does little more than parrot statutory language in its regulation and then claims that it is interpreting the regulation rather than the statute, the agency is not entitled to *Auer* deference. *Gonzales v. Oregon*, 546 U.S. 243, 257 (2006).

An agency's interpretation of statutory text is generally entitled to either *Chevron* or *Skidmore* deference, depending on whether Congress gave the agency the power to act with force of law procedures and the agency used those procedures in crafting its interpretation. A process includes "force of law" procedures when "Congress has delegated legislative power to the agency and [] the agency intended to exercise that power in promulgating the rule." *American Mining Congress v. Mine Safety & Health Administration*, 995 F.2d 1106, 1109 (D.C. Cir. 1993). Hence, if the agency interpreted the statute during notice and comment rulemaking, formal rulemaking, or formal adjudication, then *Chevron* deference would be appropriate. *Christensen v. Harris County*, 529 U.S. 576, 587 (2000). According to the majority in *Christensen*, agency actions having the force of law include more formal actions such as formal adjudication, formal rulemaking, and notice and comment rulemaking. Agency actions lacking the force of law include less formal actions such as "opinion letter[s] . . . policy statements, agency manuals, and enforcement guidelines[.]" *Id.* *Chevron* deference is warranted when the agency makes interpretations using force of law procedures. *Id.* Generally, interpretations made without force of law warrant *Skidmore* deference. *Id.*

However, in a later case, the Court suggested that there may be times that *Chevron* deference is warranted even when an agency fails to use such procedures. *United States v. Mead Corp.*, 533 U.S. 218 (2001). The Court stated that "[d]elegation of [force of law procedures] may be shown in a variety of ways, as by an agency's power to engage in adjudication or notice-and-comment rulemaking, *or by some other indication of a comparable congressional intent.*" *Id.* at 227 (emphasis added). The Court added, "[A]s significant as notice-and-comment is in pointing to *Chevron* authority, the want of that procedure . . . does not decide the case, for we have sometimes found reasons for *Chevron* deference even when no such administrative formality was required and none was afforded." *Id.* at 231.

Finally, in *Barnhart v. Walton*, 535 U.S. 212 (2002), the Court identified what types of "other indications" might be sufficient to warrant *Chevron* deference. To determine whether Congress intended for courts to defer under *Chevron* deference, a court should consider the following five factors: (1) the interstitial nature of the legal question, (2) the relevance of the agency's expertise, (3) the importance of the question to the administration of the statute, (4) the complexity of the statutory scheme, and (5) the careful consideration the agency has given the question over a long period of time. *Id.* at 222.

Chevron deference and *Skidmore* deference differ as follows. When *Chevron* applies, courts use the traditional tools of statutory interpretation to ask whether Congress has spoken to the precise issue before the court. *Chevron U.S.A., Inc. v. Natural Resources Defense Council, Inc.*, 467 U.S. 837, 843 (1984). This is *Chevron*'s first step. If Congress has so spoken, then the analysis is complete, for Congress has the authority to interpret its own statutes however it so chooses. But, if Congress has not directly spoken to the precise issue, or if Congress has left a gap or impliedly delegated to the agency, then *Chevron*'s second step applies. Courts will determine whether the agency's interpretation is reasonable in light of the underlying statute. When *Skidmore* deference applies, courts apply what are known as "the power-to-persuade factors" to evaluate the soundness of the agency's interpretation. An agency's interpretation may be entitled to deference based on the following factors: (1) the consistency in the agency interpretation over time; (2) the thoroughness of the agency's consideration; and (3) the soundness of the agency's reasoning. *Skidmore v. Swift & Co.*, 323 U.S. 134, 140 (1944).

Understanding the difference between *Chevron* and *Skidmore* in application is not always so easy. Professor Gary Lawson has offered a way of thinking of the difference, which he defines as the difference between legal deference and epistemological deference. *Chevron* deference is a form of legal deference earned based on the identity of the interpreter and the method of interpretation. Gary Lawson, *Mostly Unconstitutional: The Case Against Precedent Revisited*, 5 Ave Maria L. Rev. 1, 9 (2007). When an institution earns legal deference, the decision of whether to defer depends entirely on the identity of the interpreter. *Chevron* deference is a form of legal deference: agencies earn deference simply because they interpreted a statute using a particular process. In contrast, *Skidmore* deference is a form of epistemological deference earned based on the soundness of the agency's reasoning, not earned because agencies made the decision. *Id.*

8.02. For agency findings of fact and policy made during *informal* rulemaking and informal adjudication, the relevant standard of review is whether the agency's findings are arbitrary and capricious. APA § 706(2)(A). Under the arbitrary and capricious standard, a court examines whether the agency considered the relevant factors (as Congress identified) and whether the agency made a clear error of judgment. *Citizens to Preserve Overton Park, Inc. v. Volpe*, 401 U.S. 402, 416 (1971). The issue for the reviewing court is whether there was a rational connection between the facts the agency found and the policy choice it made. *Motor Vehicle Manufacturers Ass'n v. State Farm Mutual Automobile Ins. Co.*, 463 U.S. 29, 42–43 (1983).

For agency findings of fact and policy made during *formal* rulemaking and formal adjudication, the standard is whether the agency's findings were supported by substantial evidence. APA § 706(2)(E). Under the substantial evidence standard, a court examines whether the record contains "[such] evidence as a reasonable mind might accept as adequate to support a conclusion." *Consolidated Edison Co. v. NLRB*, 305 U.S. 197, 229 (1938). While these two standards originally differed, today, they tend to converge, and the distinction is "largely semantic." *Ass'n. of Data Processing Serv. Org. v. Bd. of Governors*, 745 F.2d 677, 684 (D.C. Cir. 1984) (citation omitted) (internal quotation marks omitted).

Finally, Congress may expressly provide that the substantial evidence standard in APA § 706(2)(E) applies in the enabling statute.

8.03.   **Answer (A) is correct.** At *Chevron's* first step, the reviewing court should determine whether Congress has spoken to the precise issue before the court. As the Court noted in its opinion, the reviewing court should employ the traditional tools of statutory interpretation when making this determination. *Chevron U.S.A., Inc. v. Natural Resources Defense Council, Inc.*, 467 U.S. 837, 843 n.9 (1984).

   Answer (B) is not correct. While the statute's text is very relevant to determining whether Congress has spoken to the precise issue before the court, it is not solely dispositive.

   Answer (C) is not correct. While the statute's legislative history may be relevant to determining whether Congress has spoken to the precise issue before the court, it is not solely dispositive.

   Answer (D) is not correct. Courts look to the reasonableness of the agency's interpretation at *Chevron's* second step.

8.04.   **Answer (D) is correct.** Courts look to the reasonableness of the agency's interpretation at *Chevron's* second step. *Chevron*, 467 U.S. at 843–44.

   Answer (A) is not correct. At *Chevron's* first step, courts look to the clarity of the legislature's intent as identified using the traditional tools of statutory interpretation. *Id.* at 843, n.9.

   Answer (B) is not correct. While the statute's text is very relevant to determining whether Congress has spoken to the precise issue before the court, it is not solely dispositive.

   Answer (C) is not correct. While the statute's legislative history may be relevant to determining whether Congress has spoken to the precise issue before the court, it is not solely dispositive.

8.05.   **Answer (C) is correct.** When an agency sends an informal letter to an entity to resolve a legal question, that action lacks force of law. Although, *Chevron* deference may still be appropriate even when an agency does not act with force of law, a court would need to apply the *Barnhart* factors to determine whether *Chevron* deference was warranted. *Barnhart v. Walton*, 535 U.S. 212, 222 (2002). Answer (C) assumes that these factors are not present. Thus, because the action lacks force of law and the *Barnhart* factors are not present, the agency's interpretation would likely be given *Skidmore* deference.

Answer (A) is not correct. This answer restates *Chevron* deference. However, *Chevron* deference is unwarranted when an agency does not act using force of law procedures.

Answer (B) is not correct. The facts indicated that the agency interpreted a statute in its letter. Agency interpretations of regulations are generally entitled to *Auer* deference, not *Chevron* deference

Answer (D) is not correct. While the agency has not acted with force of law procedures, the agency may still be entitled to *Skidmore* deference.

8.06. **Answer (D) is correct.** *Chevron* deference is a two-step process. At step one, a court examines whether Congress has spoken directly to the precise issue before the court. In doing so, the court should examine the text of the statute, the legislative history, and the purpose of the statute. In other words, the court should employ all the traditional tools of statutory interpretation to determine whether Congress has already decided the issue. *Chevron v. Natural Resources Defense Council, Inc.*, 467 U.S. 837, 843 n.9 (1984). Hence, a court should turn to step two, which requires the court to examine the reasonableness of the agency's interpretation, only when Congress has not directly spoken to the issue.

Answer (A) is not correct. This answer is incomplete. The court should examine the text of the statute in determining whether Congress has spoken to the precise issue before the court. An examination of the text alone may or may not resolve this question. The court should also look at legislative history and statutory purpose. Hence, in some cases where text is ambiguous or not ambiguous, the court will review the reasonableness of the agency's interpretation; however, in other cases where the text is ambiguous or not ambiguous, the court will not review the reasonableness of the agency's interpretation. In short, the ambiguity of the text is relevant, but not determinative.

Answer (B) is not correct. This answer is incomplete. While the court should examine the text of the statute in determining whether Congress has spoken to the precise issue before the court, ambiguity of text alone does not resolve *Chevron*'s first step.

Answer (C) is not correct. Whether the text of the regulation is ambiguous is not relevant to a court's determination of whether Congress has resolved the issue before the court — a step one question. It may be relevant to a court's determination of whether the interpretation is reasonable — a step two question.

8.07. **Answer (B) is correct.** This Answer applies the *Chevron* deference test, which would be the appropriate test in this case because the agency used force of law procedures to interpret ambiguous statutory language. In applying *Chevron*, a court would likely find that Congress did not speak to the precise issue *before* the court because the text is ambiguous, the legislative history silent, and the purpose non-dispositive. Further, under *Chevron*'s second step, a court would likely find the SSA's interpretation reasonable. *See Barnhart v. Thomas*, 540 U.S. 20 (2003) (holding that the agency's interpretation was an entirely reasonable interpretation of the text).

Answer (A) is not correct. Although the APA directs courts to decide all relevant questions of law, the Supreme Court historically, and more explicitly in *Chevron v. Natural Resources Defense Council, Inc.*, 467 U.S. 837, 843–44 (1984), recognized that it is appropriate to defer to an executive agency's construction of a statutory scheme it is entrusted to administer.

Answer (C) is not correct. The plainly wrong standard is the *Auer* deference standard. It applies when an agency interprets its own regulation, not when an agency interprets statutory language. *Auer v. Robbins*, 519 U.S. 452 (1997).

Answer (D) is not correct. The power to persuade standard is the *Skidmore* deference standard. It generally applies when *Chevron* deference is unwarranted. *Skidmore v. Swift & Co.*, 323 U.S. 134, 140 (1944).

8.08. **Answer (D) is correct.** Because the SSA acted without force of law procedures and because the *Barnhart* factors do not compel a court to use *Chevron* deference, the SSA would be entitled to *Skidmore* deference at best. Answer (D) identifies *Skidmore*'s power to persuade test.

Answer (A) is not correct. Although the APA directs courts to decide all relevant questions of law, the Supreme Court historically, and more explicitly in *Chevron v. Natural Resources Defense Council, Inc.*, 467 U.S. 837, 843–44 (1984), recognized that it is appropriate to defer to an executive agency's construction of a statutory scheme it is entrusted to administer.

Answer (B) is not correct. This answer articulates the *Chevron* deference standard. *Chevron* deference is not appropriate when the agency does not act with force of law and when the *Barnhart* factors do not suggest otherwise.

Answer (C) is not correct. The plainly wrong standard is the *Auer* deference standard. It applies when an agency interprets its own regulation, not when an agency interprets statutory language. *Auer v. Robbins*, 519 U.S. 452 (1997).

8.09. **Answer (C) is correct.** The Supreme Court has explained that when Congress leaves ambiguities and gaps, Congress intended implicitly to delegate the resolution of those ambiguities and gaps to the agency that has been entrusted to administer that statute. Resolution of these gaps and ambiguities involves reconciling conflicting policies. Agency officials, who are politically accountable and have more expertise, are in a better position than courts to make these decisions. *Chevron v. Natural Resources Defense Council, Inc.*, 467 U.S. 837, 865 (1984).

Answer (A) is not correct. *Chevron*'s first step is a search for legislative intent and clarity. Courts use all the tools of statutory interpretation to determine whether Congress had an intent on the precise issue before the court. *Id.* at 843, n.9. Step one is not simply a search for textual clarity. Linda D. Jellum, *Chevron's Demise: A Survey of Chevron from Infancy to Senescence*, 59 ADMIN. L. REV. 725, 761 (2007).

Answer (B) is not correct. This answer is incomplete and slightly inaccurate. A court should defer to an agency, but only when the court has determined that Congress did not have an intent regarding the issue. Congress intends to delegate when Congress *explicitly* or *implicitly* leaves a gap for the agency to fill. When the delegation is explicit, the court generally applies arbitrary and capricious review to agency decision making; when the delegation is implicit, the court may apply *Chevron* deference.

Answer (D) is not correct. Deferring to agency interpretations of statutes does not violate separation of powers. Because agencies have expertise and are politically accountable and because Congress may explicitly or impliedly delegated interpretive power to an agency, the Supreme Court held in *Chevron* that courts should, in some cases, defer to agencies' interpretations. *Id.*

8.10.   Agencies are more likely to prevail at step two of the *Chevron* analysis. At step one, agencies are not accorded any deference. At step one, courts are simply engaging in statutory interpretation — *i.e.*, using tools of statutory interpretation to determine whether Congress had an intention on the issue before the court. *Chevron v. Natural Resources Defense Council, Inc.*, 467 U.S. 837, 843 n.9 (1984). A court proceeds to step two of the analysis only if the court determines that Congress did not have an intention as to that issue. And, at step two, courts are deferential to the agency; *i.e.*, courts will uphold the agency's interpretative rule if the rule is reasonable, or permissible. According to one empirical study that is somewhat dated (1995–96), agencies prevail at step one 42% of the time and at step two 89% of the time. Orin S. Kerr, *Shedding Light on Chevron: An Empirical Study of the Chevron Doctrine in the U.S. Courts of Appeals*, 15 YALE J. REG. 1, 31 (1998).

8.11.   In *Christensen v. Harris County*, 529 U.S. 576, 587 (2000), the Supreme Court stated that agency actions having the force of law include more formal actions such as formal adjudication, formal rulemaking, and notice and comment rulemaking. Agency actions lacking the force of law include less formal actions such as "opinion letter[s] . . . policy statements, agency manuals, and enforcement guidelines[.]" *Id. Chevron* deference is warranted when the agency makes interpretations using force of law procedures. *Id.* Generally, interpretations made without force of law warrant *Skidmore* deference. *Id.*

However, in a later case, the Court suggested that there may be times that *Chevron* deference is warranted even when an agency fails to use such procedures. *United States v. Mead Corp.*, 533 U.S. 218, 227 (2001). The Court stated that "[d]elegation of [force of law procedures] may be shown in a variety of ways, as by an agency's power to engage in adjudication or notice-and-comment rulemaking, *or by some other indication of a comparable congressional intent.*" *Id.* at 227 (emphasis added). The Court added, "[A]s significant as notice-and-comment is in pointing to *Chevron* authority, the want of that procedure . . . does not decide the case, for we have sometimes found reasons for *Chevron* deference even when no such administrative formality was required and none was afforded." *Id.* at 231.

Finally, in *Barnhart v. Walton*, 535 U.S. 212 (2002), the Court identified what types of "other indications" might be sufficient to warrant *Chevron* deference. To determine whether Congress intended for courts to defer under *Chevron* deference, a court should consider the following five factors: (1) the interstitial nature of the legal question, (2) the relevance of the agency's expertise, (3) the importance of the question to the administration of the statute, (4) the complexity of the statutory scheme, and (5) the careful consideration the agency has given the question over a long period of time. *Id.* at 222.

8.12.   Under APA § 706(2), courts may set aside "agency action, findings, and conclusions" if the court finds them to be:

   (A) arbitrary, capricious, or an abuse of discretion;

   (B) contrary to a constitutional right, power, privilege, or immunity;

   (C) inconsistent with statutory mandates;

   (D) in violation of required procedure;

   (E) unsupported by substantial evidence in a case subject to formal rulemaking procedures; or

   (F) unwarranted by the facts — in a case where the facts may be tried de novo by the reviewing court.

Courts are completely non-deferential when reviewing agencies' actions fall under subsections (B), (D), and (F). That is, when deciding whether a rule should be set aside for the reasons designated in (B), (D), or (F), the court decides the matter "de novo" — without giving any deference to the agency. Courts give no deference because the reasons set forth in (B) and (D) require an assessment of whether the agency violated the law. In these cases, no deference is appropriate.

In contrast, Courts are deferential when reviewing agencies actions under subsections (A) and (E). These subsections require a court to give deference to the agency's actions.

Courts are both deferential and non-deferential when making a decision under subsection (C). Subsection (C) is *Chevron*'s two step analysis. *Chevron v. Natural Resources Defense Council, Inc.*, 467 U.S. 837, 843 (1984). Step one of *Chevron* — which asks whether Congress had directly spoken to the precise issue before the court — involves no deference to the agency. Step two — which asks whether the agency's interpretation is reasonable — is very deferential.

Subsection (F) appears to have no application under the Supreme Court's current jurisprudence, following the Court's holding in *Citizens to Preserve Overton Park, Inc. v. Volpe*, 401 U.S. 402, 415–17 (1971), that the standard was inapplicable.

8.13. **Answer (A) is correct.** Although both standards are similar, "hard look" review is less deferential because this standard provides a vehicle for a court to set aside agency action even when the agency action is reasonable. That is, the court scrutinizes the explanation more closely and may set the rule aside if the agency's explanation for its choice is inadequate. *See, e.g., Motor Vehicle Mfrs. Ass'n of United States v. State Farm Mutual Automobile Ins. Co.*, 463 U.S. 29, 50–51 (1983) (rejecting the Department of Transportation's decision not to require air bags in automobiles).

Answer (B) is not correct. Neither standard is *de novo* review. Although step one of *Chevron v. Natural Resources Defense Council, Inc.*, 467 U.S. 837 (1984), may be characterized as *de novo* review, because the court determines for itself whether Congress has indicated its intent regarding the statutory issue, step two of *Chevron* is very deferential to agency determinations. Further, "hard look" review is either the equivalent of or a form of arbitrary and capricious review, which is, therefore, deferential.

Answer (C) is not correct. Although both standards are deferential, "hard look" review is less deferential than deference under *Chevron*'s second step because hard look review provides a vehicle for the court to set aside agency action even when the rule is reasonable. That is, the court scrutinizes the explanation and may set the rule aside if the explanation is inadequate.

Answer (D) is not correct. Although some scholars have suggested that analysis at *Chevron*'s step two is the same as the analysis under arbitrary and capricious review, others disagree. *Compare* Ronald M. Levin, *The Anatomy of Chevron: Step Two Reconsidered*, 72 CHI.-KENT L. REV. 1253, 1254–55 (1997) (suggesting that there should be no difference between *Chevron*'s second step and arbitrary and capricious review under APA § 706(2)(a)); Mark Seidenfeld, *A Syncopated Chevron: Emphasizing Reasoned Decision-Making in Reviewing Agency Interpretations of Statutes*, 73 TEX. L. REV. 83, 128 (1994) (same); with LINDA D. JELLUM, MASTERING STATUTORY INTERPRETATION 291 (2d ed. 2013) (stating that reasonableness review and arbitrary review are different).We believe that the analysis modeled by the Court in *Chevron* is distinct from the analysis modeled by the Court in *Motor Vehicle Mfrs. Ass'n of United States v. State Farm Mutual Automobile Ins. Co.*, 463 U.S. 29 (1983).

8.14.   **Answer (C) is correct** because it is *not* a valid concern. In "hard look" review, a court is not permitted to impose a heightened evidentiary standard to factual findings. Rather, "hard look" review requires a court to focus on the agency's explanation: is there a rational connection between the facts found and the policy choice the agency made.

Answer (A) is not correct because it is a valid concern. Allowing courts to scrutinize the adequacy of an agency's explanation for a policy choice opens the door for courts to set aside an agency choice due to bias, such as politics, and to justify doing so by pointing to minimal gaps in the agency's explanation.

Answer (B) is not correct because it is a valid concern. Because hard look review allows courts to set aside agency choice due to bias and to justify doing so by pointing to minimal gaps in the agency's explanation, agencies are unlikely to know in advance whether their policy choices will be upheld.

Answer (D) is not correct because it is a valid concern. Although under the APA agencies need not provide reasoned explanations for their policy choices on the record, if agencies fail to do so, judges may remand the matter for the agency to explain the choice. *Citizens to Preserve Overton Park, Inc. v. Volpe*, 401 U.S. 402, 416 (1971) (holding that the record for informal proceedings is the evidence that the agency actually considered in making its decision). Such after the fact rationalizations may be viewed with skepticism. Thus, "hard look" review does, in essence, impose a new procedural requirement that is not in the APA: agencies must contemporaneously explain how they carefully considered whether their rule flows logically from the findings of fact. Arguably, this new procedural requirement violates *Vermont Yankee Nuclear Power Corp. v. Natural Resources Defense Council, Inc.*, 435 U.S. 519, 523–24 (1978) (holding that courts cannot impose procedural requirements beyond those required in the APA).

8.15.   When an agency either relies on factors that Congress did not intend for it to consider or when the agency failed to adequately explain its rule, courts will remand the rule back to the agency and, in essence, allow the agency an opportunity to cure the defect. *See, e.g., SEC v. Chenery Corp.*, 318 U.S. 80, 94–95 (1943) (explaining that a reviewing court may only review the justification made by the agency, and may not supply its own). Generally, the court will either void the rule or stay its application pending the remand.

8.16.   **Answer (A) is correct.** When applying the substantial evidence standard, a court should review the "whole record" before the agency, meaning the evidentiary record created by the hearing procedures specified in APA §§ 556–557. APA § 706.

Answer (B) is not correct. As noted in the response to Answer (A), the entire record must be considered, not just the evidence that supports or does not support the agency's decision.

Answer (C) is not correct. As noted in the response to Answer (A), the entire record must be considered, not just the evidence that supports or does not support the agency's decision.

Answer (D) is not correct. While testimonial and derivative evidence is part of the evidentiary record and must be considered, there may be other evidence as well. All of the evidence must be considered under APA § 706.

8.17.   **Answer (D) is correct.** Agencies are entitled to *Chevron* deference when they interpret a statute they are charged with administering using force of law procedures. Informal adjudication and non-legislative rulemaking generally do not involve force of law procedures; hence, agency interpretations made during these types of procedures typically do not receive *Chevron* deference. Moreover, a court will defer to an agency's interpretation at step two only if the court first finds that Congress did not have an intent regarding the issue before the court at step one and, second, finds that the agency's interpretation is reasonable. Agencies do not get deference for interpreting the APA. Thus, all of the answers offered are incorrect, so Answer (D) is the best choice.

Answer (A) is not correct. As noted in the response to Answer (D), informal adjudication and non-legislative rulemaking generally do not involve force of law procedures; hence, agency interpretations made during these types of procedures typically do not receive *Chevron* deference.

Answer (B) is not correct. As noted in the response to Answer (D), agencies do not get *Chevron* deference for interpreting the APA or for interpreting statutes without using force of law procedures. Additionally, if a court finds that Congress was clear about its intent at step one, that is the end of the analysis.

Answer (C) is not correct. As noted in the response to Answer (B), if a court finds that Congress was clear about its intent at step one, that is the end of the analysis. As noted in the response to Answer (A), informal adjudication and non-legislative rulemaking generally do not involve force of law procedures; hence, agency interpretations made during these types of procedures typically do not receive *Chevron* deference.

8.18.   **Answer (B) is correct.** Agency interpretations made during non-legislative rulemaking typically receive *Skidmore* deference. However, the Supreme Court suggested in *Barnhart v. Walton*, 535 U.S. 212 (2002), that there may be times when *Chevron* deference should apply. To determine whether Congress intended for courts to defer under *Chevron* deference, a court should consider the following five factors: (1) the interstitial nature of the legal question, (2) the relevance of the agency's expertise, (3) the importance of the question to the administration of the statute, (4) the complexity of the statutory scheme, and (5) the careful consideration the agency has given the question over a long period of time. *Id.* at 222.

Despite creating this five-factor test, the Supreme Court has not applied *Chevron* deference to an agency interpretation that was made without force of law procedures since *Barnhart* was decided. However, some lower courts have done so. *Compare Schuetz v. Banc One Mortg. Corp.*, 292 F.3d 1004, 1011–13 (9th Cir. 2002) (holding that *Chevron* applied to a HUD Statement of Policy), *and Kruse v. Wells Fargo Home Mortg., Inc.*, 383 F.3d 49, 61 (2d Cir. 2004) (same), *with Krzalic v. Republic Title Co.*, 314 F.3d 875, 879 (7th Cir. 2002) (holding that *Chevron* did not apply to an HUD Statement of Policy).

Answer (A) is not correct. As noted in the response to Answer (B), *Chevron* deference may be warranted in some cases; however, it is not the standard that typically applies.

Answer (C) is not correct. *Auer* deference applies to agency interpretations of regulations, not agency interpretations of statutes.

Answer (D) is not correct. Agencies do receive some deference for their interpretations contained in non-legislative rules, so this answer is incorrect.

8.19.   **Answer (B) is correct.** The statute requires only that the agency issue rules "after hearing." In the rulemaking context, the Supreme Court has held that formal APA requirements are triggered only upon clear congressional intent that the determination be based on a closed record. *See, e.g., U.S. v. Florida Coast Railway Co.*, 410 U.S. 224 (1973). This issue involves an agency's policy choice. A court will review an agency's policy choice made as a result of notice and comment rulemaking under the arbitrary and capricious standard of review. APA § 706(2)(A).

Answer (A) is not correct. This response includes the wrong standard of review. The substantial evidence standard would be correct if the agency promulgated its rule using formal rulemaking or formal adjudication. The agency used notice and comment rulemaking, so the correct standard of review is arbitrary and capricious.

Answer (C) is not correct. The response includes the standard of review for agency interpretations of statutes made without force of law, otherwise known as *Skidmore* deference. Because the issue involved was an issue of policy, was not a question of law, and because the agency used force of law procedures, *Skidmore* deference would be inappropriate.

Answer (D) is not correct. The response includes the standard of review for agency interpretations of statutes made with force of law, otherwise known as *Chevron* deference. Because the issue involved was an issue of policy not a question of law, *Chevron* deference would be inappropriate.

8.20.   **Answer (C) is correct.** Agencies review the decisions of their ALJs using a *de novo* standard. "On appeal from or review of the [ALJ] initial decision, the agency has all the powers which it would have in making the initial decision . . . ." APA § 557(b).

Answer (A) is not correct. The substantial evidence standard would apply were the court reviewing the agency's policy or evidentiary findings made via formal rulemaking or formal adjudication. It does not apply to the agency's review of the ALJ's decision.

Answer (B) is not correct. The arbitrary and capricious standard would apply were the court reviewing the agency's policy or evidentiary findings made via notice and comment rulemaking or informal adjudication. It does not apply to the agency's review of the ALJ's decision.

Answer (D) is not correct. *Chevron* deference would apply were the court reviewing the agency's interpretation of statutory language made via force of law procedures. It does not apply to the agency's review of the ALJ's decision.

8.21.   **Answer (C) is correct.** The regulation provides that residents must "be enrolled in an approved teaching program and be assigned to the portion of the hospital providing patient care . . . ." 42. C.F.R. § 412.105(g)(ii). The issue is whether residents who are performing research are providing patient care. Hence, the language in the regulation the agency is interpreting is "providing patient care."

Answer (A) is not correct. While the word "enrolled" is included in the regulation, the issue does not relate to whether residents are enrolled.

Answer (B) is not correct. While the phrase "approved teaching program" is in the regulation, the issue does not relate to whether the teaching program was approved.

Answer (D) is not correct. The word "resident" is not even in the regulation, so it cannot be the word being interpreted.

8.22. **Answer (A) is correct.** Because the agency is interpreting its own regulation, *Auer* deference is the appropriate standard of review. Under *Auer*, courts defer to agency interpretations of regulations unless they are plainly wrong. *Auer v. Robbins*, 519 U.S. 452, 461 (1997).

Answer (B) is not correct. Reasonableness review is step two of *Chevron* deference. *Chevron* does not apply when an agency interprets its own regulation.

Answer (C) is not correct. Arbitrary and capricious review applies when agencies make policy decisions and findings of fact in notice and comment rulemaking and informal adjudications. It does not apply when an agency interprets its own regulation.

Answer (D) is not correct. The clearly erroneous standard, while similar to *Auer* deference, is not the same articulation. Courts defer to agency interpretations of their own regulations unless the interpretation is "plainly wrong."

8.23. **Answer (A) is correct.** Because the standard of review is *Auer* deference, the agency's interpretation should prevail unless that interpretation is plainly wrong. If the agency's interpretation is contrary to the text of the regulation, it would be plainly wrong.

Answer (B) is not correct. While this might be a good argument, it would not be the best argument.

Answer (C) is not correct. While this might be a good argument, it would not be the best argument.

Answer (D) is not correct. It is unlikely that the rule of lenity would apply in this case. The rule of lenity applies only when criminal, or possibly civil, penalties apply. That is not the case here.

8.24. **Answer (D) is correct.** Under the APA § 706(2)(E), the "substantial evidence" standard of review applies for questions of policy and fact in formal rulemaking and formal adjudication. Because none of the answers offer either of these two options, Answer (D) is correct.

Answer (A) is not correct. *Chevron* deference applies to questions of law in formal adjudication and rulemaking.

Answer (B) is not correct. *Chevron* deference applies to questions of law in formal adjudication and rulemaking.

Answer (C) is not correct. The arbitrary and capricious standard would apply to questions of fact during non-legislative rulemaking. APA § 706(2)(A).

8.25. **Answer (A) is correct.** Formal adjudication is only required when the enabling statute requires that the issue "be determined on the record after opportunity for an agency hearing . . . ." The Supreme Court held that formal APA requirements would be triggered only upon clear congressional intent that the determination be based on a closed record. *See United States v. Florida Coast Railway Co.*, 410 U.S. 224, 238 (1973); *United States v. Allegheny-Ludlum Steel Corp.*, 406 U.S. 742, 757 (1972). Clear congressional intent would be found where this exact language was used; however, few statutes contain this "magic language." When the exact language is not used, court have, at least in the adjudication context, held that agency decisions regarding the formality of the proceeding are entitled to deference under *Chevron v. Natural Resources Defense Council, Inc.*, 467 U.S. 837 (1984). *Chemical Waste Management, Inc. v. EPA*, 873 F.2d 1477, 1482 (D.C. Cir. 1989); *Dominion Energy v. Johnson*, 443 F.3d 12 (1st Cir. 2006).

Answer (B) is not correct. While the statement contained in Answer (B) is correct, it is irrelevant in this context. The issue for the court is whether the agency interpreted the statute reasonably, not whether *Vermont Yankee* was triggered.

Answer (C) is not correct. The response to Answer (A) explains why the Supreme Court has not interpreted the APA to require formal rulemaking in most cases. If Congress wants the agency to use formal rulemaking, Congress must be very clear about that intent.

Answer (D) is not correct. Arbitrary and capricious review does not apply when an agency interprets a statute; *Chevron* deference is the appropriate standard of review.

8.26.   **Answer (B) is correct.** In this case, *Chevron* is the appropriate standard to apply because Congress delegated authority to the agency generally to make rules carrying the force of law and the relevant agency interpretation was promulgated in the exercise of that authority. *Gonzales v. Oregon*, 546 U.S. 243, 255–56 (2006); *United States v. Mead Corp.*, 533 U.S. 218, 226–27 (2001). Under *Chevron*, if a court finds that Congress did not speak to the precise issue before the court at step one, then the court will examine the agency's interpretation to determine whether it is reasonable at step two. If the court finds the agency's interpretation to be reasonable at step two, then the court must defer to that interpretation. *See Estate of Gerson v. C.I.R.*, 507 F.3d 435, 437 (6th Cir. 2007) (from which the facts of this question were drawn).

Answer (A) is not correct. Agencies are not entitled to deference when they interpret statutes they do not administer. However, the fact that the agency administers a statute alone is not sufficient for courts to defer to the agency's interpretation. Rather, the issue at *Chevron*'s second step (assuming Congress did not speak to the issue before the court at *Chevron*'s first step) is whether the agency's interpretation is reasonable.

Answer (C) is not correct. At *Chevron* step one, a court applies the traditional tools of statutory interpretation to decide whether Congress spoke to the precise issue before the court or left a gap or ambiguity to be filled by the agency. If the plain meaning of the text of a statute is clear and leaves no ambiguity, then a court will not turn to *Chevron*'s second step. It does not matter that the agency issued its interpretation using force of law procedures.

Answer (D) is not an accurate statement. In part, this answer is not accurate for the reason explained in the response to Answer (C), but it is also not accurate because, on the facts of this problem, the IRS used force of law procedures, specifically notice and comment rulemaking.

8.27.   **Answer (B) is correct.** It is possible for a court to apply *Chevron* deference even when an agency does not use force of law procedures to reach its statutory interpretation. Specifically, a court should examine the *Barnhart* factors to determine whether the interpretation is one that Congress would want courts to decide or would want courts to the agency. To determine whether Congress intended for courts to defer under *Chevron* deference, a court should consider the following five factors: (1) the interstitial nature of the legal question, (2) the relevance of the agency's expertise, (3) the importance of the question to the administration of the statute, (4) the complexity of the statutory scheme, and (5) the careful consideration the agency has given the question over a long period of time. *Id.* at 222. Despite creating this five-factor test, the Supreme Court has not applied *Chevron* deference to an agency interpretation that was made without force of law procedures since *Barnhart* was decided. However, some lower courts have done so. *Compare Schuetz v. Banc One Mortg. Corp.*, 292 F.3d 1004, 1011–13 (9th Cir. 2002) (holding that *Chevron* applied to a HUD Statement of Policy), *and Kruse v. Wells Fargo Home Mortg., Inc.*, 383 F.3d 49, 61 (2d Cir. 2004) (same), *with Krzalic v. Republic Title Co.*, 314 F.3d 875, 879 (7th Cir. 2002) (holding that *Chevron* did not apply to an HUD Statement of Policy).

Although it is possible that a non-legislative rule might be afforded *Chevron* deference, because the Supreme Court has not yet done so, *Skidmore* deference is the most likely the appropriate standard of review.

Answer (A) is not correct. As noted in the response to Answer (B), although *Chevron* deference may be appropriate, it is not the most likely standard of review to be applied.

Answer (C) is not correct. *Auer* deference is the standard of review to apply when an agency interprets its own regulations. Here, the agency interpreted a statute.

Answer (D) is not correct. Arbitrary and capricious review is the appropriate standard of review for when an agency makes policy choices or factual determinations in notice and comment rulemaking or informal adjudication. Here the agency interpreted a statute, which is a question of law. Arbitrary and capricious review is not the appropriate standard.

GOVERNMENT ACQUISITION OF PRIVATE INFORMATION: INSPECTIONS, SUBPOENAS, & REPORTS

9.1.   **Answer (D) is correct** because it includes all of the other answers.

      Answer (A) is correct but incomplete. Agencies conduct inspections, require the filing of reports, and issue subpoenas for a variety of reasons, including to obtain information that they need to set policy through the promulgation of rules and regulations and to keep Congress advised of their regulatory agenda.

      Answer (B) is correct but incomplete. Agencies also conduct inspections, require the filing of reports, and issue subpoenas to gain information needed to enforce their own and other agencies' regulatory requirements.

      Answer (C) is correct but incomplete. Agencies also conduct inspections, require the filing of reports, and issue subpoenas to gain information needed to prosecute regulated entities for civil and criminal violations.

9.2.   **Answer (D) is correct** because it includes all of the other answers. Answers (A), (B), and (C) all include instances when inspections are appropriate.

      Answer (A) is correct but incomplete. State health inspectors need the ability to enter and inspect restaurant practices to ensure that the restaurants are meeting applicable health standards.

      Answer (B) is correct but incomplete. When a state welfare agency receives a complaint that a child is being abused or neglected by the child's parents, the welfare officials need to enter and inspect the home to determine whether the complaint is valid.

      Answer (C) is correct but incomplete. Employers must provide safe working environments for their employees. Federal Occupational Safety and Health Administration inspectors must visit worksites to ensure that the employers are meeting the standards.

9.3.   **Answer (C) is correct.** In *See v. City of Seattle*, 387 U.S. 541, 545–46 (1967) and *Camara v. Municipal Court*, 387 U.S. 523, 538 (1967), the Court held that even though administrative inspections are conducted for health and safety reasons, the Fourth Amendment prohibition against "unreasonable searches and seizures" still applies; however, the standard is lower. *See Marshall v. Barlow's, Inc.*, 436 U.S. 307, 320 (1978) (explaining that the "[p]robable cause justifying the issuance of a warrant [in the administrative context] may be based not only on specific evidence of an existing violation but also on a showing that reasonable legislative or administrative standards for conducting an . . . inspection are satisfied."). For example, in *Camara v. Municipal Court*, 387 U.S. at 538, the Court held that inspectors did have to get a warrant before they could search an apartment for violations of a city housing code; however, the inspectors did not have to show cause that they would find violations at the particular apartment they wanted to inspect. Rather, the inspectors had to show that the inspection complied with "reasonable legislative or administrative standards." In other words, the inspection could occur without evidence of wrongdoing.

Answer (A) is not correct because the Fourth Amendment prohibition against unreasonable searches and seizures does apply to administrative inspections, as explained in the response to Answer (C).

Answer (B) is not correct because *Camara* and *See* made clear that although the Fourth Amendment does require agencies to obtain a warrant, the standard for getting that warrant is much easier to meet than the probable cause standard. In *Camara v. Municipal Court*, 387 U.S. 523, 537–38 (1967), the Court held that, because administrative searches and inspections do not involve searches for evidence of criminal activity, the probable cause requirement can be modified to require that the agency show that it has a reasonable inspection plan and proof that it is time to inspect under that plan (as opposed to the ordinary requirement of proof that the fruits or instrumentalities of evidence of crime exist and can be found at the place to be searched).

Answer (D) is not correct. The standard required for administrative searches is less than, not greater than, the probable cause standard for criminal searches.

9.4.   **Answer (D) is correct.** When an agency uses an administrative search to look for evidence of criminal activity, the agency must obtain a warrant, and likely must meet the criminal probable cause standard. The Court in *New York v. Burger*, 482 U.S. 691, 716–17 n.27 (1987), said that an administrative inspection cannot be used as a "pretext" for a traditional law enforcement search for evidence of a crime.

Answer (A) is not correct because no warrant is necessary when emergency circumstances exist requiring an agency to act immediately. This answer includes one such emergency.

Answer (B) is not correct because the search identified in this answer is not a search under the Fourth Amendment. When individuals do not have a reasonable expectation of privacy in the searched location, the Fourth Amendment does not apply. *See, e.g., Air Pollution Variance Board v. Western Alfalfa Corp.*, 416 U.S. 861, 864–65 (1974) (upholding an inspection of a factory when emissions from the factory smokestacks were visible from the public grounds).

Answer (C) is not correct. The Supreme Court rejected this argument in *United States v. Martinez-Fuerte*, 428 U.S. 543, 561–62 (1976). The Court reasoned that it would be impracticable for the border patrol officers to a seek warrant for every vehicle they choose to search and that to do so would eliminate any deterrent effect. The Court concluded that the intrusion to motorists was minimal, while the government and public interest was substantial.

9.5.   **Answer (D) is correct.** The Supreme Court has held that businesses that are closely — the Court also uses the term pervasively — regulated have lower expectations of privacy than other businesses. This exception was also known as the *Colonnade-Biswell* exception. Moreover, such businesses have a long tradition of close supervision by the state. Hence, warrants are unnecessary. The closely regulated exception to the warrant requirement is essentially an outgrowth of the waiver/consent doctrine: by voluntarily engaging in a heavily regulated business, business owners give up their privacy expectations. To date, the following businesses have been found to be closely regulated: *Colonnade Catering Corp. v. United States*, 397 U.S. 72, 77 (1970) (liquor dealers); *United States v. Biswell*, 406 U.S. 311, 315 (1972) (weapon dealers); *Donovan v. Dewey*, 452 U.S. 594, 602–03 (1981) (mining companies);

New York v. Burger, 482 U.S. 691, 707 (1987) (junkyards engaging in vehicle dismantling).

Answer (A) is not correct. Administrative searches of ordinary businesses do require a warrant; however, the standard for that warrant is less than the criminal probable cause standard. *See v. City of Seattle*, 387 U.S. 541, 545–46 (1967).

Answer (B) is not correct. Administrative searches of homes do require a warrant; however, the standard for that warrant is less than the criminal probable cause standard. *Camara v. Municipal Court*, 387 U.S. 523, 538 (1967).

Answer (C) is not correct. It is not enough that Congress provide in a statute that an agency has the authority to conduct a warrantless search. *Marshall v. Barlow's Inc.*, 436 U.S. 307, 316 (1978) (holding that the agency did not have power to conduct warrantless searches despite an explicit grant to do so in the statute). The Fourth Amendment limits Congress' authority to allow warrantless searches, even administrative searches.

9.6. **Answer (C) is correct.** According to *New York v. Burger*, 482 U.S. 691, 702–03 (1987), the Fourth Amendment applies, but it does not require either a warrant or probable cause. Rather the standard for a valid warrantless search is threefold: (1) the regulatory scheme has to be justified by a substantial governmental interest, (2) warrantless inspections must be necessary to further the regulatory scheme, and (3) the terms of the inspection must provide a constitutionally adequate substitute for a warrant. This third requirement requires that the scheme be detailed enough to put regulated entities on notice that they are subject to periodic inspections and the scheme must limit the inspector's discretion, requiring the inspector to act reasonably.

Answer (A) is not correct. The Supreme Court has held that businesses that are closely (or pervasively) regulated have lower expectations of privacy than other businesses. Moreover, closely regulated businesses have a long tradition of close supervision by the state. Hence, warrants are unnecessary.

Answer (B) is not correct. When an inspection complies with reasonable legislative or administrative statutory standards, then a warrant will be issued. In other words, the standard provided in this answer substitutes for probable cause, not for a warrant.

Answer (D) is not correct. This answer is both incomplete and inaccurate. Answer (C) includes all of the elements established in the Court's most recent case on this issue: *New York v. Burger*, 482 U.S. 691, 702–03 (1987)

9.7. **Answer (B) is correct.** Because administrative proceedings are civil in nature, the exclusionary rule does not generally apply. *United States v. Janis*, 428 U.S. 433, 459–60 (1976); *see INS v. Lopez-Mendoza*, 468 U.S. 1032, 1033 (1984); *Pennsylvania Bd. of Probation & Parole v. Scott*, 524 U.S. 357, 363 (1998). When a civil penalty is involved, however, some lower courts have held that the exclusionary rule does apply. *See, e.g., Trinity Industries, Inc. v. OSHRC*, 16 F.3d 1455, 1461–62 (6th Cir. 1994); *Lakeland Enter. Of Rhinelander, Inc. v. Chao*, 402 F.3d 739, 744–45 (7th Cir. 2005).

Answer (A) is not correct. Generally, the exclusionary rule does not apply in administrative adjudications; however, some lower courts have applied the rule when civil fines were to be imposed. *See, e.g., Trinity Industries, Inc. v. OSHRC*, 16 F.3d 1455, 1461–62 (6th Cir. 1994); *Lakeland Enter. Of Rhinelander, Inc. v. Chao*, 402 F.3d 739, 744–45 (7th Cir. 2005).

Answer (C) is not correct. Although the Court has held that the Fourth Amendment alone may be the basis for excluding from federal *criminal* trials evidence seized by a federal officer in violation solely of that Amendment, *Weeks v. United States*, 232 U.S. 383, 391–92 (1914), the exclusionary rule generally does not apply in the administrative context. *United States v. Janis*, 428 U.S. 433, 459–60 (1976).

Answer (D) is not correct. This statement is simply incorrect. If the exclusionary rule applies, it would apply at all stages of the proceedings, not just during appeals.

9.8.   **Answer (C) is correct.** Absent an exception to the warrant requirement, agencies must always obtain a warrant prior to a search, even when a statute provides authority to the agency to search. Indeed, if the statute did not provide the agency with authority to search, then even if the agency obtained a warrant, the search would be invalid. In this case, OSHA has statutory authority to conduct a limited scope inspection when it receives a complaint. Assuming the statute also granted OSHA the authority to conduct comprehensive inspections, such inspections must be based on neutral criteria. *Marshall v. Barlow's, Inc.*, 436 U.S. 307, 321 (1978). Employee complaints cannot serve this purpose. *Trinity Industries, Inc. v. OSHRC*, 16 F.3d 1455, 1460 (6th Cir. 1994).

Answer (A) is not correct. This statement is only partially true. OSHA must get a warrant, but the statute limits the scope of the inspection.

Answer (B) is not correct. Because there is no emergency, just a complaint, the emergency exception would not apply to these facts.

Answer (D) is not correct. There is nothing in the facts to suggest that the employer is a business that is so heavily regulated that it would have a lower expectation of privacy than owners of ordinary businesses. Hence, the closely regulated business exception would not apply to these facts.

9.9.   The inspector would likely not need a warrant. According to *New York v. Burger*, 482 U.S. 691, 702–03 (1987), the standard for a valid warrantless search of a closely (or pervasively) regulated industry is threefold: (1) the regulatory scheme has to be justified by a substantial governmental interest, (2) warrantless inspections must be necessary to further the regulatory scheme, and (3) the terms of the inspection must provide a constitutionally adequate substitute for a warrant. This third requirement requires that the scheme has to be detailed enough to put regulated entities on notice that they are subject to periodic inspections and the scheme must limit the inspector's discretion, requiring the inspector to act reasonably. Here, the government has a substantial interest in regulating nuclear energy, because it is very dangerous and could be harmful to the public if not handled safely. Warrantless searches would further the government's regulatory scheme because if such businesses knew the government was on its way to inspect their facilities, such businesses might try to hide the regulatory violations. Assuming the terms of the inspection are reasonable and limit the inspector's discretion, a warrant is likely unnecessary.

9.10.   **Answer (A) is correct.** Unlike the other three examples, the Supreme Court has not yet held that a search of hospital employees who work with small children would justify a warrant exception.

Answer (B) is not correct. In *Skinner v. Railway Labor Executives' Ass'n*, 489 U.S. 602 (1989), the Court upheld agency regulations mandating blood and urine testing of railway employees who were involved in major train accidents. The Court noted that the "governmental interest in ensuring the safety of the traveling public and of the employees themselves plainly justifie[d] prohibiting covered employees from using alcohol or drugs on duty." *Id.* at 621. Also, because alcohol and drugs are quickly eliminated from the body, the Court believed any delay caused by the need to obtain a warrant might result in evidence being destroyed. Hence, the Court concluded that the government interest in testing without a showing of individualized suspicion was compelling. In contrast, the Court reasoned that the employees had a diminished expectation of privacy due to the nature of their jobs and that the search was considered minimal.

Answer (C) is not correct. In *National Treasury Employees Union v. Von Raab*, 489 U.S. 656, 666 (1989), using much the same reasoning as in *Skinner*, the Court held that the Customs Service could test the urine of its employees who were being considered for transfer or promotion to positions involving drug interdiction or involving possession of firearms.

Answer (D) is not correct. In *Vernonia School District 47J v. Acton*, 515 U.S. 646, 664–65 (1995), the Court held that public school *student athletes* could be subject to urinalysis because they elected to participate in school activities. This holding was extended over a strong objection to all public school students who wished to participate in after school activities in *Board of Education of Pottawatomie County v. Earls*, 536 U.S. 822, 837–38 (2002). In *Pottawatomie*, the Court reasoned that students' privacy interests are limited when they attend public school and they voluntarily choose to participate in afterschool activities. Additionally, the degree of intrusion is minimal, while the government's interest in preventing children from using drugs is very strong.

9.11. Although the Fourth Amendment requires an agency to obtain a warrant based on probable cause before it conducts an administrative inspection, few inspections are actually based on a warrant. Rather, an individual or business usually gives consent to a search. Indeed, many trade and industry groups advise their members to consent to searches absent unusual circumstances that might justify refusal. In this case, if the plant owner consents, then a warrant is unnecessary. Given that this situation does not present an emergency, the inspector may wish to try obtaining consent. Importantly, with consent, the inspector may be able to inspect the whole plant and its processing. However, assuming the statute allows the FDA to inspect when complaints are lodged, generally the scope of the search is limited to the allegations in the complaint. So, the search would be narrower without consent.

9.12. **Answer (C) is correct.** While statutory authorization is required, that authorization can be explicit or implicit.

Answer (A) is not correct because agencies do not have inherent authority under the Constitution to impose recordkeeping or reporting requirements.

Answer (B) is not correct because the authorization to impose recordkeeping or reporting requirements need not be express.

Answer (D) is not correct. If agencies do not have statutory authority, they cannot grant themselves such authority by regulation.

9.13. **Answer (D) is correct** Other requirements in the Paperwork Reduction Act, 44 U.S.C. §§ 3501–3521, are as follows: (A) The Act regulates the "collection of information" by agencies including "the obtaining, causing to be obtained, soliciting, or requiring the disclosure to third parties or the public, of facts or opinions by or for an agency, regardless of form or format," calling for answers from 10 or more persons; (B) the Act requires agencies to review each proposed collection information requirement to ensure that it contains an evaluation of the need for collection of the information; and (C) the Act requires a specific objectively supported estimate of the burden the collection will impose on persons (measured in hours).

Answer (A) is not correct. The National Environmental Policy Act requires agencies to complete an Environmental Impact Statement; the Paperwork Reduction Act does not.

Answer (B) is not correct. The Unfunded Mandates Act requires agencies to analyze the impact of regulations on State, local, and tribal governments; the Paperwork Reduction Act does not.

Answer (C) is not correct. The Regulatory Flexibility Act requires agencies to analyze the impact of regulation on small businesses and consider less burdensome alternatives; the Paperwork Reduction Act does not.

9.14.   **Answer (B) is correct.** Agencies may issue subpoenas but may not engage in a fishing expedition to find relevant information. *Endicott Johnson Corp. v. Perkins*, 317 U.S. 501, 509–10 (1943) (holding that the DOL was not on a fishing expedition with its subpoena); *Oklahoma Press Publishing Co. v. Walling*, 327 U.S. 186, 214 (1946) (stating that subpoenas may be sued to develop facts, even when the agency is not yet certain it has a case).

Answer (A) is not correct. Agencies have no power to impose sanctions when their subpoenas are ignored. Rather, the Department of Justice will file suit on behalf of an agency, which must then defend the validity of its subpoena in court.

Answer (C) is not correct. An agency must have some knowledge that a violation has occurred before it issues a subpoena.

Answer (D) is not correct. The Ninth Circuit had held that agencies may not issue subpoenas when less drastic information-gathering techniques are available, but the Supreme Court reversed this holding in *Civil Aeronautics Board v. Hermann*, 353 U.S. 322 (1957) (*per curiam*).

9.15.   Because the purpose of the self-incrimination privilege is to protect individuals from testifying against themselves, it does not apply to corporations or its officers. In sum, the privilege against self-incrimination is available only to natural persons and cannot be asserted on behalf of a regulated entity. *Bellis v. United States*, 417 U.S. 85, 100 (1974). Moreover, the privilege applies only to compelled testimonial utterances, not to other communications, such as the act of providing corporate records. *Couch v. United States*, 409 U.S. 322, 329 (1973); *Fisher v. United States*, 425 U.S. 391, 400 (1976). Finally, the privilege only applies for sanctions that are criminal rather than civil. *United States v. Ward*, 448 U.S. 242, 248 (1980).

9.16.   **Answer (D) is correct.** All of the statements in Answers (A), (B), and (C) are correct; thus, Answer D is the best answer because it includes all the other answers.

Answer (A) is correct but it is incomplete.

Answer (B) is correct but it is incomplete.

Answer (C) is correct but it is incomplete.

TOPIC 10:	ANSWERS
PUBLIC ACCESS TO GOVERNMENT INFORMATION & RECOVERY OF ATTORNEY'S FEES	

10.1. **Answer (D) is correct.** The FOIA is designed for use by anyone who wants information from the federal government. "Any person" can file a FOIA request, including U.S. citizens, foreign nationals, organizations, associations, and universities. The FOIA's purpose is to ensure the citizenry is informed. One way the FOIA accomplishes its purpose is to allow individuals and businesses to obtain information from agencies. Pursuant to 5 U.S.C. § 552(a)(3)(A), when an agency receives a request that reasonably describes the records sought, the agency shall make the records promptly available. Additionally, in some situations, agencies may impose reasonable charges for their costs in searching and copying records. 5 U.S.C. § 552(a)(4)(A)(ii). For example, agencies may charge reasonable fees for document search, duplication, and review, when records are requested for commercial use. 5 U.S.C. § 552(a)(4)(A)(ii)(I).

Answer (A) is not correct. First, the agency need not provide the records within 20 days; rather, the agency need only notify the requester within 20 working days whether the agency will comply with the request. 5 U.S.C. § 552(a)(6)(i). Assuming it will comply, the agency must then "promptly" make the records available to the requester. 5 U.S.C. § 552(a)(3)(A). Additionally, the agency may impose a fee for the search and duplication costs it incurs. An agency must first determine the projected use of the records sought by the FOIA request and the type of requester asking for the documents. Because the FOIA was intended to promote the public's access to information, news media organizations and educational institutions are excused from certain fees. 5 U.S.C. § 552(a)(4)(A)(ii).

Answer (B) is not correct because requesters need not describe the documents being sought specifically. The records need only be "reasonably describe[d]." 5 U.S.C. § 552(a)(3). Moreover, the agency may charge fees in specific cases.

Answer (C) is not correct. First, the agency must notify the requester within 20 days whether the agency will comply with the request. Assuming it will comply, the agency must then "promptly" make the records available to the requester; in reality, agencies often do not respond promptly to FOIA requests. In 1996 and 2007, Congress amended the FOIA to try to speed up agency response times. Specifically, in 1996, Congress allowed multitrack processing so that simple FOIA requests could leap frog over more complex requests. 5 U.S.C. § 552(a)(6)(D)(i). And in 2007, Congress amended the FOIA to prohibit agencies from collecting fees when they fail to promptly comply. 5 U.S.C. § 552(a)(4)(A)(vii).

10.2. **Answer (D) is correct.** It is the best answer because Answers (A), (B), and (C) are all correct.

Answer (A) is an accurate statement, but it is not the correct answer. An agency must notify the requester within 20 working days whether the agency will comply with the request. 5 U.S.C. § 552(a)(6)(i).

Answer (B) is an accurate statement, but it is not the correct answer. An agency must provide reasons for denying any request. 5 U.S.C. § 552(a)(6)(i). Further, the agency must notify the requester of the requester's right to appeal any adverse determination.

Answer (C) is an accurate statement, but it is not the correct answer. An agency must make a determination with respect to any appeal of a denial within 20 working days after the receipt of such appeal. 5 U.S.C. § 552(a)(6)(ii).

10.3. **Answer (D) is correct.** It is the best answer because Answers (A), (B), and (C) are all correct. There are nine exceptions in total: (1) classified information; (2) internal agency personnel rules and practices; (3) matters that another statute specifically exempts from disclosure; (4) trade secrets and commercial or financial information that the agency obtained from someone other than the requester; (5) inter-agency or intra-agency memoranda and letters, not otherwise available through discovery in a civil action against the agency; (6) personnel files, medical files, and similar files, the disclosure of which would constitute a clearly unwarranted invasion of personal privacy; (7) records and information compiled for law enforcement purposes; (8) matters related to the regulation of banks and other financial institutions; and (9) geological and geophysical information.

Answer (A) is not correct, but it is an exception to FOIA. 5 U.S.C. § 552(b)(1)(B).

Answer (B) is not correct, but it is an exception to FOIA. 5 U.S.C. § 552(b)(2).

Answer (C) is not correct, but it is an exception to FOIA. 5 U.S.C. § 552(b)(4). but it is an exception to FOIA. 5 U.S.C. § 552(b)(4).

10.4. **Answer (B) is correct** because agencies can charge commercial requester fees designed to allow them to recover the direct cost of searching, duplicating, and reviewing commercial requests. 5 U.S.C. § 552(a)(4)(A)(ii)(I).

Answer (A) is not correct. Agencies may charge non-commercial requesters (who are not educational, scientific, or news institutions) reasonable standard charges for document search and duplication. 5 U.S.C. § 552(a)(4)(A)(ii)(III).

Answer (C) is not correct. Under the FOIA today, agencies may not charge educational or scientific institutions any fees so long as the requester's purpose is for scholarly or scientific research. Additionally, agencies may not charge representatives of the news media any fees. 5 U.S.C. § 552(a)(4)(A)(ii)(II).

Answer (D) is incorrect. Because Answer (A) and Answer (C) are incorrect, Answer (D), which states that "all of the above" are correct, is necessarily incorrect.

10.5. **Answer (B) is correct.** When an agency denies a FOIA request, the requester may seek judicial review under the FOIA directly, not under APA § 706. 5 U.S.C. § 552(a)(4)(B). Pursuant to this section, the agency has the burden to prove that it denied the request legitimately. Additionally, the standard of review is *de novo*. Finally, the FOIA authorizes a court to award attorney's fees and costs if the requester substantially prevails.

Answer (A) is not correct. A requester seeks review under FOIA, not the APA.

Answer (C) is not correct. A requester seeks review under FOIA, not the APA.

Answer (D) is not correct. A requester seeks review under FOIA.

10.6. **Answer (A) is correct.** Pursuant to 5 U.S.C. § 552(a)(4)(B), the agency has the burden to prove that it denied the request legitimately, and the standard of review is *de novo*.

Answer (B) is not correct. Under the FOIA, the burden is on the agency denying the records, not on the requester.

Answer (C) is not correct. The standard of review is *de novo* under the FOIA. APA § 706(C) and *Chevron* deference do not apply.

Answer (D) is not correct. The standard of review is *de novo* under the FOIA. APA § 706(A), arbitrary and capricious review, does not apply.

10.7. An agency has the burden to prove that information is exempt from disclosure under the FOIA. 5 U.S.C. § 552(a)(4)(B). To prove a document is exempt, the agency may have to disclose more information that would maintain the document's confidentiality. There are two ways to solve this problem. First, the FOIA specifically authorizes a court to review withheld records *in camera*. *Id.* Second, because a requester cannot argue that the records are not exempt when the requester knows nothing about the records, a reviewing court may require the agency to file an index of the supposedly exempt records instead of providing them *in camera*. These indices are called *"Vaughn"* indices, after the case in which the procedure was developed. *Vaughn v. Rosen*, 484 F.2d 820 (D.C. Cir. 1973), *cert. denied*, 415 U.S. 977 (1974). In a *Vaughn* index, the agency must describe each exempt record in enough detail to convince the court that the record does fall within one or more of the FOIA exemptions. Further, the index must identify, for each record, which exemptions the agency is claiming apply. The requester receives a copy of the index so that he or she can challenge the agency's exemption claims.

10.8. **Answer (C) is correct** because a requester need not show that he or she needs to receive documents; however, the purpose behind the request may impact the amount of the fees an agency can charge for fulfilling the request. The purpose may also relate to whether the requested information falls within one of the exceptions.

Answer (A) is not correct because no showing of need is required.

Answer (B) is not correct because no showing of need is required.

Answer (D) is not correct because no showing of need is required and requesters generally need not address the issue of privilege.

10.9. **Answer (B) is correct** because the FOIA explicitly requires the requester to "reasonably describe" the records sought. 5 U.S.C. § 552(a)(3)(A)(i). According to the legislative history, this phrase means that "a professional employee of the agency who was familiar with the subject area of the request [would be able] to locate the record with a reasonable amount of effort." *See, e.g., Ruotolo v. DOJ*, 53 F.3d 4, 10 (2d Cir. 1995) (quoting this legislative history).

Answer (A) is not correct because the FOIA includes a specific standard, identified in Answer (B).

Answer (C) is not correct because the FOIA includes a specific standard, identified in Answer (B).

Answer (D) is not correct because the FOIA includes a specific standard, identified in Answer (B).

10.10. **Answer (C) is correct** because the Sunshine Act requires "every portion of every meeting at an agency . . . be open to public observation." 5 U.S.C. § 552b(b). In addition, the Act requires agencies to give advance public notice of their meetings. 5 U.S.C. § 555b(e). However, the Act defines "agency" narrowly to include only agencies "headed by a collegial body composed of two or more individual members, a majority of whom are appointed to such position by the President and with the advice of the Senate." 5 U.S.C. § 552(a)(1). Hence, the Act applies to the so-called independent agencies only, such as the Federal Communications Commission, the Securities and Exchange Commission, the Federal Trade Commission, etc.

      Answer (A) is not correct because the Food and Drug Administration is not headed by a multi-member body. It is also considered an executive, not an independent, agency.

      Answer (B) is not correct because the Environmental Protection Agency is not headed by a multi-member body. It is also considered an executive, not an independent, agency.

      Answer (D) is not correct because the Justice Department is not headed by a multi-member body. It is also considered an executive, not an independent, agency.

10.11. The Sunshine Act applies when the FTC holds a "meeting." Meeting is defined in the Act as "the deliberations of at least the number of individual agency members required to take action on behalf of the agency where such deliberations determine or result in the joint conduct or disposition of official agency business." 5 U.S.C. § 552b(a)(2). This definition incudes three requirements for a gathering of commissioners to be considered a meeting: (a) the number of agency members must constitute a quorum; (b) the agency members must deliberate; and (c) the deliberations must determine agency business.

      Here, because all the commissioners meet during both meetings, a quorum would be present. Further, the facts state that the commissioners "fully vet relevant agency business" at the first meeting and make decisions at the second; hence, the agency members are deliberating at both meetings. Finally, the fact that the commissioners do not actually decide issues at the first meeting does not insulate it from the Sunshine Act open meetings requirement. A meeting can occur even when that meeting does not lead to official agency actions or decisions. It is enough if the discussions are "sufficiently focused . . . as to cause or be likely to cause the individual participating members to form reasonably firm positions regarding matters pending or likely to arise before the agency." *FCC v. ITT World Communications, Inc.*, 466 U.S. 463, 471 (1984). The first meeting deliberations "effectively predetermine official agency actions" and are likely to cause the commissioners to form firm positions. For these reasons, both meetings are likely subject to the Sunshine Act.

10.12. FACA imposes a variety of open-meeting and disclosure requirements on groups that meet the definition of an "advisory committee." Pursuant to the FACA, an "advisory committee" means "any committee, board, commission, council, conference, panel, task force, or other similar group, or any subcommittee or other subgroup thereof . . . , which is: . . . established or utilized by the President . . . in the interest of obtaining advice or recommendations . . . . " 5 U.S.C. § 3(2). Importantly, the statute specifically excludes "any committee that is composed wholly of full-time, or permanent part-time, officers or employees of the Federal Government . . . . " *Id.*

      Here, there is no dispute that the president appointed only federal government officials to the group. However, private lobbyists, who are nonfederal employees, regularly attended and participated in the meetings, suggesting that they were actually *de facto* members of the committee. If accurate, then the group may be an advisory committee not subject to the exception (meaning all documents must be made public). *Ass'n of American Physicians & Surgeons, Inc. v. Clinton*, 997 F.2d 898, 904–05 (D.C. Cir. 1993). Because of concerns about separation of powers, the United States Circuit Court for the District of Columbia recently interpreted this provision in FACA very narrowly, to include only individuals who could vote or participate in consensus decision making. *In re Cheney*, 406 F.3d 723, 729 (D.C. Cir. 2005). Because the private lobbyists here had no authority to vote or veto the decisions made by the group members, the group would likely not be an advisory group subject to FACA requirements.

10.13. **Answer (B) is correct** because it is an untrue statement. In many other countries, the losing party pays not only damages, but also the prevailing party's attorney's fees. The United States, however, has traditionally followed the "American rule" regarding attorney's fees, meaning that each party generally must bear its own legal expenses. *See Alyeska Pipeline Service Co. v. Wilderness Society*, 421 U.S. 240, 247 (1975). Numerous statutes (for example, the FOIA) explicitly permit prevailing parties to recover some or all of the costs, fees, and other expenses, including attorney's fees.

Answer (A) is not correct because it is a true statement. As noted in the response to Answer (B), unless a statute provides otherwise, all litigants generally pay their own fees and costs, even if they prevail.

Answer (C) is not correct because it is a true statement. One means for encouraging the enforcement of federal regulatory schemes is to allow private citizens to bring lawsuits against the federal agency and to include specific authorization to award costs and attorney's fees, when appropriate, to a prevailing or substantially prevailing party. For example, the Safe Drinking Water Act authorizes judges to award such fees. 42 U.S.C. § 300j–8(d).

Answer (D) is not correct because it is a true statement. Contingency fee arrangements are permitted. They are often used in cases where the claimant is bringing a suit against a federal agency to recover a monetary benefit. Traditionally, however, Congress has been hostile to contingency fees in these benefits suits. For this reason, Congress often limits the amount of recoverable attorney's fees. *See, e.g., Walters v. Nat'l Ass'n of Radiation Survivors*, 473 U.S. 305, 307 (1985) (upholding a statute that limited attorney's fees in veteran's cases to $10).

10.14. **Answer (D) is correct** because it is not accurate. The EAJA authorizes judges to award fees and expenses in *formal* agency adjudications in which the government is represented by counsel. 5 U.S.C. § 504(b)(1)(C)(i). The EAJA does not authorize courts to award such fees and expenses in informal adjudications, even if the government is represented by counsel. *See Ardestani v. INS*, 502 U.S. 129, 139 (1991).

Answer (A) is not correct because it is accurate. The EAJA specifically authorizes judges to award fees and expenses to prevailing parties for judicial review of agency action. 28 U.S.C. § 2412(d). This provision also waives the sovereign immunity of the United States.

Answer (B) is not correct because it is accurate. The EAJA authorizes judges to award fees and expenses when agencies bring actions to enforce a party's compliance with a statutory or regulatory requirement. *See* 5 U.S.C. § 504(a)(4).

Answer (C) is not correct because it is accurate. The EAJA specifically excludes proceedings involving ratemaking and license grants/renewals from its coverage. 5 U.S.C. § 504(b)(1)(C)(i).

10.15. Answer (D) is correct. These were the facts in *Buckhannon Board and Care Home, Inc. v. West Virginia Dep't of Health and Human Resources*, 532 U.S. 598, 610 (2001). In that case, the Court rejected the catalyst theory, which posits that a plaintiff is a prevailing party if the plaintiff achieves the desired result because the lawsuit brought about a voluntary change in the defendant's conduct. In *Buckhannon*, the Court held that a party is a prevailing party only if a court is somehow involved in the final outcome, whether by litigated judgment or by judicially-approved settlement.

Answer (A) is not correct. As noted in the response to Answer (D), the Supreme Court specifically rejected the "catalyst" approach to defining a prevailing party.

Answer (B) is not correct. This answer simply restates the catalyst approach without using the catalyst language. And as noted in the response to Answer (D), the Supreme Court specifically rejected the "catalyst" approach to defining a prevailing party.

Answer (C) is not correct. Contrary to this answer, a prevailing party need only prevail on the merits of at least some of its claims through a judgment or consent decree. It need not prevail on all of its claims.

10.16. Answer (A) is correct. The EAJA applies to *formal* APA adjudications, meaning only those adjudications in which the relevant statute includes the language "on the record after opportunity for a hearing." Thus, the EAJA does not apply to information adjudications (however adversarial or formal they may actually be).

Answer (B) is not correct. It is correct to say that the EAJA does not apply in adjudications involving ratemaking or granting or renewing a license. 5 U.S.C. § 504(C)(i). However, the EAJA applies in other licensing actions, so long as formal adjudication procedures apply.

Answer (C) is not correct. It is correct to say that the EAJA allows recovery only when the government is represented by counsel; however, in addition, the Act requires that the underlying action be formal adjudication. 5 U.S.C. § 504(C)(i).

Answer (D) is not correct. It is correct to say that fees are awarded to the prevailing party; however, the type of proceeding is very relevant. 5 U.S.C. § 504(C)(i). The Act defines "adversary adjudication" as "an adjudication under section 554 [the APA] in which the position of the United States is represented by counsel or otherwise, but excludes an adjudication for the purpose of establishing or fixing a rate or for the purpose of granting or renewing a license." *Id.*

10.17. Answer (D) is correct. Under 28 U.S.C. § 2412(d)(1)(A), a court shall award to a prevailing party fees and expenses incurred in any civil action (except a case sounding in tort) brought by or against the United States, including judicial review of agency action. When a party loses at the agency level but then prevails on judicial review, § 2412(d) permits an award of expenses and costs incurred at both the agency and judicial levels, but only if 5 U.S.C. § 504 would have permitted a recovery of expenses and costs at the agency level. In other words, the EAJA allows recovery of costs incurred at the agency level only in cases of agency formal adjudication, whether the party won at the agency level or lost at the agency level but prevailed on judicial review. Because the facts state that the hearing at the lower level was a formal hearing and because the hearing addressed license revocation (a type of license action not exempt from the EAJA), then fees and expenses are available at the agency level, unlike in the last question, and are available at the trial level.

Answer (A) is not correct. As noted in the response to Answer (D), Becky meets all the requirements in the EAJA. The agency hearing was a formal adjudication, she prevailed at the trial level, and the type of licensing action is not exempt from coverage. So an award of fees and expenses for both the agency and the trial level is appropriate.

Answer (B) is not correct. For the reasons noted in response to Answer (D), an award of fees and expenses for both the agency and the trial level is appropriate.

Answer (C) is not correct. For the reasons noted in response to Answer (D), an award of fees and expenses for both the agency and the trial level is appropriate.

10.18. **Answer (B) is correct.** 5 U.S.C. §§ 504(a)(4) and 2412(d)(1)(D) apply to enforcement actions brought by the government against a private party, either in an agency formal adjudication or in federal court. A defendant's right to recover fees when the defendant loses is triggered when (i) the Government's demand was substantially in excess of the agency decision or judicial judgment it finally obtains, or when (ii) the Government's demand was unreasonable when compared with such judgment. These provisions were added by 1996 amendments to EAJA. In such cases, the agency or the court can award fees and other expenses related to defending against the excessive demand unless the defendant has committed a willful violation of law or otherwise acted in bad faith or special circumstances make an award unjust.

Answer (A) is not correct. The EAJA does not require a showing that the agency acted in bad faith; rather, the agency's demand is unreasonable when the fine ultimately awarded is substantially smaller than the fine initially assessed.

Answer (C) is not correct. It is not necessary for the business to successfully defend the enforcement action; rather, the issue is whether the fee initially assessed was substantially in excess of that ultimately awarded.

Answer (D) is not correct. While the statement that the EAJA does not apply to informal agency adjudications, the facts are clear that the hearing was a formal hearing. The facts state that the civil hearings were to be "on the record after an opportunity for a hearing."

10.19. **Answer (C) is correct.** According to Supreme Court precedent, the position of the United States is "substantially justified" if it is " 'justified in substance or in the main' — that is, justified to a degree that could satisfy a reasonable person. That is no different from . . . [having a] 'reasonable basis both in law and fact.' " *Pierce v. Underwood*, 487 U.S. 552, 565 (1988). The Court also noted that "a position can be substantially justified even though it is not correct, . . . it can be substantially (i.e., for the most part) justified if a reasonable person could think it correct, that is, if it has a reasonable basis in law and fact." *Id.* at 566 n.2.

Answer (A) is not correct. The standard articulated in this answer is not the one the Supreme Court adopted in *Pierce*.

Answer (B) is not correct. The standard articulated in this answer is not the one the Supreme Court adopted in *Pierce*.

Answer (D) is not correct. The standard articulated in this answer is not the one the Supreme Court adopted in *Pierce*.

10.20. **Answer (D) is correct** because both Answers (B) and (C) are correct statements.

Answer (A) is not correct. The EAJA provides that the agency "that conducts an adversary adjudication shall award, to a prevailing party other than the United States, fees and other expenses incurred by that party in connection with that proceeding . . . . " 5 U.S.C. § 504(a)(1). However, the award is qualified; it must be provided "unless the adjudicative officer of the agency finds that the position of the agency was substantially justified or that special circumstances make an award unjust." *Id.*

Answer (B) is not correct because it is not the only correct statement. This statement is correct. The EAJA provides that the agency "shall award, to a prevailing party . . . fees and other expenses . . . unless the adjudicative officer of the agency finds that the position of the agency was substantially justified or that special circumstances make an award unjust." *Id.*

Answer (C) is not correct because it is not the only correct statement. This statement is correct. The EAJA provides that when the agency "appeals the underlying merits of the adversary proceeding, no decision on an application for fees and other expenses . . . shall be made . . . until a final and unreviewable decision is rendered by the court on appeal or until the underlying merits of the case have been finally determined . . . . " 5 U.S.C. § 504(a)(2).

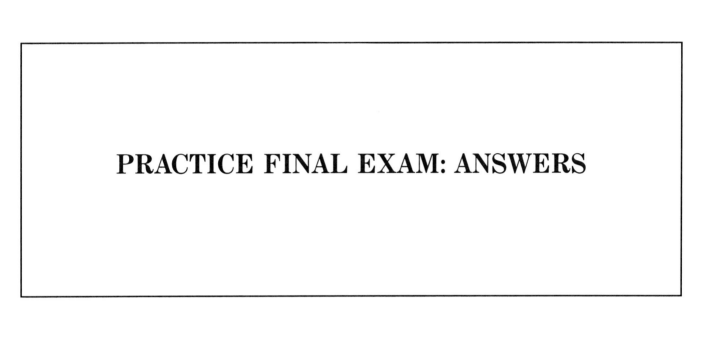

PRACTICE FINAL EXAM: ANSWERS

1.   **Answer (C) is correct.** The court will likely void the rule, but an agency can always try again. In trying again, an agency would do well to follow required procedures.

Answer (A) is not correct. This statement is inaccurate. If an agency fails to follow a procedural rule, any ensuing regulation is generally void, regardless of why the agency failed to follow procedure.

Answer (B) is not correct. While the court will most likely void the rule, the agency remains free to try to promulgate the rule again.

Answer (D) is not correct. The failure of an agency to follow procedures when promulgating an informal regulation does not lead to the agency having to use formal procedures should it wish to try to promulgate the same rule again. Formal procedures are required only when the enabling statute requires formal procedures to be used.

2.   **Answer (C) is correct** because it is not an accurate statement. The president, not OIRA, has this authority. E.O. 12866 § 6(b)(3) requires the Administrator of OIRA to provide a written explanation when OIRA returns a proposed regulatory action to the agency for "further reconsideration." Further, if the agency head disagrees with OIRA and the two cannot resolve their disagreement, the president or the vice president acting at the request of the president, with the relevant agency head (and, as appropriate, other interested government officials), shall resolve any conflict between OIRA and the specific agency. E.O. 12866 § 7.

Answer (A) is not correct because it is an accurate statement. E.O. 12866 § 2(b) provides that OMB shall coordinate review of agency rulemaking to ensure that rulemaking is consistent with applicable law, the president's priorities, and the principles set forth in the order, and OMB shall ensure that decisions of one agency do not conflict with the policies or actions of another agency.

Answer (B) is not correct because it is an accurate statement. E.O. 12866 § 1(a) provides that agencies should assess all costs and benefits of available regulatory alternatives, including the alternative of not regulating, and should select regulatory approaches that maximize net benefits, broadly defined. Further, E.O. 12866 § 6(a)(3)(B) directs each agency to provide this cost benefit analysis to OIRA.

Answer (D) is not correct because it is an accurate statement. E.O. 12866 § 5(a) directs agencies to submit to OIRA a program under which the agency will periodically review its existing, significant regulations to determine whether any such regulations should be modified or eliminated so as to make the regulatory program more effective, less burdensome, or more in-line with presidential priorities.

3.   **Answer (A) is correct.** The APA requires formal, trial-like procedures only when the statute authorizing the rulemaking requires the determination to be made "on the record" after an opportunity for a hearing. *United States v. Florida East Coast Railway Co.*, 410 U.S. 224,

241 (1973); *United States Et Al. v. Allegheny-Ludlum Steel Corp.*, 406 U.S. 742, 756–57 (1972). Congress has rarely used the specific language necessary to trigger formal APA procedures in the rulemaking context.

Answer (B) is not correct. As it does for rulemaking, the APA requires formal, trial-like procedures only when the statute authorizing the adjudication requires the determination to be made "on the record" after an opportunity for a hearing. *Dominion Energy Brayton Point, LLC v. Johnson*, 443 F.3d 12, 14–15 (1st Cir. 2006) (applying *Chevron* deference to review an agency's decision to not use formal APA procedures); *Chemical Waste Management, Inc. v. EPA*, 873 F.2d 1477, 1481–82 (D.C. Cir. 1989) (same). Hence, the equivalent of a clear statement is needed from Congress before formal procedures are required in rulemaking or adjudication.

Answer (C) is not correct. An agency may avoid notice and comment rulemaking and use non-legislative procedures only in certain situations, which are identified in APA § 553.

Answer (D) is not correct. The APA identifies when formal rulemaking procedures are required. In all other situations, the APA requires the agency to use either informal rulemaking or non-legislative procedures. Additionally, Congress may require the agency to use procedures separate from those required by the APA. That is, the agency may be required to follow what is sometimes referred to as "hybrid" procedures.

4. The phrase "non-legislative rules" refers to some types of rules that administrative agencies issue without following the APA's formal or informal rulemaking procedures. Congress, however, has ordinarily required publication of all rules — including rules that are exempt from rulemaking procedures. Section 552(a)(1), part of the Freedom of Information Act, requires agencies to publish the following rules in the *Federal Register*: rules of procedure; substantive rules of general applicability; statements of general policy or interpretation of general application; and any amendments or revisions of such rules. *See also* § 553(d) (requiring publication of substantive rules 30 days prior to their effective date; and exempting certain other rules from the 30-day requirement, but not from the publication requirement).

5. **Answer (D) is correct.** The Equal Access to Justice Act (EAJA) provides that a "judgment for costs . . . not including the fees and expenses of attorneys *may* be awarded to the prevailing party in any civil action brought by or against the United States or any agency." 28 U.S.C. § 2412(a)(1). The statute is discretionary, not mandatory, and does not allow the prevailing party to recover attorney's fees. Additionally, the answer correctly notes that this subsection does not include an exception should the court find that the non-prevailing party's position was substantially justified. *Id.* The "substantially justified" language is in another subsection of the EAJA. So, the court may award costs to the agency regardless of whether either side's position is substantially justified.

Answer (A) is not correct. The EAJA provides that a court *shall* award to a prevailing party "other than the United States" fees and costs other than attorney's fees "unless the court finds that the position of the United States was substantially justified." 28 U.S.C. § 2412(d)(1)(A). The statute defines the "United States" as including "any agency and any official of the United States acting in his or her official capacity." 28 U.S.C. § 2412(d)(2)(C). Thus, a court may not award attorney's fees, other expenses, and costs to an agency under this subsection. Second, the exception for "substantially justified" refers to whether the agency's position was substantially justified, not the claimant's position.

Answer (B) is not correct. As noted in the response to answer (A), subsection (d)(1)(A) of the EAJA requires a court to award "costs . . . but not including the fees and expenses of attorney" to a prevailing party other than the agency. 28 U.S.C. § 2412(d)(1)(A). Additionally, the exception for "substantially justified" refers to whether the agency's position was substantially justified, not the claimant's position.

Answer (C) is not correct. As noted in the response to Answer (D), the EAJA permits a court to make an award "for costs . . . not including the fees and expenses of attorneys . . . to the prevailing party in any civil action brought by or against the United States or any agency." 28 U.S.C. § 2412(a)(1). However, there are two problems with this answer. First, this subsection does not include the "substantially justified" exception. Second, attorney's fees would not be recoverable. It is correct that section 2412(b) allows a court to award attorney's fees "to the same extent that any other party would be liable under the common law or under the terms of any statute which specifically provides for such an award." 28 U.S.C. § 2412(b). In the United States, each party in litigation typically bears its own legal expenses. Subsection (b) waives the government's immunity from paying such fees (sovereign immunity), and thus puts the federal government in the same position as a private entity in terms of its liability for and recovery of attorney's fee awards under this subsection. Importantly, subsection (b) does not create a new right to attorney's fees. Rather, to receive attorney's fees, a prevailing party, including an agency, would have to identify a separate statute, common law doctrine, or rule allowing the court to make such an award. The facts state that there is no other statute, rule, or common law doctrine.

6.   **Answer (C) is correct.** Courts will review an agency's denial of a petition, but the review is very deferential. Courts hesitate to second-guess an agency's decision especially if the decision hinges on priority setting among important agency concerns. *See Northern Spotted Owl v. Hodel*, 716 F. Supp. 479, 483 (W.D. Wash. 1988) (overturning an agency decision only "where the agency spurns unrebutted expert opinions without itself offering a credible alternative explanation").

Answer (A) is not correct. APA § 553(e) requires an agency to give prompt notice of a denial of a petition. Further, APA § 706(a) allows a reviewing court to "compel agency action unlawfully withheld or unreasonably delayed," and APA § 551(13) defines "agency action" as including an agency's failure to act.

Answer (B) is not correct. As noted in the response to Answer (A), APA § 706(a) allows a reviewing court to "compel agency action unlawfully withheld or unreasonably delayed," and APA § 551(13) defines "agency action" as including an agency's failure to act. A failure to act on a petition for rulemaking may become unreasonable after several years. *See Telecommunications Research & Action Center v. FCC*, 750 F.2d 70, 80 (D.C. Cir. 1984) (establishing a six-step analysis for determining whether an agency has unreasonably delayed action).

Answer (D) is not correct. APA § 553(e) provides that, in addition to providing prompt notice of a denial of a petition, an agency must provide a brief statement of the reasons for that denial.

7.   **Answer (B) is correct.** APA § 553(d) states that "the required publication of a substantive rule shall be made not less than 30 days before its effective date." None of the exceptions in subsection (d) apply in this case. Hence, because the ride occurred before January 31, and therefore, the Final Rule was not yet in effect, the citations would not be valid.

Answer (A) is not correct. As discussed below, publication in the *Federal Register* is not the only requirement relating to the effectiveness of an agency rule.

Answer (C) is not correct. While APA § 552(a) allows an agency to enforce or apply a rule against persons with actual notice, APA § 552(d) still applies in cases of actual notice. An agency must wait a minimum of 30 days to enforce a new rule, unless one of the exceptions applies.

Answer (D) is not correct. The enabling statute requires only that the NPS promulgate rules "after hearing." This language is insufficient to trigger formal rulemaking. *U.S. v. Florida Coast Railway Co.*, 410 U.S. 224, 234–35 (1973).

8. The term "executive agencies" is often used to refer to both "departments" and agencies within "departments." Departments and agencies within departments are generally headed by individual people, who are appointed by the president, with the advice and consent of the Senate, and who serve at the pleasure of the president. Because they serve at the president's pleasure, agency heads can generally be fired without cause. Accordingly, the President can exert greater influence over "executive agencies." Independent agencies, in contrast, are not part of a department. Further, they are not headed by a single person but, rather, are headed by a multi-member group, such as a commission, board, or council. Members of the commission, board, or council have greater insulation from presidential influence because they generally can be removed only "for cause." Political disagreement generally is insufficient cause for removal. Additionally, although the President may have authority to appoint members of the groups heading independent agencies, these members generally serve for a term of years; because the terms are staggered, the president generally is unable to replace all members at one time. All of these features help make independent agencies more politically insular from the president.

9. **Answer (C) is correct.** Rulemaking is the "agency process for formulating, amending, or repealing a rule." APA § 551(5). A rule is "the whole or part of an agency statement of general . . . applicability and future effect." APA § 551(4). A city's decision to tax property owners and its decision regarding the amount to tax is rulemaking.

    Answer (A) is not correct because it describes agency adjudication. Adjudication is an "agency process for the formulation of an order." APA § 551(7). An order is the "whole or part of a final disposition . . . of an agency in a matter other than rulemaking but including licensing." APA § 551(6). Adjudication, then, is the agency process for formulating a decision of particular applicability and present effect. An agency is defined to include any authority of the government. APA § 551(1). Because the facts state that the APA applies even though this is state action, a police officer working for the City of Chicago would be considered as working for a state agency. Hence, ticketing a car for illegally parking would be adjudication. The police officer made a determination about a particular car and the decision has a present, or immediate, effect. Adjudications need not be elaborate processes.

    Answer (B) is not correct because it describes agency adjudication. The FHA's determination is a finding that a particular entity, Capital Mortgage, Inc., is no longer authorized to participate in a federal program, and that determination has a present, or immediate effect.

    Answer (D) is not correct because it describes agency adjudication. The NTSB's determination about a particular individual's right to continue providing flight instruction and that determination has a present, or immediate effect.

10.   The Supreme Court has held that businesses that are pervasively — the Court also uses the term "closely" — regulated have lower expectations of privacy than other businesses. Moreover, such businesses have a long tradition of close supervision by the state. Hence, warrants are unnecessary. The pervasively regulated exception to the warrant requirement is essentially an outgrowth of the waiver/consent doctrine: by voluntarily engaging in a heavily regulated business, business owners give up their privacy expectations. To date, the following businesses have been found to be pervasively regulated: *Colonnade Catering Corp. v. United States*, 397 U.S. 72 (1970) (liquor dealers); *United States v. Biswell*, 406 U.S. 311 (1972) (gun dealers); *Donovan v. Dewey*, 452 U.S. 594 (1981) (mining company); *New York v. Burger*, 482 U.S. 691 (1987) (auto dismantlers).

Additionally, warrantless searches are permitted when there is an emergency and the agency cannot wait to secure a warrant and when securing a warrant would be impracticable. *United States v. Martinez-Fuerte*, 428 U.S. 543, 561–62 (1976) (holding that border patrol officers need not seek a warrant for every vehicle they search). And warrantless searches are permitted when regulated entities do not have a reasonable expectation of privacy. *See, e.g., Air Pollution Variance Board v. Western Alfalfa Corp.*, 416 U.S. 861, 864–65 (1974) (upholding an inspection of a factory when emissions from the factory smokestacks were visible from the public grounds).

11.   **Answer (D) is correct.** APA § 553(b)(3) requires "notice" of a rulemaking to include "either the terms or substance of the proposed rule or a description of the subjects and issues involved." Courts have held that when a final rule deviates from the proposed rule, the notice should be found adequate when the final rule represents "a logical out-growth" of the proposed notice and comments or when the notice was sufficient to serve the policies underlying the notice requirement. *See, e.g., Chocolate Manufacturer's Ass'n v. Block*, 755 F.2d 1098, 1105 (4th Cir. 1985). If the final rule is a logical outgrowth of the proposed rule, the final rule is valid despite the changes.

Answer (A) is not correct. This answer simply states an inaccurate test. The appropriate test is the logical outgrowth test identified in the response to Answer (D).

Answer (B) is not correct. This answer simply states an inaccurate test. The appropriate test is the logical outgrowth test identified in the response to Answer (D).

Answer (C) is not correct. This answer simply states an inaccurate test. The appropriate test is the logical outgrowth test identified in the response to Answer (D).

12.   **Answer (B) is correct.** There has been a lot of debate about whether agencies should be allowed to articulate policy adjudicatively or whether they should be required to do so legislatively. Many commentators argue that legislative procedures are preferable because they allow greater participation in rulemaking processes by those subject to those processes. Nevertheless, an administrative agency "is not precluded from announcing new principles in [the] adjudicative proceeding and . . . the choice between rulemaking and adjudication lies in the first instance within the [agency's] discretion." *NLRB v. Bell Aerospace Co.*, 416 U.S. 267, 294 (1974). *See also, SEC v. Chenery Corp.*, 332 U.S. 194, 202–203 (1947). But like all grants of discretion, "there may be situations where the [agency's] reliance on adjudication would amount to an abuse of discretion . . . . " *Bell Aerospace Co.*, 416 U.S. at 294. The question is where to draw the line. On that point, the Supreme Court has avoided black-

letter rules. Assuming the enabling statute grants authority to an agency to act via both rulemaking and adjudication, the agency has broad authority to choose which process to use. *SEC v. Chenery Corp.*, 332 U.S. at 203. In *Chenery*, the SEC noted that agencies sometimes must create new standards in adjudication and that necessarily has some retroactive effect. "But such retroactivity must be balanced against the mischief of producing a result which is contrary to a statutory design or to legal and equitable principles. If that mischief is greater than the ill effect of the retroactive application of a new standard, it is not the type of retroactivity which is condemned by law." *Id.* The agency's choice becomes an abuse of discretion when this balance is upset. To determine whether there has been an abuse of discretion, a court may consider whether the issue is very specialized, such that adjudication would be appropriate and whether the regulated entity would be unfairly penalized. *See, e.g., Bell Aerospace Co.*, 416 U.S. at 292–93.

The Ninth Circuit has held that agencies may proceed by adjudication to enforce discrete violations of existing laws where the effective scope of a rule's impact will be relatively small; however, an agency must proceed by rulemaking if it seeks to change the law and establish rules of widespread application. *Patel v. INS*, 638 F.2d 1199, 1205 (9th Cir. 1980). *See e.g., Ford Motor Co. v. FTC*, 673 F.2d 1008 (9th Cir. 1981) (holding setting aside an FTC order reached via adjudication for this reason). While this approach provides a clearer line, the Supreme Court has not adopted this approach to date.

Answer (A) is not correct. The benefits to the public of rulemaking are not factors courts consider when determining whether an agency's choice to use adjudication rather than rulemaking was legitimate. A court will balance the agency's interests and the individual regulated entity's interest.

Answer (C) is not correct. Whether the new policy will be broadly applicable is not a factor courts consider when determining whether an agency's choice to use adjudication rather than rulemaking was legitimate. A court will balance the agency's interests and the individual regulated entity's interest.

Answer (D) is not correct. Whether the public has requested a rulemaking is not a factor courts consider when determining whether an agency's choice to use adjudication rather than rulemaking was legitimate.

13.   **Answer (D) is correct.** The delegation, or non-delegation doctrine requires Congress to provide an "intelligible principle" when Congress delegates quasi-legislative power to an agency. The Supreme Court articulated the intelligible principle test in *J.W. Hampton, Jr., & Co. v. United States*, 276 U.S. 394, 409 (1928). The test was refined in *Panama Refining Co. v. Ryan*, 293 U.S. 388 (1935) (the hot oil case) and *A.L.A. Schechter Poultry Corp. v. United States*, 295 U.S. 495 (1935) (the sick chicken case). In both cases, the Court struck down provisions in the National Industrial Recovery Act (NIRA) on delegation grounds. Many believe that these two cases reflected the Court's skepticism of President Roosevelt's New Deal legislation.

Answer (A) is not correct because it is not accurate. As noted in the response to Answer (D), Congress can delegate quasi-legislative power to agencies so long as it cabins that delegation.

Answer (B) is not correct because it is not accurate. Congress can delegate quasi-legislative power to agencies so long as it cabins that delegation. *See, e.g., Mistretta v. United States*, 488 U.S. 361 (1989).

Answer (C) is not correct. Congress can delegate both quasi-legislative and quasi-judicial power to agencies.

14. **Answer (C) is correct.** This question explores what due process requires regarding neutral decision-making for adjudications. In *Withrow v. Larkin*, 421 U.S. 35 (1975), the Supreme Court held that litigants must overcome "a presumption of honesty and integrity in those serving as adjudicators." *Id.* at 47. The D.C. Circuit held that where the decision-maker already decided the facts of a case, bias exists. *Texaco v. FTC*, 336 F.2d 754, 760 (D.C. Cir. 1964), *vacated and remanded on other grounds*, 381 U.S. 739 (1965). In that case, the Chairman of the Federal Trade Commission (FTC) gave a speech while an adjudication was pending against Texaco and said that the FTC was aware of Texaco's illegal practices. The court noted that a disinterested person "could hardly fail to conclude that [the Chairman] had in some measure decided that Texaco had violated the Act." *Id.* In other words, the speech showed that the agency head's action indicated case-specific predisposition.

Answer (A) is not correct. This answer provides the wrong standard for determining whether the decision-maker is neutral.

Answer (B) is not correct. This answer provides the wrong standard for determining whether the decision-maker is neutral.

Answer (D) is not correct. This answer is incorrect because there were no ex parte communications. APA § 551(14) defines ex parte communications as "oral or written communication not on the public record." Speeches by a chairperson to the public are not ex parte communications.

15. **Answer (B) is correct.** Because neither argument would have merit, the court should rule in favor of the SEC. See the response to Answers (C) and (D) below to understand why neither claim has merit.

Answer (A) is not correct. Because Author Anderson was found to have engaged in criminal misconduct and will have its audit released to the public, Author Anderson would have a direct injury from the SEC's action and would have standing to challenge the rule.

Answer (C) is not correct. Because challenged rules are "rules of agency . . . procedure or practice," the SEC is not required to use notice and comment rulemaking procedures to promulgate them. APA § 553(b)(3)(A). The test to determine whether a rule is procedural and is thus exempt from notice and comment rulemaking is to determine whether the rule encodes a substantive value judgment and substantially alters the rights of the parties. *See JEM Broadcasting Co., Inc. v. FCC*, 22 F.3d 320, 328 (D.C. Cir. 1994). Rules that limit evidence in an adjudication to written submissions only do not encode a substantive value judgment because the agency remains free to agree with the regulated entity and such rules do not substantially alter the rights of the parties even if adjudication is simply more difficult.

Answer (D) is not correct. Because the relevant statute requires that such hearings be held "on the record," formal adjudication procedures are likely not required. Formal adjudications are required only when Congress provides a clear statement that such procedures are necessary. *Dominion Energy Brayton Point, LLC v. Johnson*, 443 F.3d 12, 17 (1st Cir. 2006) (applying *Chevron* deference to review an agency's decision to not use formal APA procedures); *Chemical Waste Management, Inc. v. EPA*, 873 F.2d 1477, 1480 (D.C. Cir. 1989) (same).

16.   A case must be ripe for judicial review for a court to hear it. The ripeness doctrine predates
       the APA, and unlike finality and exhaustion, ripeness was not codified in the APA. Hence, it
       remains a judicially developed doctrine. To determine whether a case is ripe, courts look to
       two factors: (1) whether the issue is fit for judicial review, and (2) whether the parties would
       suffer hardship if court consideration were withheld. The rationale for the ripeness doctrine
       is to prevent courts from entangling themselves in abstract disagreements "[and] to protect
       [] agencies from judicial interference until an administrative decision has been formalized
       and its effects felt in a concrete way . . . . " *Abbott Laboratories v. Gardner*, 387 U.S. 136,
       148 (1967). Ripeness issues generally arise in pre-enforcement review cases.

       In this case, the precise substantive issue is purely legal — what is the effect of the 1966
       amendments to the FLSA on coin-operated laundries. Moreover, the coin-operated
       employers would suffer significant hardship. The letter also comes from the head of the
       agency, suggesting that this interpretation is authoritative. Employers who violate the
       FLSA can suffer significant monetary, as well as possible criminal, penalties. The letter
       from the agency thus places the trade association's members in a dilemma, either they can
       comply with the letter or they can choose to not comply and face sanctions. Hence, the case
       is ripe for review. *See National Automatic Laundry and Dry Cleaning Council v. Shultz*,
       443 F.2d 689, 703 (D.C. Cir. 1971) (finding ripeness on similar facts).

17.   **Answer (C) is correct.** The issue in this fact pattern relates to the ex parte communications.
       APA § 551(14) defines ex parte communications as "oral or written communication not on the
       public record with respect to which reasonable prior notice to all parties is not given, but it
       shall not include requests for status reports . . . . " While the comments made to the FTC
       seem to be more than status reports because they were intended to influence the FTC's
       decision making and because the comments were not on the record or docketed after they
       occurred, the comments are ex parte communications. However, the APA only expressly
       prohibits ex parte communications in formal adjudication and rulemaking. APA § 557(d)(1).
       This proceeding was not formal rulemaking; hence, the comments were not impermissible.
       But see Home Box Office v. FCC, 567 F.2d 9, 35–6 (D.C. Cir. 1977) (suggesting that agencies
       cannot engage in ex parte communication with interested persons during notice and
       comment rulemaking). Because *Home Box Office* was decided one year before the Supreme
       Court held that courts could not add procedural requirements beyond those mandated by
       the APA in *Vermont Yankee v. NRDC*, 435 U.S. 519, 524 (1978), *Home Box Office* is likely
       wrong.

       Answer (A) is not correct. Even though the FTC may choose to docket the comments in the
       interest of fair disclosure, absent a statute or regulation requiring docketing, docketing is
       not required. *See, e.g., Sierra Club v. Costle*, 657 F.2d 298, 403 (D.C. Cir. 1981) (finding that
       the Clean Air Act required docketing for notice and comment rulemaking).

       Answer (B) is not correct. The issue is whether the OMB's influence would be found to be
       undue influence. The president has constitutional authority to influence agency policy-
       making; indeed, we elect presidents specifically to choose and direct policy choices. Having
       said this, the agency's policy choice must be supported by its record and cannot be arbitrary
       and capricious. In this case, the facts state that the record would have supported either
       choice; hence, the agency's decision is not arbitrary and capricious.

       Answer (D) is not correct. Although status reports are specifically exempted from the
       APA's definition of ex parte communications, APA § 551(14), a court would likely find that the

OMB comments were more than status reports; the comments were intended to influence the FTC's decision making.

18. The objection is not valid. Assuming the enabling statute so provides, the NTSB has the authority to seek relevant records from Chrysler. Chrysler is using FOIA as a shield to prevent required disclosure to the NTSB. FOIA, APA § 552, requires the government to fully or partially disclose previously unreleased information and documents it controls. Assuming none of the nine exceptions in APA § 552(b) apply, the NTSB would be required to disclose Chrysler's proprietary information. However, FOIA is a disclosure statute designed to provide the public with information about regulated entities. Congress did not intend for regulated entities to use the statute as a shield to prevent regulated entities from complying with the government's valid requests for information. As a result, the objection is invalid.

19. **Answer (B) is correct.** APA § 551(1) defines an agency as any "authority of the Government of the United States . . . but does not include" identified exceptions. The Central Intelligence Agency and the Office of Management and Budget are authorities of the United States and are not included within any of the exceptions.

Answer (A) is not correct. National Public Radio and the Republican Party are not authorities of the United States Government, although they may receive public funding. Although the president is not specifically excepted in the APA from the definition of agency, the Supreme Court has held that, because of separation of powers concerns, the president is not an agency. *Franklin v. Massachusetts*, 505 U.S. 788, 800–01 (1992).

Answer (C) is not correct. This answer is not correct because, in addition to including the two correct agencies, it also includes the president. As noted in the response to Answer (A), the president is not an agency.

Answer (D) is not correct. Although the Office of Management and Budget is an agency, the Central Intelligence Agency is also an agency. This answer omits the latter.

20. **Answer (B) is correct.** The EAJA provides for the award of attorney's fees and other expenses to eligible individuals and small entities that are parties to litigation against the government. An eligible party may receive an award when the party prevails over the government, unless the government's position was "substantially justified." The EAJA defines eligible parties as individuals whose net worth "[does] not exceed $2,000,000 at the time the civil action was filed" and businesses with no more than 500 employees and a net worth that "[does] not exceed $7,000,000 at the time the civil action was filed." 28 § 2412(d)(2)(B)(ii); 5 U.S.C. § 504(b)(1)(B)(ii). A business with 800 employees and a net worth of $8 million exceeds both limits.

Answer (A) is not correct. Individuals with a net worth of $2 million and less qualify. An individual with a net worth of $1 million meets this requirement.

Answer (C) is not correct. Non-profit organizations qualify regardless of their net worth. 5 U.S.C. § 504(b)(1)(B)(ii); 28 U.S.C. § 2412(d)(2)(B)(ii).

Answer (D) is not correct. A "unit of local government" qualifies if its net worth did not exceed $7 million and it had no more than 500 employees at the time the adversary adjudication was initiated. 5 U.S.C. § 504(b)(1)(B)(ii); 28 U.S.C. § 2412(d)(2)(B)(ii). A city government with 400 employees and a net worth of $3 million meets these requirements.

21.   **Answer (B) is correct.** The key inquiry in deciding whether a rule falls within the APA exception for rules of "agency organization, procedure or practice" is (1) whether the rule is essentially a "housekeeping measure" or a rule that merely alters the manner in which parties present themselves to the agency; or (2) whether the rule affects, in a more substantive way, the rights and interests of regulated parties (encodes a substantive value judgment). *See JEM Broadcasting Co. v. F.C.C.*, 22 F.3d 320, 326–27 (D.C. Cir. 1994). While the rule at issue here affects the Hospital, it does not do so in a sufficiently substantive way. Moreover, the rule does not change Medicare's substantive reimbursement standards but rather, governs merely the timing of submissions and the efficiency of the appeals process. *See, e.g., Inova Alexandria Hosp. v. Shalala*, 244 F.3d 342, 349–50 (4th Cir. 2001).

       Answer (A) is not correct. Although an exception to notice and comment procedures exists for rules that merely prescribe the manner in which the parties present themselves to the agency, the exception does not hinge on the concept of impracticality. *See* APA § 553(b)(3)(A) & (B).

       Answer (C) is not correct. The right to an appeal granted by the Medicare Act is a "substantive" right. Further, although Congress also granted authority to the Board to establish "procedures" to implement the provider right to appeals, procedural rules often have an impact on substantive rights. In cases such as this, the issue is whether the effect on the substantive right to a hearing is sufficiently grave so that notice and comment may be deemed necessary as a safeguard. Here, the interest impacted by the rule is a hospital's interest to an unlimited time within which to submit its "position papers." Courts would not likely find that interest to be so weighty that public notice and comment would be necessary. *See JEM Broadcasting Co. v. F.C.C.*, 22 F.3d 320 (D.C. Cir. 1994) (holding that a license applicant's right to notice and an opportunity to correct errors in the license application was not so significant as to have required the agency to use notice and comment procedures for a procedural rule eliminating that right).

       Answer (D) is not correct. In 1990, the Court of Appeals for the District of Columbia suggested that an agency's adoption of a comprehensive penalty scheme required notice and comment procedures because the scheme encoded a value judgment on the appropriate balance between a defendant's rights to adjudicatory procedures and the agency's interest in an efficient prosecution. *Air Transport Ass'n of America v. DOT*, 900 F.2d 369, 383 (D.C. Cir. 1990). However, in a later case, the court backed away from this narrow definition of "procedure" rules in favor of the reasoning discussed in the response to Answer (B). *JEM Broadcasting Co. v. FCC*, 22 F.3d 320, 328 (D.C. Cir. 1994) (finding that an FCC rule allowing the agency to dismiss with prejudice a regulated entity's incomplete application for a license was a procedural rule).

22.   **Answer (A) is correct.** Under APA § 704, regulated entities must exhaust administrative remedies only in two situations: (1) when a statute requires exhaustion, or (2) when an agency by regulation requires exhaustion and stays the effect of the agency's action during the administrative appeal. *Darby v. Cisneros*, 509 U.S. 137, 148 (1993). Here, the ESA requires the ranchers to exhaust administrative remedies. It is irrelevant that the statute does not stay the agency's action pending the administrative challenge. If it were an agency rule, then a stay would be required.

       Answer (B) is not correct. APA § 702 creates a cause of action for persons suffering legal wrong or persons adversely affected or aggrieved by *agency action.* APA § 551(13) defines agency action to include, "the whole or a part of an agency rule, order, license, sanction, relief, or the equivalent or denial thereof, or failure to act." Here, the agency's decision to limit grazing on federal lands would likely be considered a discrete agency action. *Bennett v. Spear*, 520 U.S. 154, 177–78 (1997). Also, the agency's decision to limit permits for 20 specific federal lands is discrete agency action.

Answer (C) is not correct. The ripeness doctrine helps ensure that claims are not brought to court prematurely. This doctrine is not found in the APA; rather, it is judicially created. *See, e.g., Abbott Laboratories v. Gardner*, 387 U.S. 136, 148 (1967). To determine whether a case is ripe, courts look to two factors: (1) whether the issue is fit for judicial review, and (2) whether the parties would suffer hardship if court consideration were withheld. Here, the issue is ripe because the question of whether the statute required the agency to follow certain procedures is a legal question "fit for judicial review." Additionally, the ranchers will likely suffer hardship because they may not be able to have their cattle graze if the case is not heard. Hence, the case is ripe.

Answer (D) is not correct. Pursuant to APA § 702, any person who is "adversely affected or aggrieved by agency action within the meaning of a relevant statute" has a cause of action. Pursuant to this language, courts require plaintiffs to be within the zone of interests that the relevant statute protects. The zone of interests test is resolved using statutory interpretation analysis: who or what did Congress intend to protect when it enacted the statute at issue? *Air Courier Conference of America v. American Postal Workers Union, AFL-CIO*, 498 U.S. 517, 526 (1991) (holding that postal workers were not within the zone of interests of a statute that created the U.S. Postal Service as a monopoly). The relevant statute for the zone of interest inquiry is the ESA, not the APA.

23. **Answer (D) is correct.** Arguably, a lawyer working for the General Counsel's office in the Department of Transportation represents the government generally, the president more specifically, and the Secretary of the Department of Transportation most specifically and directly. Thus, all of the above is the best answer. But the other answers are accurate as well; they are just incomplete.

Answer (A) is not correct because it is incomplete.

Answer (B) is not correct because it is incomplete.

Answer (B) is not correct because it is incomplete.

24. **Answer (C) is correct.** This question raises the issue of whether the Johnsons can assert a liberty interest that would trigger a right to procedural due process. On the facts of the question, the more precise issue is whether the Johnsons can satisfy the "stigma-plus" test recognized by the Supreme Court. A liberty interest may be implicated where a person's good name, reputation, honor, or integrity is at stake because of a state agency's actions, but only where a resulting stigma has foreclosed in some way a future pursuit qualifying for liberty interest protection and/or where the agency action has altered or extinguished a right or status previously recognized by state law. *See Paul v. Davis*, 424 U.S. 693, 724 (1976); *Board of Regents v. Roth*, 408 U.S. 564, 573 (1972); *Wisconsin v. Constantineau*, 400 U.S. 433, 437 (1971). Cases satisfying the standard generally involve agency activity involving a finding of a disputed fact bearing on a person's honor or integrity, where that finding is made public pursuant to the regulatory scheme or will be accessible in such a way as to create a reasonable likelihood of an infringement on future rights. Here, the Johnsons

can demonstrate both stigma (they have been mistakenly labeled as child abusers) and the plus factor (they cannot work or volunteer at a community center for children). *See Humphries v. County of Los Angeles*, 554 F.3d 1170, 1186–1192 (9th Cir. 2009) (concluding that the "plus-test" is satisfied if a regulatory scheme creates a stigma and a tangible burden on an individual's employment opportunities).

Answer (A) is not correct. Here, listing occurs if it is determined by an investigating agency that allegations of suspected child abuse or neglect is "not unfounded." Although the requisite finding is not that the person is guilty, it nonetheless is a finding that would call into question the person's good name, reputation, honor, or integrity.

Answer (B) is not correct. Although it is true that all future job opportunities may not be foreclosed, many specific types of jobs will be foreclosed because the information is available for "pre-employment" background investigations (including specific opportunities that the Johnsons have stated that they want to pursue) and especially because many background checks are also required by state law.

Answer (D) is not correct. The availability of a defamation suit is irrelevant: the issue is whether "stigma plus" is present.

25.   **Answer (D) is correct.** The court would likely find a violation of due process. Although the state has a strong interest in preventing child abuse, the Johnsons' interest in not being included on the list by mistake is very strong, and additional safeguards (such as an informal hearing by which a listed person can ask for reconsideration upon an appropriate showing) would lower the risk of erroneous deprivation and would not be too burdensome for the state. *Mathews v. Eldridge*, 424 U.S. 319, 334–35 (1976) (directing courts to balance the private interest affected, the risk of erroneous deprivation without the additional safeguards, and the governmental interest in additional procedures). *See Humphries v. County of Los Angeles*, 554 F.3d 1170, 1193–1201 (9th Cir. 2009) (concluding that, although the state did not have to provide additional procedures prior to listing persons on the CACI, that state did need to provide "some kind of hearing" by which a listed person could challenge the inclusion).

Answer (A) is not correct. This response does not reflect the appropriate test from *Mathews*.

Answer (B) is not correct. This answer does not include the appropriate test from *Mathews*, although it does include some of the *Mathews* factors. While the state does have a strong interest in preventing child abuse and the CACI index may be efficient, the burden on the state to provide a method to correct errors is minimal.

Answer (C) is not correct. The response described still fails to faithfully apply *Mathews* and address whether additional safeguards would lessen the risk of error and whether such additional procedures are feasible.

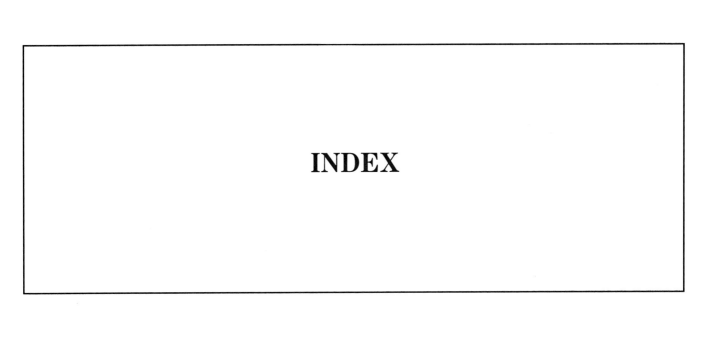

INDEX

INDEX